Improving the Student Experience

The landscape of higher education (HE) has dramatically altered in the past 30 years as more students are attending universities and colleges than ever before. In such a competitive market, the quality of the student experience is pivotal to an institution's ability to attract students. However, the increasing costs of delivering higher education teamed with a reduction in government funding means that creating a high standard of student experience has never been more challenging.

The Student Experience Practitioner Model discussed in this book recognises the need for all staff, at all levels, to develop and implement initiatives to improve and enhance the student experience. It provides an organised and detailed structure that can be orchestrated in a cost-effective and highly adaptable manner. It guides practitioners in the identification of what they must deliver, who it is delivered to and when they need to deliver by working through the six key stages of the Practitioner Model's new student lifecycle:

- First contact and admissions;
- Pre-arrival;
- Arrival and orientation;
- Induction to study;
- Reorientation and reinduction (returners' induction);
- Outduction (preparation for life after study).

Packed with working solutions and both UK and internationally based case studies, this book includes chapters from Liz Thomas, Diane Nutt, Marcia Ody, Christine Keenan (UK), Mary Stuart Hunter (USA), Kerri-Lee Krause and Duncan Nulty (Australia). The authors show how practitioners can adapt and customise the 40 case studies presented to help them improve and enhance the experience of the undergraduate students in their own institution, and also to support their students' progression and retention while engaging their colleagues in the activity. It is an indispensible manual for higher education practitioners of all levels.

Michelle Morgan is a Learning and Teaching Coordinator and Student Experience Manager at Kingston University, UK.

Improving the Student Experience

A practical guide for universities and colleges

Edited by Michelle Morgan

Routledge
Taylor & Francis Group

LONDON AND NEW YORK

First published 2012
by Routledge
2 Park Square, Milton Park, Abingdon, Oxon OX14 4RN

Simultaneously published in the USA and Canada
by Routledge
711 Third Avenue, New York, NY 10017

Routledge is an imprint of the Taylor & Francis Group, an informa business

British Library Cataloguing in Publication Data
A catalogue record for this book is available from the British Library

Library of Congress Cataloging in Publication Data
Improving the student experience : a practical guide for universities and colleges /
[edited by] Michelle Morgan. -- 1st ed.
p. cm.
1. College students--Services for. 2. Counseling in higher education. 3. College student orientation. 4. School improvement programs. I. Morgan, Michelle.
LB2343.I45 2011
378.1'98--dc23
2011021781

ISBN: 978-0-415-59878-1 (hbk)
ISBN: 978-0-415-59879-8 (pbk)
ISBN: 978-0-203-81751-3 (ebk)

Typeset in Galliard and Gill Sans
by GreenGate Publishing Services, Tonbridge, Kent

Printed and bound in Great Britain by the MPG Books Group

In memory of Dr Sandra Winn, University of Brighton.

This book is dedicated to all my colleagues who, over the years, have helped me improve the student experience.

Contents

8 Outduction: preparing to leave, graduation and beyond 126

APRIL L. PERRY, UNIVERSITY OF CANTERBURY, NEW ZEALAND

PART 3
Core activities in the student Experience Practitioner Model 143

9 Academic student support and development 145

MARCIA ODY, UNIVERSITY OF MANCHESTER, UK

10 Supporting staff to be supporters 164

GLYN JONES, KINGSTON UNIVERSITY, UK

11 Supporting learning and teaching: improving academic engagement

LIZ THOMAS, EDGE HILL UNIVERSITY, UK

12 Student evaluation and feedback

DUNCAN NULTY, GRIFFITH UNIVERSITY, AUSTRALIA

13 Future developments in higher education and the student experience

MICHELLE MORGAN AND GLYN JONES, KINGSTON UNIVERSITY, UK

Figures and tables

Figures

Tables

Contributors

Akbar Aboutorabi is Deputy Dean of the Faculty of Engineering at Kingston University. He has more than 30 years' experience in higher education in the UK from research into the failure of engineering structures to the design of UG and PG courses and the development of a number of international collaboration projects. For the past few years he has been involved with the development and implementation of learning and teaching strategies with a particular focus on students' experiences.
Email: a.aboutorabi@kingston.ac.uk

Deborah Anderson is Principal Lecturer at Kingston Business School, Kingston University, where she teaches marketing communications to both undergraduates and postgraduates. Her research interests relate to her role as faculty learning and teaching coordinator. She is involved in pedagogic research and has a particular interest in innovative teaching practices and assessment and feedback. Recent projects include the development of interactive workshops based on social theories of learning.
Email: d.anderson@kingston.ac.uk

Erica Arthur is International Development Manager (North America), University of Birmingham. She was formerly Study Abroad Manager at Keele University, where she authored and produced 'Tick Off to Take Off' (TOTTO), an interactive online pre-departure guide. TOTTO has been licensed to other UK and international institutions, and was awarded the AUA Award for Excellence in Higher Education Management and Administration 2007. Erica was formerly Chair of the British Universities Transatlantic Exchange Association (BUTEX), an association of 80 UK higher education institutions with active transatlantic links and interests.
Email: e.d.arthur@bham.ac.uk

Katie Barnes is Admissions and International Liaison Officer in the Faculty of Engineering at Kingston University. She currently deals with both UG and PG applications and is the contact for international students in the faculty. The Faculty of Engineering collaborates with many industrial and educational partners in both the UK and abroad so the admissions process involves liaising with many different parties. She has been in this role at KU for four years, building on her previous experience of helping international students apply to UK universities.
Email: k.barnes@kingston.ac.uk

Barry J. Beggs is Senior Lecturer in Telecommunications at Glasgow Caledonian University and has had a long interest in enhancing the student experience in higher education. He has initiated and led a significant number of UK- and EC-funded research projects in

educational technology and related areas. Although appreciating and realising the importance of theoretical studies in educational research, he is very strongly in the empirical research camp.
Email: bjbe@gcu.ac.uk

Sally Brown is widely published and has edited more than a dozen volumes for Routledge/ Kogan Page, her most recent being *Beyond Bureaucracy: a Practical Guide to University and College Management* (2010 Routledge), edited with Steve Denton. Her best known publications include *Internationalising Higher Education* (2007 Routledge), edited with Elspeth Jones; *Towards Inclusive Learning* (2006 Routledge), edited with Mike Adams; and *Assessing Learners in Higher Education* (1994 Kogan Page), with Peter Knight. She was the founding series editor for the Kogan Page series on *Staff and Educational Development* until July 1999 and edited the book *Internal Audit in Higher Education* (2000 Routledge) with Alison Holmes.
Email: s.brown@leedsmet.ac.uk

Lynn Burnett is Senior Lecturer in higher education at the University of Western Sydney. Lynn works at the institution level with senior members of the university to ensure timely and strategic implementation of top-down and bottom-up initiatives to inform both policy and practice. Her research experience and interests include first-year student experience, student experience, women's studies, feminist research methods (in particular, memory work methodology), qualitative research and identity formation. Lynn was previously employed at Griffith University (2007–10) as a lecturer in higher education and was the university's first-year advisor (FYA) coordinator.
Email: l.burnett@uws.edu.au

William Carey is Teaching and Learning Adviser within the University of Manchester's central Teaching and Learning Support Office. With specific responsibility for the operational activity of the 'Students as Partners' programme, William works directly with faculties and schools to ensure the programme's implementation through appropriate student engagement, training, consultation and staff development.
Email: william.carey@manchester.ac.uk

Andrew Casey is Academic Quality and Student Support Officer for London South Bank University's Faculty of Engineering, Science and the Built Environment. He coordinates the implementation, monitoring and enhancement of quality assurance processes within the faculty as well as working on ways to improve the student experience. Prior to this he worked for over two years in a student-facing role in Kingston University Students' Union, collaborating with the university to develop the course representation scheme and run projects on student learning, along with being part of the university's Change Academy Project team.
Email: ardcasey@gmail.com

Beverly Christy is Director of the Career Resource Center at Westminster College in Salt Lake City. She has been with the college for 20 years, 14 of which have been in this position. She is an active member of many professional organisations within the career services field. In November 2009, she was awarded the Priscilla A. Scotlan Award for Distinguished Service from the American Association for Employment in Education.
Email: bevchristy@comcast.net

Elaine Clafferty is Senior Lecturer in Analogue Electronics at Glasgow Caledonian University who has worked as a first-year tutor in engineering programmes. She has developed and

published her innovative student experience paradigm called the 'Triple C Model'. Elaine has completed external consultancies for QAA Scotland and for the HEA Engineering Subject Centre of which she is an associate.
Email: esm@gcu.ac.uk

Karen Clarke is Senior Lecturer in the School of Surveying & Planning, Kingston University, where she teaches construction and applications of construction to both undergraduates and postgraduates. As part of her role she has developed a cross-faculty academic skills centre with her colleague Maia Ibsen from Civil Engineering to enable academic skills support for all students studying construction, property and engineering courses.
Email: k.clarke@kingston.ac.uk

Kevin C. Clarke is Program Coordinator for Faculty Development and Assessment for University 101 Programs at the University of South Carolina, where he is responsible for developing and facilitating faculty training, workshops and support resources for the instructors, peer leaders and graduate leaders of the first-year seminar. In addition to teaching, Kevin is responsible for developing lesson plans, assignments and tools to further enhance the first-year seminar curriculum.
Email: kclarke@mailbox.sc.edu

Becka Colley is Dean of Students at the University of Bradford. She is passionate about the student experience and is using new technologies and social networking in order to engage with students more effectively. Her work has led to an innovative approach to skills development across the sector and includes the introduction of social networking to support student transition and the creation of a Skills and Personal Development Reflective Activity (SaPRA).
Email: b.colley@bradford.ac.uk

James Denholm-Price is from the Faculty of Computing, Information Systems and Mathematics at Kingston University (he's from the maths side) and has been a keen proponent of the pedagogical use of educational technology since becoming Learning and Teaching Coordinator in 2005. He also does research in meteorology, mathematics and computing, most recently mixing databases with HIV and parasitological data, and speech recognition technology with maths.
Email: j.denholm-price@kingston.ac.uk

Ginny DeWitt is currently serving as Associate Director of the START Center (academic advising, FYE) and Director of Disability Services for students. She has been with the college for 25 years, 15 years in the START Center and also ten years with Disability Services. She is an active member of NACADA (National Academic Advising Association) and served on the Utah Association of Orientation and Advising Advisory Board from 2006–8. She is also a member of AHEAD (Association on Higher Education and Disability).
Email: gdewitt@westminstercollege.edu

Elisabeth Dunne is Head of Project Development: Education Enhancement. She is currently directing funded projects on students as change agents, audio-feedback, developing a protocol for converting programmes to distance learning and a major project on integrating technology across the University of Exeter Business School. Her career has been devoted to the promotion of innovation, change and strategic development in education. She has coordinated and directed many major research, development and evaluation projects on aspects of learning and teaching of national interest.
Email: e.j.dunne@exeter.ac.uk

Pam Fearnley is Staff Development Coordinator for the Registrar and Secretary's Office at Leeds Metropolitan University. Pam has been employed by the university for 20 years in a variety of roles and was Project Manager of the graduation ceremonies at Leeds Metropolitan University both in the UK and Hong Kong from 2004–9. Pam was runner-up in 2007 for the AUA Award for Excellence in Higher Education and Administration and has contributed to the publication *Beyond Bureaucracy: a Practical Guide to University and College Management* (2010 Routledge).
Email: p.fearnley@leedsmet.ac.uk

Chris Ford studied geography at Kingston University and went on to be Vice President of the Students' Union for two years. He worked as Student Experience and Support Officer for engineering, working closely with Michelle Morgan to enhance the student experience. Chris's current position (Student Support Liaison within Student Services and Administration) has an overarching role of developing initiatives to integrate student support and enhance the student experience. This includes the implementation, analysis and reporting of internal student satisfaction surveys and the National Student Survey to obtain feedback from students and looking at the induction experience for new students, centrally. Chris has presented papers at several conferences on the student voice and leadership at the Association of University Administrators (AUA) and internationally at the International Convention for Student Quality Control Circles where he also received the award for Young Leader of the Year.
Email: chris.ford@kingston.ac.uk

Brad Garner is Assistant Dean for Teaching and Learning at Indiana Wesleyan University in the United States. His greatest passion is the creation of engaging instructional techniques that can be easily transported into the classroom. He authors *The Toolbox*, an electronic newsletter designed to assist faculties in the creation of engaging and motivating classroom learning experiences.
Email: brad.garne@indwes.edu

Nancy Giardina is Assistant Vice President for Academic and Student Affairs and Professor of Movement Science at Grand Valley State University. She holds a Doctorate of Education from Teachers College, Columbia University in curriculum and instruction. Her career in education spans 36 years. Throughout these years she has been engaged as a researcher, author and advisor with experience in university administration, curriculum/programme development activities, programme assessment and evaluation, as well as faculty and staff development activities. Most recently, Nancy initiated and coordinated student success initiatives to increase student persistence and timely completion of degrees. In 2009–10 she was selected as a fellow in the American Council on Education (ACE) Fellows Program.
Email: giardinn@gvsu.edu

Mary Stuart Hunter is Associate Vice President at the University of South Carolina. Her work centers on providing educators with resources to develop personal and professional skills while creating and refining innovative programs to increase undergraduate student learning and success. She is extensively published in the area of student experience. In 2001 she was honoured as the Outstanding Alumni by USC's Department of Higher Education and Student Affairs; in 2010 she was awarded a Doctor of Humane Letters degree by Queens University of Charlotte; and in 2011 was named a 'Pillar of Our Profession' in the *Journal of College Orientation and Transition* published by the National Orientation Directors Association.
Email: shunter@sc.edu

Maia Ibsen is Senior Lecturer in Civil Engineering and Construction at Kingston University. She has set up and now manages two academic skills centres to support engineering and construction students at each of their study sites. The centres provide a drop-in service where one-to-one advice and guidance can be given on draft assignments by trained student staff. This work led to winning a joint first prize university award in 2009–10.
Email: m.ibsen@kingston.ac.uk

Darlena Jones is Director of Education and Program Development for Educational Benchmarking (EBI). She received her PhD at Oklahoma State University and has been a faculty member in the physics department at both The Ohio State University and Missouri State University. Currently, Darlena conducts research on EBI's studies and has published her findings in journals such as *BizEd*, *Perspectives* and *E-SOURCE for College Transitions*.
Email: darlena@webebi.com

Glyn Jones is Head of Student Affairs in the Student Services and Administration department at Kingston University. He has experience of both being a lecturer and researcher in faculties and working in academic quality and student support services. In addition to publications in his PhD field of French administrative reform, Glyn has also written articles on student complaints and student discipline in higher education in *Perspectives* published by Routledge.
Email: g.r.jones@kingston.ac.uk

Christine Keenan is Learning and Teaching Fellow at Bournemouth University where she is involved in learning and education development and also has teaching responsibilities. Christine has been conducting research into the first-year student experience, in particular student transition to university, since 2002. The relationship between freshers and the 'university as institution' is the topic of her doctoral work. Christine's work has been disseminated widely at conferences, seminars and through consultancy work.
Email: ckeenan@bournemouth.ac.uk

Kerri-Lee Krause is Chair in Higher Education, Director of the Griffith Institute for Higher Education and Dean (Student Outcomes) at Griffith University, Australia. Her research expertise and experience spans broadly across higher education policy areas. Her particular research focus is the student experience in higher education and implications for policy and practice. She is extensively published, an award winning author and an international reviewer for the Scottish Quality Assurance Agency. She also leads a number of quality enhancement initiatives at Griffith University in areas, such as assessment and teaching quality.
Email: k.krause@griffith.edu.au

Louise Livesey is Widening Participation Officer at Stockport College. She was the first appointee of the new role within one of the North of England's largest colleges. She is responsible for pilot projects in higher education mentoring and peer mentoring, and is on the steering group for the recently launched 'Supporting Life's Journeys' national campaign to increase awareness of mentoring and befriending. She also coordinates Aimhigher Associates Scheme and organises in-house master classes for Year 10 pupils from local schools. She delivers and coordinates higher education study skills programmes for Level 3 apprentices and other students, and is a member of a national group (fdfMEG) promoting progression for Level 3 apprentices. She holds the post of Chair of the HE&A Student Council and is lead on the development of an Alumni Association.
Email: louise.livesey@stockport.ac.uk

Beverley Matthews has been working in higher education at the University of Derby for 14 years and currently heads the department responsible for student attendance monitoring and advice on progression through study. The centralised student attendance monitoring system at Derby means that Beverley works closely with academic staff and students and her work over the past two years has been in developing robust systems as a supportive mechanism for re-engaging students with study.
Email: b.j.matthews@derby.ac.uk

Tim May is Head of Student Systems as the University of Sussex. He has been in this post since 2001 and previously worked at the Coventry University. Tim spearheaded the fast-track registration process in 2002 and in 2003 he introduced direct online registration for all new undergraduate students. In 2004, he expanded the system to include all new and returning students at undergraduate and postgraduate level.
Email: t.a.may@sussex.ac.uk

Frances McNally is Team Leader of the International Student Support Service (ISSS) at Glasgow Caledonian University (GCU). An honours graduate with three years' hands-on experience supporting and working with international students, Frances is passionate about enhancing the experience of international students at GCU. The team's efforts are recognised as GCU's international students consistently rank ISSS as a top support service. They are also reigning winner of the *Times Higher Education Supplement*'s award for Outstanding Support for Overseas Students.
Email: frances.mcnally@gcu.ac.uk

Michelle Morgan is Learning and Teaching Coordinator and Student Experience Manager at Kingston University. During her career she has been a senior faculty administrative manager, researcher and academic. Her various roles have given her good insight into academic and support working practices. Michelle is a highly respected student experience practitioner both nationally and internationally. In 2004 she was 'highly commended' in the Association of University Administrators (AUA) Inaugural National Excellence Awards, in recognition of her outstanding achievements in higher education, management and administration in the field of the student experience. In 2009, she was made a fellow of the AUA.
Email: michelle.morgan@kingston.ac.uk/practitionermodel@hotmail.co.uk

Richard Mullendore is Professor of College Student Affairs Administration at the University of Georgia (UGA) and Fellow of the National Resource Center for the First-Year Experience and Students in Transition at the University of South Carolina. Richard served as a student affairs administrator for 30 years, including five years as Vice President for student affairs at UGA. He is a frequent writer, presenter, speaker and consultant on student affairs, orientation and college parents.
Email: richardm@uga.edu

Ian Munton is Head of Student Support Services at Keele University. Ian has a wide and varied remit for supporting and developing the student experience. His main areas of interest and responsibility include peer-assisted support, student transitions, responses to harassment and crisis management. He has previously worked in student services settings at the University of Sheffield, De Montfort University and the University of Birmingham.
Email: i.munton@acad.keele.ac.uk

Duncan Nulty is Senior Lecturer at the Griffith Institute for Higher Education at Griffith University, Brisbane, Australia. He has nearly 20 years of experience in teaching, course

and programme evaluation obtained in several large universities. He has also conducted many educational evaluation consultancies in Australia and overseas.
Email: d.nulty@griffith.edu.au

Diane Nutt is Learning and Teaching Consultant and University Teaching Fellow at Teesside University. She has worked closely with a range of staff across the institution to develop more holistic approaches to student support and student learning. She set up the student retention team at Teesside and has led several research projects into retention related issues, including two funded by the European Social Fund. Diane is Chair of the European First-Year Experience Conference Organising Committee; she set up the European First-Year Experience Network and is co-editor of *International Perspectives on the First-Year Experience*.
Email: diane.nutt@tees.ac.uk

Marcia Ody has worked at the University of Manchester since 2001, currently employed as a Teaching and Learning Manager within the central Teaching and Learning Support Office. The areas of work she is currently involved in include induction and transition, developing the independent learner, peer support, student initiative, student representation, student consultation and engaging students as partners in curriculum development. Marcia has an excellent national and international reputation and has disseminated her work at a number of prestigious conferences.
Email: marcia.ody@manchester.ac.uk

Diana Pace holds a PhD in psychology and serves as Associate Dean of Students at Grand Valley State University in Allendale, Michigan. She is a licensed psychologist and was Director of the Counseling Center for many years at Grand Valley State University. She is a co-founder of WISE, a living–learning community for female students in science and maths. She has received a number of awards at Grand Valley State University including the Maxine Swanson Award for Outstanding Female Staff/Faculty Member and the Administrative/Professional Award for Outstanding Staff Member. She also received the Outstanding Publication Award from Michigan College Personnel Association. She is author of *The Career Fix-It Book* (2000 Sourcebooks) and has authored a number of articles on the link between academic affairs and student affairs.
Email: paced@gvsu.edu

April L. Perry is currently finishing her PhD at the University of Canterbury in Christchurch, New Zealand. As an international student, originally from Oklahoma, USA, she is pursuing a degree in higher education within the School of Educational and Human Development Studies. Previous to pursuing her doctorate, April worked at the University of Central Oklahoma in Student Affairs and Leadership Development Programs. April is specifically researching the post-university transition of recent graduates. She is passionate about student development in the college years and lives by the motto that the only thing better than watching someone grow is helping them grow.
Email: aprilperry2@gmail.com

Gabriela Peschiera-Carl is Assistant Director of Study Abroad, International Programs, at the University of South Carolina (USC). She holds an MA degree in socio-cultural studies of education from Western Michigan University and a BA from Kalamazoo College in psychology, Spanish and Latin American studies. She has worked in the field of international education at Western Michigan University and Kalamazoo College prior to coming to the USC. At USC she has primary responsibility for developing, facilitating and coordinating faculty-led programmes in education abroad.
Email: gpcarl@sc.edu

Georgy Petrov is Senior Lecturer at Kingston Business School, Kingston University, where he teaches organisational behaviour to both undergraduates and postgraduates. Prior to joining Kingston in 2008, Georgy was a research fellow at the Centre for Leadership Studies at the University of Exeter Business School. His research interests relate to leadership and leadership development, workforce development and employer engagement with higher education and higher education reform in transitional countries.
Email: g.petrov@kingston.ac.uk

Clare Philp completed her undergraduate degree in sociology in 1997 at the University of Surrey. She has worked in higher education since then and currently works at Kingston University as a Student Affairs Advisor within the Student Services and Administration department. Clare has worked at Kingston for seven years, investigating student complaints about the university as well as responding to issues concerning student behaviour. Clare has recently jointly authored an article on challenging student behaviour for *Perspectives* published by Routledge.
Email: c.philp@kingston.ac.uk

Matthew Semple has a varied background in education and IT having worked as a school teacher and in information services at a large international bank before moving to the University of Bristol to work in student systems. Matthew has developed and implemented systems changes for Bristol's student records' database and implemented their systems for managing the new PBS processes. Matthew has recently moved to work in finance services at the University of Bristol.
Email: matthew.semple@bristol.ac.uk

Juliette Stephenson has been involved with education all her working life. She has taught adult literacy; EFL; secondary education in Ghana, inner London and rural Devon; and was previously Chair of Devon Development Education. For the past ten years she has been Head of Student Learning across disciplines and also Director of Education Economics at the University of Exeter Business School. All these contexts have in common a passion for engaging with students in their learning. She is actively involved with a number of projects, including enhancing learning and teaching with an increasingly internationalised student body.
Email: j.stephenson@exeter.ac.uk

Liz Thomas is Director of the Widening Participation Research Centre at Edge Hill University. She is also Senior Adviser for Widening Participation at the Higher Education Academy, and Lead Adviser working with institutions for Action on Access, the national widening participation coordination team for England. Liz has 12 years' experience of undertaking and managing widening participation and lifelong learning research, and is committed to using research to inform policy and practice at all levels. Liz is currently directing a three-year research and evaluation programme to improve student retention and success on behalf of the Higher Education Funding Council for England and the Paul Hamlyn Foundation. She has recently undertaken a review of widening participation strategic assessments prepared by all English higher education institutions, and contributed to a similar review in Wales in 2009. Liz is author and editor of ten books on widening participation and enhancing the student experience.
Email: liz.thomas@edgehill.ac.uk

Jayne Tidd has worked at Teesside University since 2002, where she is now Senior Lecturer in Education. She is course leader for the MA in Education and also teaches PGCE students.

Her research centres on the study of non-traditional students in higher education, an interest which has been informed by her own prior experience as a mature student. She has both published and presented on a variety of issues relating to the scholarship of learning and teaching, both in the UK and further afield.
Email: j.tidd@tees.ac.uk

Christopher Tucker has worked for the University of Sussex for eight years as the Residential Student Support Manager and in the field of higher education for over 13 years both in the UK and the US. Christopher began his career in academia as a residential advisor many years ago and has since worked both for university managed accommodation and student housing association settings. Currently he manages the welfare and discipline of 4,300 residential students supported by a team of 90 residential advisors. Christopher also has an MSc in mediation and conflict resolution and provides dispute resolution training at student housing associations and universities across the UK.
Email: c.tucker@sussex.ac.uk

Margaret Ward has worked in student support services within the HE sector for the past 16 years, having spent the last six years at Glasgow Caledonian University (GCU), in the roles of Head of International Student Support Service and, presently, Student Advice and Wellbeing Services Manager. Margaret is dedicated to developing and managing the wellbeing services, i.e. for the International Student Support, Funding, Disability and Health and Wellbeing Service and recognising and ensuring the delivery of exceptional student support services to all GCU students, so they sense a truly memorable student experience.
Email: margaret.ward@gcu.ac.uk

Marion Webb joined Kingston University in 1997 and became Head of Learning and Teaching Development in 2006. Marion leads a National Teaching Fellowship project called 'Outduction: improving the final year experience'. Marion is on the executive committee of the Staff and Educational Development Association (SEDA) and the general council of South East England Consortium (SEEC). She has published on the links between widening participation and learning and teaching at the institutional level and on foundation degrees. Before joining Kingston, Marion worked in further education where she was involved in teacher education and staff development.
Email: m.webb@kingston.ac.uk

Emma Weber is Program Coordinator in the Office of Global Education and Partnerships at Millersville University, Pennsylvannia. She is responsible for working with outgoing and inbound study abroad students (from initial interest to re-entry post-study abroad: 'soup to nuts'); working with exchange partners that Millersville University has established to grow links and increase the number of students studying abroad (both outgoing and inbound); and she helps facilitate international faculty visits from existing and potential partner institutions.
Email: emma.weber@millersville.edu

Wendy J. Wenner is Dean of the Brooks College of Interdisciplinary Studies at Grand Valley State University. Her research focuses on the eighteenth-century novel and teaching of reading and writing. As Associate Provost at Grand Valley she was responsible for improvements in student retention, leading the university's First-Year Retention Task Force and supporting the university's Greater Expectations and Claiming a Liberal Education initiatives.
Email: wennerw@gvsu.edu

Andrew West is Director of Student Services at the University of Sheffield. His remit has a wide scope covering the whole student 'journey' including recruitment, registry and student support. Andrew is the Vice Chair of the Association of University Administrators (AUA) and the Chair of AMOSSHE, the student services organisation. Andrew has published a number of professional journal articles on HE management issues, including a chapter on strategy in student services within UNESCO's 2009 guide to best practice in student affairs.
Email: a.west@sheffield.ac.uk

Patricia Willer is Associate Vice President for International Programs at the University of South Carolina. She holds masters and bachelor degrees from the University of Kansas and has worked in international education for 25 years. She has served professionally in leadership roles and has recently been named Chair for the NAFSA: Association of International Educators annual conference in 2012. Her most recent publication appears in *Student Affairs and Services in Higher Education: Global Foundations, Issues and Best Practices* (2009 UNESCO).
Email: pwiller@sc.edu

Laurie Witucki has been teaching organic and bioorganic chemistry at Grand Valley State University since 2000. She is the author of numerous scientific papers in bioorganic chemistry and has won several awards during her tenure at Grand Valley including the GVSU Outstanding Teaching Award (2004) and the GVSU Women's Impact Award (2009). Her interests are in the education of women in the sciences and providing a positive academic experience for female students as they enter and progress through college. She established the first all-female living and learning community at Grand Valley in 2006 (WISE).
Email: wituckil@gvsu.edu

Trudi Woodhouse completed an undergraduate degree in multimedia and women's studies at the University of Gloucestershire. Since then she has gained ten years' experience of working at UCAS: as a customer service adviser, a curriculum database officer and, for the past three years, as a multimedia editor. Her job involves providing editorial for UCAS' written publications and online information, aimed at higher education applicants, universities and colleges, advisers and parents.
Email: t.woodhouse@ucas.ac.uk

Sherry A. Woosley is Associate Director of Institutional Effectiveness at Ball State University. She is responsible for numerous university-wide assessment activities and provides assessment consulting to academic and student affairs departments. She has overseen the MAP-Works project at Ball State for more than ten years and has been actively involved in the on-going development of MAP-Works at a national level. Formally the Associate Director of Institutional Effectiveness at Ball State University, Sherry joined EBI as the Director of Analytics and Research in 2011.
Email: swoosley@webebi.com

Acknowledgements

To my first boss, Professor Gordon McBeth, who helped shape the way I think about higher education.

To Mary Stuart, who, all those years ago, had the vision to create a Student Experience Manager post and to employ me in that role!

To Peter Mason and Akbar Aboutorabi; thank you for trusting me to do my job and believing in the importance of the student experience. Your passion and support made my job so much easier.

To Professor Julius Weinberg; thank you for taking the time to provide valuable feedback.

To my family and friends for all their love and support but especially to Anne and Mrs P, Mark, David and Zoe, Rob and Anne, JanJan, Lucy, Jan and Mike, Steve, Sue and Prof Townsend.

And lastly, a huge thank you to Professor Sally Brown for having the faith in me to write this book and being a fantastic mentor.

Foreword

Michelle Morgan was a contributing author to a volume I co-edited with Steve Denton, *A Practical Guide to University and College Management: Beyond Bureaucracy*. The quality of her writing was such that I encouraged her to consider editing a book of her own, and so I am delighted to welcome here the fruits of her endeavours.

The volume is timely, written at a period when universities globally are rethinking the ways in which we support students in higher education. International competition for students is strong at a point in time when Anglophone universities can no longer assume a monopoly of students wishing to study in English and when students (and their fee-paying parents) are querying, ever more frequently, the value that is being provided to learners in the course of their studies.

This book's focus on how best to enhance experiences across the student lifecycle, from initial enquiry about programmes until graduates' emergence into the wider world, provides useful guidance to managers, administrators, faculty academics and members of professional services teams including those working in student support, libraries, disability services, IT services and quality assurance.

The proposed Student Experience Practitioner Model will be invaluable to all who are involved in systematically planning how best to engage students and to foster their effective learning. Much has been written to good effect in recent years on improving the first-year experience, but this book takes a holistic approach to the whole undergraduate experience, proposing a toolbox of interventions at each stage within the lifecycle. The benefit to students from such an approach is likely to be substantial and this, in turn, will lead to market advantage as students become better satisfied with their studies.

Invaluable practical guidance and advice is provided by thoughtful and experienced contributors from the UK, Australia and the United States, who draw on extensive relevant literature to support their arguments. Scholarship is supported by invaluable case studies, which demonstrate how theory is implemented in practice, offering realm solutions to live and current issues.

It has been a pleasure to watch this volume develop from proposal to publication, and to review its development from idea to execution under the guiding hand of the capable and engaging editor. I commend this volume to readers, hoping you will benefit from reading it as much as I have from monitoring it in the course of production.

Sally Brown
Emeritus Professor, Leeds Metropolitan University (UK)
Adjunct Professor, University of the Sunshine Coast (Queensland, Australia)
Visiting Professor, University of Plymouth (UK)

Preface

My motivation for writing this book has been to provide colleagues who are responsible for improving the student experience, whether it is in a particular area or across the entire student lifecycle, with a working manual that is interesting to read and helpful in their work.

For many years, I have been responsible for developing practical initiatives to improve the student experience for a diverse student body across the student lifecycle. Although there is a lot of research and advice available on improving the student experience, I have struggled over the years to find an array of published practical initiatives that cover all areas and stages of the student lifecycle as well as information and guidance to help me, as a practitioner, to organise and structure my work.

My response has been to develop the Student Experience Practitioner Model which enables me to organise and map out the different types of support I need to provide to different students at particular times throughout their journey at university or college. It is a model that I have developed over the years as the student body I have been responsible for has grown and diversified. I have used my administrative, academic, research and managerial knowledge and experience to develop the model. I hope that as you read through the book, you understand the reasons for the 'stages' in the Student Experience Practitioner Model and how the 'themes' enable the practitioner to develop initiatives by addressing a range of questions and interlinking critical activities.

The practical case studies that I have selected for each stage and theme in the Student Experience Practitioner Model have been done on the basis of transferability and adaptability between different types of students and institutions. Although each case study has been allocated a stage or activity within the book, each one cuts across the different stages, themes and activities.

I hope that you find this book interesting to read and helpful in your work, and that the Student Experience Practitioner Model provides you with a valuable structure, as it has done me, in helping to improve the student experience.

Michelle Morgan

Part I

Setting the scene

Introduction

Higher education (HE) has changed dramatically in the past 30 years and it continues to evolve and change. Globally, more students than ever before are entering HE and attending university (university or college) at undergraduate and postgraduate level (UNESCO, 2009). The increase in diversity of the student body entering HE in terms of social background, age, gender and race, plus changes in curriculum design, delivery, assessment and evaluation has added complexity to the delivery of the efficient and effective provision of HE. It is no longer acceptable, if it ever was, to treat students entering this level of study as a homogenous group. Nor can we assume that what students need if they are to thrive, is what they received in the past.

Supporting and enhancing the 'student experience' throughout the student lifecycle (from first contact through to becoming alumni) is critical to success in higher education today for both the student and the institution. The student experience encompasses all aspects of student life (i.e. academic, social, welfare and support) with the academic imperative at the heart of it. As the HE market becomes increasingly competitive and as students become more demanding and better informed, providing an excellent quality student experience is crucial to organisational survival. It can increase the 'retention' of students by reducing withdrawal rates and aiding student progression as well as being pivotal to a higher education institution's (HEI) ability to attract students. However, the increasing costs of delivering HE, the reduction in government/state funding and resource constraints means delivering an excellent quality student experience has never been more challenging.

In recent years, undergraduate research and initiatives looking at the student experience have tended to focus on the 'first-year' experience (with subsequent years being neglected); learning and teaching or assessment and feedback. However, there is increasing recognition that the student experience involves more than just the first-year and 'academic' experience (Tinto, 2006; Thomas and Quinn, 2006; Morgan and Brown, 2009; Hunter *et al.*, 2010).

The aim of this book

This book will assist managers, academics and members of the professional service teams within universities to improve the student experience throughout the entire student lifecycle. It is a working manual and introduces a new model, the 'Student Experience Practitioner Model' that interlinks the key activities of academic, welfare and support. There are

40 practical case studies outlining real solutions to actual problems. The introductory chapter identifies those involved in improving and enhancing the student experience; it explains the purpose and direction of the book and describes why the landscape of HE today is so different to that of 30 years ago. It is essential that senior university managers, who were educated at a time before mass participation in HE, recognise the situation facing modern students today and understand that students, their family, friends and society will critically appraise their entire university experience.

Chapter 1

The context of learning in higher education

Michelle Morgan, Kingston University, UK

Who improves and enhances the student experience within HE?

As students progress through the student lifecycle at university, they need a range of academic and personal services plus advice and support in order to succeed. This requires the input, collaboration and coordination of a range of key service providers consisting of academic and professional service staff (non-academic staff) from across an institution at university level, and also the student's academic home unit with whom they tend to identify (referred to as the home unit hereafter). The home unit can be at faculty, department, school or course level. Professional service staff, although not directly involved in the academic strand of the student experience are essential contributors through their various roles and functions, such as student support and student funding.

Enhancing the student experience today is an important activity for all staff within HE. With the increasing pressures on HE, such as increased student numbers and declining resources, trying to improve and enhance the experience of the undergraduate student across the student lifecycle is often challenging, frustrating and confusing for staff. The student expects and demands support, advice and guidance which meets their specific needs (academic and personal) throughout their studies. For an institution that may have between 8,000 and 20,000 other students for whom they also need to provide a quality student experience, this is not only a major challenge but can seem impossible. There is the danger that an institution will minimise a change in student experience strategy if it does not appear to offer immediate monetary gain.

There are also contested themes within HE today. There is a growing concept of the student being a 'customer' rather than a 'consumer' of education, and a drive for students to be 'clients' and 'partners' with their institutions in their learning process. This is a substantial move away from the traditional delivery of HE. However, the benefits of making the student and institution face up to their joint responsibilities are beneficial to both. They must recognise that there is a myriad of issues, pressures and challenges in delivering and enjoying an excellent quality student experience.

Providing targeted individual support that leaves the student satisfied is a complex activity to comprehend and deliver. As a result, it is understandable why an institution, central support units or the student's home unit may adopt the fall-back position of the 'one size fits all' approach. This limited approach enables them to provide a range of basic services to all students as well as being seen to be doing 'something' to improve the student experience. However, this is not suitable for today's HE environment or the needs of the modern student.

The practitioner in higher education

Staff at all levels, and across all areas within an institution, are developing and implementing initiatives to improve and enhance the student experience whether they are directly engaging with students or on the periphery, thus making them all 'practitioners' in the student experience. This could include the admissions administrator improving the information available for potential applicants; the academic improving his/her feedback to students; or central welfare departments ensuring that their services are being advertised and supported within a student's home unit. Often, these changes are small and incremental and they have occurred because of feedback arising out of a specific activity by certain groups, such as students, staff or applicants. Sometimes, initiatives are university-wide and large scale, driven by external and internal requirements. Both processes can be informed by internal, national and international research and both make an important contribution to improving and enhancing the student experience. Regardless of how small or large the initiative, it is critical that any changes are at the very minimum communicated to all key service providers, staff and students and at best, and that all the key service providers are involved in the planning stage.

Purpose and direction of this book and how it can help the practitioner

The practitioner faces a huge challenge in delivering a high-quality student experience at all levels. This book will provide the practitioner with practical guidance and advice in improving the undergraduate student experience across academic, welfare and support areas. Although the case studies presented in this book are drawn from undergraduate initiatives, many can also be adapted and applied to the postgraduate student experience. The author plans to review specific postgraduate examples in a future publication.

Although there is a massive body of research which outlines the issues and problems facing higher education now (e.g. access; the first-year experience; retention and completion; and entrenching knowledge and skills) there:

- is limited research on improving the student experience across every stage of the student lifecycle;
- are few models to help the practitioner manage the student experience in, through and out of every stage of the student lifecycle;
- are few focused and dedicated practitioners' guides or handbooks designed to provide examples of good quality and evidence-based initiatives across the student lifecycle that are relevant today.

This book aims to address these issues and to be an instrument in the toolbox of the practitioner for enhancing and improving the student experience at all levels and areas within an institution. This book will provide the practitioner with:

- a brief overview of how higher education has changed, and its impact on the practitioner and the next generation of students;
- a concise way of delivering 'interlinked' academic, welfare and support activities at faculty/department/school/course and university level to support the student in their university journey;

- a new Student Experience Practitioner Model to help practitioners navigate through the maze of student diversity across all levels of study, determining what to deliver, how to deliver it and to whom;
- a range of UK and international academic, welfare and support case studies outlining real solutions that colleagues have developed to overcome actual problems they have experienced in improving and enhancing the student experience across the undergraduate student lifecycle. These case studies cover many different scenarios commonly experienced by practitioners across an institution and have been specifically chosen for their transferability and adaptability for a diverse student body;
- a positive and proactive approach to managing the student experience and future development;
- a review of texts and sources by key authors in the area so that readers can improve and enhance their knowledge and understanding of issues relating to the student experience.

Contributors have been drawn from the UK, the USA and Australia where the student experience movement is well established. The educational structures in these countries are broadly similar in terms of the composition of the student body and university structures, although there will obviously be disparity between environments and the backgrounds of students between institutions and countries. The Student Experience Practitioner Model has been developed as a result of research in the field and practical experience by the editor. For the rest of the book, the Student Experience Practitioner Model will be referred to as the 'Practitioner Model'.

The structure of the book

This book is a collection of 13 chapters. This chapter outlines the changes that have occurred in HE in the past few years and how it has impacted on the student experience and student retention. Chapter 2 will explain the rationale behind the Practitioner Model and its delivery.

The remaining chapters in Parts 2 and 3 that make up the main body of the book have been organised specifically to explore the particular stages, themes and core activities in the Practitioner Model. Each chapter contains an introduction and conclusion by a leading authority in the area who will introduce four practitioners' case studies.

This book is not designed to be an overview of the research undertaken in the field but chapter authors highlight any relevant research where appropriate. The book does not cover aspiration activities for 14–18-year-old students (see HEFCE, 2001; Thomas and Slack, 1999) or best assessment and feedback practices (see Race, 2010; Gibbs, 2010), as these areas already have a vast range of dedicated texts. However, details of some of these have been included in the further reading list at the back of this book for those wishing to explore further detailed texts relating to accessibility, retention and withdrawal rates, and student success. It also includes key texts by the founding father of the student experience, Vincent Tinto (USA), as well as other prominent researchers including Liz Thomas, Mantz Yorke, Thomas Woodrow and David Watson (UK), Kerri-Lee Krause, Craig McInnis, Michael Long and Margaret Heagney (Australia) and Mary Stuart Hunter, John Gardner and Richard Mullendore (USA).

The changing face of the HE student body

To put our challenges as practitioners into context, it is useful to have a broad overview of how the student of today is different from that of ten years ago. As a practitioner, I strongly suggest that practitioners can only improve the experience of the undergraduate student if they understand the student body entering university today, the educational system they have come from and are about to enter and the nature of the courses offered.

There are two major changes in HE impacting on us as practitioners. The first is massification. Since the 1970s, higher education in the Western world has massified (Trow, 1973). The biggest global expansion in higher education as a result of governments' commitment to widening access to HE has occurred since the late 1990s (UNESCO, 2009). For many governments, their commitment to higher education is the result of them seeking to improve their industrial competitive global position (DTI, 1998) and their position in the global market of higher education (DfES, 2003). The latter phenomenon has arisen 'due to the increasing mobility of students and graduates worldwide' (Kumar, 2008:5).

However, some argue that 'education within a competitive global economy can encourage new forms of racial and social exclusion' (Tomlinson, 2003:213) and that:

> The perception of higher education as an industry for enhancing national competiveness and as a lucrative service that can be sold in the global market place has begun to eclipse the social and cultural objectiveness of higher education generally encompassed in the conception of higher education as a 'public good'.
>
> (Naidoo, 2003:250)

Massification

Massification of higher education has been a global phenomenon with the biggest increase between 2000 and 2008 with 51.7 million new students enrolling (UNESCO, 2009). Thirty years ago, one in two students in higher education studied in North America or western Europe. Today, they only account for one in every four students (UNESCO, 2009). In the UK in the 1960s, approximately seven per cent of the population went to university (Pugsley, 2004). In 2010, the percentage of 18–30 year olds participating in HE was 45 per cent (DBIS, 2010). In Australia, the participation rate in 2000 was 33.5 per cent (DEST, 2002).

Massification leads to more graduates. More graduates result in there being a larger pool from which employers can recruit. Wolf (in Wakeling, 2005:506) suggests that the massification of undergraduate degrees is the reason for the increase in the postgraduate population because 'as the bachelor degree becomes ubiquitous, its relative advantage in the labour market is diminishing'.

Wide-ification

The second change is that HE has experienced what I call *wide-ification*, which is the widening of the student body in terms of demographics. The undergraduate student body today, both nationally and internationally, is more diverse than ever before in terms of student demographics, study mode and entry qualifications. Consequently, this has added to the complexity of enhancing and improving the student experience for practitioners. Thirty years ago, practitioners only had to contend with home students from a limited range of backgrounds and ability, and no concept of the student experience. By contrast, today's practitioners have to develop initiatives, provide support and deliver a quality student experience for a diverse student population which includes 'students from different ethnic groups and non-English speaking backgrounds, international, lower socio-economic backgrounds, mature aged students, students with disabilities, as well those for whom higher education is the first family experience' (Crosling *et al.*, 2008:1).

Change in study patterns

For a variety of reasons, including the need to supplement study loans with paid work, family responsibilities, gaining valuable skills and the cost of higher education, students are increasingly deciding to study in a more flexible manner undertaking part-time degrees; taking gap years; studying as a distance or work-based learner; entering university partway through a degree as a direct-entry or transfer student; and repeating levels to improve grades or correct failures. Part-time study is a particular mode of learning that is on the increase. In 2009/10, 43 per cent of the undergraduate study body in the UK was studying part-time (HESA, 2010), with the largest increase of 45 per cent occurring between 1996 and 2008 (DIUS, 2009). In Australia, the percentage studying part-time at undergraduate level is similar to that of the UK. As the cost of studying for a traditionally delivered university qualification continues to increase, flexible study modes will continue to be in demand.

Students today live more complex lives and, as McInnis suggests, the increase in the 'number of activities and priorities that compete with the demands of university' (McInnis, 2001:4) means that students are spending less time on campus. The traditional university experience of 30 years ago is not the norm for many students today and this fact may not be appreciated by older university academic and administrative staff.

Entry qualifications

Better access and continuation on to secondary education has increased the access to higher education across the world (UNESCO, 2009). The traditional pre-entry university qualifications have changed in terms of teaching style and assessment whether they are A levels in the UK, SATs and ACTs in the USA, or UAI, ENTER and TER qualifications in Australia. Rote learning is a common teaching and learning style, coursework has increased as a means of assessment and there is a different approach to analytical and critical thinking skills. This means that students entering HE via a traditional entry qualification route are entering with a skills base that is different from that traditionally required by a university, resulting in a skills gap.

Students are also entering university with a range of non-traditional qualifications. In the UK, during 1989–90, 77 per cent of all home-domiciled students on entry to full-time and sandwich first degree courses held A levels. By the mid-nineties, it was only 62 per cent (McGivney, 2003). This change is common across the HE sector and has been encouraged by the widening participation agenda of many governments' to increase the proportion of students from lower socio-economic groups and from other groups underrepresented in HE. Unfortunately, in the UK and Australia, the socio-economic data of students entering university shows that, despite government intentions, increased participation in HE has been due to the engagement of the middle classes and not the lower socio-economic groups which has remained relatively stable (James, 2002; DIUS, 2009). The diversity in entry qualifications means that many institutions have a course cohort with a very diverse academic skills base. The challenge for institutions and practitioners is to bridge the skills gap so that students don't fail in making the successful transition from school or college to higher education, nor are they left behind their peers, or hindered in their studies.

Student mobility

The mass expansion of HE across the world has enabled students to become mobile and access education on a global scale. Students are increasingly choosing to study for a quali-fication, or undertake a placement abroad, for a range of reasons including broadening their horizons; pursuing a particular course; wishing to study at an internationally recog-nised institution; or to escape difficult situations in their home country. However, mobility opportunities for poor students are likely to be restricted and the evidence suggests that women are less mobile than men due to expectations, family responsibilities and finan-cial issues (European Commission, 2007). The number of mobile students has grown by 53 per cent since 1999 (UNESCO, 2009). The top two countries that send students to study abroad are China, followed by India, and the largest host countries of mobile students are the USA followed by the UK (UNESCO, 2009).

Feminisation

In the past few years, there has also been a feminisation of higher education due to massification and wide-ification. Parity within HE, on a global scale of male and female participation, was reached in 2003 (UNESCO, 2009) although this is not the case in every country. Leathwood and Read state that 'in the vast majority of "developed" countries and those in transition, women are in the majority, though in sub-Saharan Africa, South and West Asia, and East Asia, men remain in the majority' (Leathwood and Read, 2009:29). Despite global parity, global gender subject stratification remains entrenched with women representing less than one-quarter of engineering, manufacturing and construction students and just over one-third of agricul-ture and science students. But over two-thirds study education, health and welfare (UNESCO, 2009). However, there are some countries where these statistics are higher than the global average: in Denmark, Pakistan and Kuwait, women in the engineering, manufacture and con-struction subjects constitute between 38 and 50 per cent (European Commission, 2007).

Standards of entry qualifications and university degrees

Discussion surrounding the educational levels of entry qualifications to HE, and the standard of degrees today, occurs across the sector and in the media. There is a lot of sensitivity around these issues and any suggestion that both have declined in standards is not well received. However, due to adjustments in primary and secondary educational approaches, it has to be accepted by institutions and governments that there has been a shift in the skills base and entry qualifications of students and, as a result, we need to adapt our practices to meet this change. This may be the reason why Anderson *et al.* suggest 'the general perception of academics is that standards are lower than they were ten or 20 years ago' (Anderson *et al.*, 2002:36). Students also need to realise that university study is another rung on the ladder of lifelong learning. A degree is no longer a passport to an automatic, well-paid graduate job.

The student body

Students entering university as a result of wide-ification routes are often referred to as 'non-traditional' or 'non-standard' students. However, these terms will become redundant as the definition of the 'traditional' student changes. Non-traditional students bring a myriad of experiences and knowledge to their student experience, thus enriching the whole process, but they also bring challenges to their institution in its efforts to provide a high-quality student experience. The student body today comprises of students from the 'Baby Boomer' generation (born mid-1940s to mid-1960s), 'Generation X' (born mid-1960s to early 1980s) and the 'Millennial' generation (born early 1980s to 2000). These students bring to university different skills in using and understanding technology and varying life experiences. This can create tensions not only between students but also between students and lecturers and support staff. For example, the Generation X student may feel that the Millennial student is not as committed to their studies or engaged in group project work as they are. The Baby Boomer student, who has worked in business for many years, may feel that they are more qualified to teach the subject of business than the lecturer who has only ever worked in a university, teaching business studies.

The changes in the student body has impacted on the way institutions have evolved and function, whether that means increasing the intake numbers on certain courses, or providing specific support. It is clear that in HE today, one size no longer fits all, and it is not possible to teach a massified and diversified student body in the same way a small percentage of the population was taught years ago.

Completion rates

With the increase in student diversity and the number of students starting university, the probability of withdrawal or non-completion increases. As a result, 'a significant concern in higher education is the retention of students in their studies. Institutions world-wide are under pressure to reduce the rates of students "dropping out", and develop new and innovative means that encourage students to continue' (Crosling *et al.*, 2008:1).

Obtaining accurate data on the real scale of non-completion is difficult because it can be a very sensitive issue. Understandably, institutions are reluctant to release the data because of the financial and political implications (Kember, 1995; McGiveny, 2003). The definitions and the registering of student withdrawal and success differ between countries as does the way statistics are recorded (Crosling *et al.*, 2008). This makes an accurate comparison of student withdrawal very difficult. Although institutions often lose a large proportion of new students within the first few weeks at university, withdrawal occurs at all levels and throughout the student lifecycle. The reasons for student withdrawal are complex and diverse.

Withdrawal from university studies can be due to a range of factors, including:

- poor subject or course choice or institutional fit;
- course structure (e.g. level of study, length of course, mode of study);
- student demographics (e.g. age, gender, social class, ethnic background, domiciled status);
- previous educational experience (e.g. disengagement with educational environment, poor-quality qualifications);

- an inadequate university experience (e.g. poor-quality and weak management of the student experience);
- personal reasons (e.g. finance, bereavement, illness, balancing demands of study with life, cultural conflict).

We need to take into account that the student experience is a personal and unique experience. Each student's personality, life experience, study experience and future plans will all impact on how successfully they make the transition in, through and out of every stage of their studies.

Rarely is it just one factor that causes withdrawal from university study. It is often a combination of factors, therefore it is important when developing initiatives to take a holistic view of the various reasons. As McInnis *et al.* state:

> From the variety of studies ... it is clear that student withdrawal is a complex and often very individualised process involving the interplay of institutional, social and personal factors. Identifying single factors influencing withdrawal is risky since the research consistently demonstrates that it is rarely the case that any one factor is the cause for a given student deciding to leave.
>
> (McInnis *et al.*, 2000:1)

Also, 'the mix of reasons that come into effect largely relates to the students' stage of life, with different reasons more important for younger and for older students' (Long *et al.*, 2006:168).

Pressure on higher education

The changes identified above have increased pressures on the delivery of higher education. They include:

- infrastructure (social, academic space, effective information systems);
- increased expectations of students and staff;
- conflicting demands on staff to respond to the needs of a diverse student body;
- the ability to provide excellent quality learning and teaching to large cohorts;
- the increased and effective utilisation of technology to support and meet the needs of all students.

How do we improve and enhance the student experience?

There are three key aspects which are critical for the practitioner in delivering a high-quality and holistic student experience. The first is that we have to support and inform students as they progress in, through and out of every stage of their academic and personal journey at university from first contact until they become alumni. Each part of the lifecycle needs to be interlinked and joined so there is a seamless progression from one stage to the next. This will be discussed in greater detail in Chapter 2.

The second important aspect to understand is that for our work as practitioners to be truly effective, services, advice, guidance and support at the university and home unit level (whether they are academic-, welfare- or support-based) must not operate in isolation or in one direction. We need to avoid providing and delivering advice, guidance and support:

- only to specific groups of students (dyslexic, mature, disabled, weak entry qualifications);
- only via central services only (e.g. academic support, student services, registry, Students' Union);
- by expecting students to seek out the support themselves.

These approaches will not meet the expectations or needs of most students nor provide a satisfying experience for them or staff. Key service providers need to talk to one another, and cooperate, coordinate and join up their activities. Examples illustrating this can be found below.

Example 1 Validation of a new course

The validation process should not concentrate only on the academic content. It should take into account all aspects of the student experience. If a new course aims to deliver a part-time course to students in the evening, the validation process should consider other questions such as:

- will the library have the resources to support the course by stocking enough books or having flexible opening hours?
- will the students have access to a canteen for food and drink during lesson breaks?
- what welfare and support services should this cohort of students be entitled to and how will they access them?
- if the university is situated in a place where there is minimal car parking and limited public transport, how will students get to and from the institution?

To lay the foundations of a satisfying student experience, the validation of a course requires input from a range of key service providers, including the learning resources (library) and catering managers, the estates department (for transport and security), and the welfare and support units as well as the academic team who have designed the content and structure of the course.

Example 2 Distribution of disability information and support

The disability unit within institutions tends to be centrally based and although it has a lot of direct contact with students who have support needs, it also needs to work closely with the home unit in identifying, assessing and supporting students with learning requirements. Although many students are aware of disability issues pre-entry, some students do not discover they have support needs until they start university. Activities to be considered should include:

- training to help colleagues within a home unit identify students with disability issues post-entry;
- support and training for academic colleagues in designing inclusive assessments instead of separate assessments for students with disabilities;
- reminding students at regular intervals of the support available;

- raising student awareness of special needs to increase the recognition of characteristics of students with these special needs and to inspire tolerance of them;
- the availability of on-site disability and medical support.

Collaboration will help develop and implement those needs via the curriculum and assessment process as well as effectively disseminating information and raising awareness about the disability unit and its role.

Example 3 The admissions process

Whether the admissions process is run and operated centrally, or by the home unit, the admissions process must involve both. It is important for the home unit to begin to build a relationship with their applicants from first contact.

Activities that should be considered include:

- running joint admissions/open days;
- ensuring that admissions and pre-arrival information is consistent and complementary;
- a seamless transfer of the student experience responsibility to the home unit after completion of the full admissions process.

Students are now very aware of information given and implied by the home unit and university websites, and their decisions on their HE course can be based on such advertising.

Successful collaboration between units should enable the effective transition of the applicant from the admissions and pre-entry stages into their studies as a student.

Conclusion

Unfortunately, it is all too common for key service providers from across an institution not to consult and collaborate. There can be the assumption that someone else is taking responsibility for the 'bigger picture' or that their involvement is not necessary. This results in a poor student experience. This is not only detrimental for the students but it affects the morale of university colleagues.

The final aspect, which is the most critical, is how do we effectively combine aspects 1 and 2 (see page 10)? How do we join up the dots of the academic and personal journey of the student with an effective and efficient service provision involving all key players? Chapter 2 will address these questions with an explanation of the Practitioner Model.

References

Anderson, D., Johnson, R. and Saha, L. (2002) *Changes in Academic Work Implications for Universities of the Changing Age: Distribution and Work Roles of Academic Staff*, Canberra: Commonwealth of Australia.

Crosling, G., Thomas, L. and Heaney, M. (2008) 'Student success and retention', in G. Crosling, L. Thomas and M. Heaney (eds) *Improving Student Retention in Higher Education: The Role of Teaching and Learning*, London: Routledge.

Department for Business, Innovation and Skills (2010). Online. Available at: http://stats.berr.gov.uk/he/Participation_Rates_in_HE_2008-09.pdf (accessed 25 November 2009).

Department of Education Science and Training (2002) *Higher Education at the Cross Roads*, Canberra: DEST.

Department of Education and Skills (2003) *Widening Participation in Higher Education*, London: DfES.

Department for Innovation, Universities and Skills (2009) *Students and Universities: The Eleventh Report of Session 2008–9*, London: DIUS.

Department of Trade and Industry (1998) 'Building the knowledge driven economy'. Online. Available at: http://www.berr.gov.uk/files/file32392.pdf (accessed 25 November 2009).

European Commission (2007) *Key Data on Higher Education In Europe*, Luxembourg: European Commission.

Gibbs, G. (2010) *Using Access to Support Student Learning*, Leeds: Leeds Metropolitan University.

Higher Education Funding Council for England (2001) *Strategies for Widening Participation in Higher Education: A Guide to Good Practice*, Bristol: HEFCE.

Higher Education Statistics Agency (2010) 'Students in 2009/10 by mode and level'. Online. Available at: http://www.hesa.ac.uk/index.php?option=com_content&task=view&id=1897&Itemid=239 (accessed 9 March 2011).

Hunter, M.S., Tobolowsky, B.F. and Gardner, J.N. (2010) *Helping Sophomores Succeed: Understanding and Improving the Second Year Experience*, San Francisco: Jossey-Bass.

James, R. (2002) *Socioeconomic Background and Higher Education Participation: An Analysis of School Students' Aspirations and Expectations*, Canberra: DEST.

Kember, D. (1995) *Opening Learning Courses for Adults: A Model of Student Progress*, Englewood Cliffs, New Jersey: Education Technology Publications.

Kumar, A. (2008) *Personal, Academic and Career Development in Higher Education: Soaring to Success*, London: Routledge.

Leathwood, C. and Read, B. (2009) *Gender and the Changing Face of Education*, Maidenhead: Open University Press.

Long, M., Ferrier, F. and Heagney, M. (2006) *Stay, Play or Give it Away? Students Continuing, Changing or Leaving University Study in First Year*, Canberra: DEST.

McGiveny, V. (2003) *Staying or Leaving the Course: Non-completion and Retention of Mature Students in Further and Higher Education*, Leicester: NIACE.

McInnis, C. (2001) *Signs of Disengagement? The Changing Undergraduate Experience in Australian Universities*, Melbourne: Centre for the Study of Higher Education, University of Melbourne.

McInnis, C., Hartley, R., Polesel, J. and Teese, R. (2000) *Non-completion in Vocational Education and Training and Higher Education: A Literature Review*, Canberra: Department of Education Training and Youth Affairs.

Morgan, M. and Brown, S. (2009) 'Commencement of the academic year', in Denton, S. and Brown, S. (eds) *Beyond Bureacracy: A Practical Guide to University and College Management*, London: Routledge.

Naidoo, R. (2003) 'Repositioning higher education as a global commodity: opportunities and challenges for future sociology of education work', *British Journal of Sociliogy of Education*, 24 (2): 249–59.

Pugsley, L. (2004) *The University Challenge: Higher Education Markets and Social Stratification*, Hants: Ashgate Publishing.

Race, P. (2010) *Making Learning Happen: A Guide for Post-compulsory Education*, London: Sage Publications.

Tinto, V. (2006) 'Resaerch and practice of college student retention: what next?' *Journal of College Student Retention*, 8 (1): 1–19.

Thomas, L. and Slack, K. (1999) *Evaluation of Aiming High 1999*, Stoke-on-Trent: Institute for Access Studies, Staffordshire University.

Thomas, L. and Quinn, J. (2006) *First Generation Entry into Higher Education: An International Study*, Buckingham: SRHE and Open University Press.

Tomlinson, S. (2003) 'Globalisation, race and education: continuity and change', *Journal of Educational Change*, 4: 213–30.

Trow, M. (1973) *Problems in the Transition from Elite to Mass Higher Education*, New York: Carnegie Commission on Higher Education.

United Nations Educational, Scientific and Cultural Organisation (2008) *Global Education Digest: Comparing Education Statistics Across the World*, Canada: UNESCO Institute for Statistics.

United Nations Educational, Scientific and Cultural Organisation (2009) *Global Education Digest: Comparing Education Statistics Across the World*, Canada: UNESCO Institute for Statistics.

Wakeling, P. (2005) 'La noblesse d'état anglasie? Social class and progression to postgraduate study', *British Journal of Sociology of Education*, 26 (4): 505–22.

Chapter 2

The Student Experience Practitioner Model

Michelle Morgan, Kingston University, UK

The challenges for the practitioner

Student success and completion is important for the student and the institution both in terms of reputation and finances. The aim is for the student to have the best possible experience at university and for the institution to experience low withdrawal and high completion rates in all the different study modes. In order to achieve this, it is important that as Noel and Levitz (in Low, 2002) state, 'retention is not a goal, retention is the result of high quality learning and professional development experiences on campus'.

As the cost of higher education increases for both student and institution, it is understandable that there is a high expectation by students to receive value for money. As Eastwood argues, 'if we are expecting students to pay high fees, they will expect higher quality not lower' (Eastwood, 2010). As a result, 'the growing trends of customer sovereignty and increased education on student rights and entitlements means that they [the institutions] need to know what their "customers" want and need' (Church, 2001). Providing a quality experience is also the correct and professional thing to do.

The challenges faced by practitioners will be driven by the needs of their particular student body. Understanding their student body and the services they need, and managing the processes that identify and deliver those services at key times, will enable the practitioner to deliver an enhanced quality student experience.

As stated earlier, there are three very important aspects which are critical in understanding the desired outcomes and delivering a high-quality and holistic student experience.

They are:

- supporting students through every stage of their academic and personal journey at university;
- identifying the key services students need to succeed at university whether they are academic-, welfare- or support-based;
- combining the two aspects above.

How can we achieve this?

The student journey

The Student Lifecycle Model is one framework used to describe the journey of students at university and it is made up of a number of stages that occur in a specific order. It can be applied to undergraduate (UG) and postgraduate (PG) students. The model in Figure 2.1 is used by many institutions and practitioners in developing initiatives to improve and enhance the student experience.

Although this model is still applicable to the individual student to broadly describe their UG or PG university journey, I would argue that the massification and wide-ification of the student body already described in Chapter 1 results in this not being detailed enough for practitioners to successfully deliver an improved and enhanced student experience at UG and PG level.

The Practitioner Model

For practitioners to be able to deliver a high-quality student experience to a more diverse student body, I believe it is essential to have a more detailed and structured framework in order to manage the process. The Practitioner Model in Figure 2.2 is one step on from the Student Lifecycle Model. It provides an organised and more detailed structure in guiding practitioners in the identification of what we have to deliver, who we need to deliver it to and when we need to deliver it.

Figure 2.1 The Student Lifecycle Model

Source: adapted from list in HEFCE, 2001:15.

The stages of the Practitioner Model

The Practitioner Model consists of the following six stages as illustrated in Figure 2.2. The key difference between the Student Lifecycle Model in Figure 2.1 and the Practitioner Model in Figure 2.2 is that the admissions and moving through stages are more detailed in the Practitioner Model. I believe these extra stages more accurately describe the journey of the student and provide more structure for the practitioner on which to develop and deliver support. These stages making up the Practitioner Model will be discussed in detail later in this chapter.

The Practitioner Model remains constant for all students whether they are studying part-time or full-time; on a distance or work-based learning course; studying at a partner institution; undertaking a degree; or studying for a one- or two-year qualification at university. Throughout the stages, aspirations, expectations, academic and social integration must be managed.

Mapping the Practitioner Model to study

Practitioners need to make sure that these stages are mapped to the length of a student's anticipated study time and that each stage links to the next one. All students must undergo every stage regardless of the level at which they enter. I use the term 'level' instead of 'year'

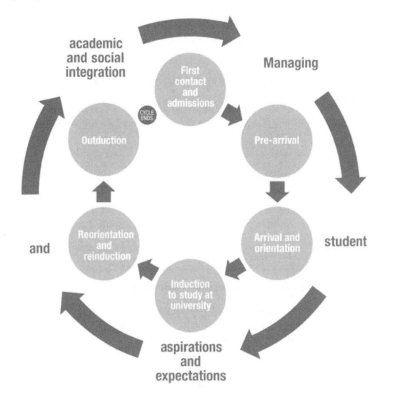

Figure 2.2 The Student Experience Practitioner Model

Source: developed from the HEFCE Student Lifecycle to demonstrate the Practitioner Model (Morgan, 2008b).

in the Practitioner Model as I feel that it more accurately describes the position of the student in their academic study. For example, a student may be in their second year at university but still studying at Level 1 because they are a part-time student. The stages of the Practitioner Model must not be linked to specific levels of academic study in the progression route. The progression route is the movement from one academic level to the next.

All students will undertake the stages of first contact and admissions, pre-arrival and arrival and orientation at the same time. The induction to study at university (referred to as induction to study hereafter), reorientation, reinduction and outduction stages will be mapped to the length of the course.

The skill of the practitioner is to ensure that every student is equipped with the necessary academic and personal skills to help them proceed through the different stages of the Practitioner Model regardless of the length or mode of the course they are studying on. They must also take into account that a student might change their study mode during their course.

So, for example, induction to study is not a stage undertaken only by a student entering Level 1: it should be undertaken by all new students regardless of the level they are entering. The induction to study stage is especially critical for direct-entry, transfer students and distance or work-based learners. Direct-entry students may not have had any previous experience of higher education and transfer students still need to learn how to study at a particular institution and for a particular qualification regardless of any previous experience. Distance and work-based learners are required to study off-site and, as a result, can feel lost and out of their depth when starting their studies.

Examples of mapping the Practitioner Model to different students

(Note: all students will undertake the stages of first contact and admissions, pre-arrival and arrival and orientation at the same time.)

Example 1 A student on a one-year course

A student on a one-year course will complete induction to study by the end of semester 1 or term 1; undertake reorientation at the start of semester 2 or term 2; reinduction in semester 2 or terms 2 and 3 and will start outduction just after the start of semester 2 or the beginning of term 3.

Example 2 A student on a three-year full-time degree

A student undertaking a full-time degree consisting of three academic levels over a three-year period will undertake induction to study during Level 1; reorientation at the start of Levels 2 and 3; reinduction in Levels 2 and 3 and start outduction midway through Level 2 and complete it in Level 3.

Example 3 A direct-entry student into Level 2

A student entering Level 2 as a direct-entry student will undertake arrival and orientation. They will undertake reorientation with the students who have progressed into

Level 2. Their induction to study will run alongside or be incorporated with reinduction activities aimed at Level 2.

Example 4 A student who has intermitted

If a student has experienced a period of intermission for over two years (e.g. one-year placement and one year through illness) then the student should undertake the same process as a direct-entry student.

Management of the Practitioner Model

In my experience, students tend to identify with their home unit (where their subject 'lives') when studying at university. Unless a student has undertaken a professional degree such as law or medicine, students tend to identify with the 'university' once they have graduated. Where a student belongs to a faculty or school that contains numerous subject-based departments or schools, students will identify with the subject-based unit. Therefore, the key to the effectiveness of the Practitioner Model is that it must be primarily managed by the subject-based home unit. This is because:

- students invariably identify with their home unit;
- the home unit tends to have the most contact with the students throughout the life-cycle on an academic and personal level. As a result, it is better placed to identify the needs of the student, and to be able to distribute and disseminate all home unit and institutional targeted information.

The home unit should act as the first port of call in the provision of academic, welfare and support (e.g. student support officers, course administrators and academic personal tutors) and be the gatekeeper referring students on to other key central university services when necessary. The home unit is the conduit through which central services can advertise their services and effectively target students. This approach makes students feel that they are receiving dedicated and not just generic support. Where a student is undertaking a joint degree and has two 'home' units, it is important that one is nominated to take responsibility for him or her.

Description of each stage in the Practitioner Model

Stage 1 First contact and admissions

Once a student considers continuing to higher education, their first contact with an institution is often when they apply. This is when aspirations and expectations are established. However, some may have had their expectations raised prior to first contact, as a result of schools and colleges encouraging their students to go to university, or through universities themselves spearheading programmes in schools/colleges designed to raise student aspirations.

The home unit must be actively involved in this stage. Any promises made in institutional literature must reflect what is deliverable within the home unit. This makes communication between a home unit and the marketing department an important activity. First impressions count, so getting correct and helpful information to applicants is vital.

It is now that an institution, especially the potential home unit, should start to shape the aspirations and expectations of applicants. Answers to commonly asked questions need to be provided. These may include:

- Why go to university?
- Why is it important to be on the 'right' course at a 'suitable' university?
- How and why will university study be different to previous types of study?
- What is expected of a university student?
- How will students be treated at university?
- What happens in each academic level of study?
- What support advice and help is available both academically and personally throughout the lifecycle?
- Is university suitable for everyone?
- Is university the only option?
- What will the university experience give students?
- How can a student's family support him or her?
- What are the options for a student after study?

As well as managing student aspirations and expectations, academic and social integration should start here. It should not just be undertaken as part of an institution's marketing strategy. Engaging applicants with newsletters, emails and the opportunities to attend university and home unit events encourages them to consider going to a specific institution and it should also help them feel part of an institution's academic and social community before they arrive. It also familiarises students with the way the institution communicates with them. All information should be targeted and easily accessed whether by hard copy information or electronic. Information overload should be avoided with a staggered approach being adopted instead.

In Chapter 3, Diane Nutt from the University of Teesside discusses the importance of the first contact and admissions stage in more detail and looks at a range of case studies designed to support and advise students through this process.

Stage 2 Pre-arrival

The pre-arrival stage is an important time for applicants who have accepted a place at an institution. The information supplied at this stage can also be useful for applicants who are still undecided.

Proactively preparing students, their parents or guardians, or their spouses and partners, for the student's university experience, starts now. Anyone who is involved in the pre-arrival stage needs to collaborate and coordinate their activities. All too often, key service providers (such as the home unit, accommodation, welfare and Students' Union) act independently resulting in students receiving a number of information packs. By collaborating and coordinating activities, the amount of information can be reduced, made more concise, and sent out together giving the impression that there is a coordinated approach in terms of service delivery.

Pre-arrival is the period when reinforcement of the questions raised and answered during the first contact and admissions stage should occur. It is also when academic and personal advice, guidance and support on pre-arrival is given. Identifying needs, providing support to students with specific requirements and giving answers to key questions are critical in the pre-arrival preparation of the student. Common questions include:

- Do I need to undertake any pre-entry academic work or reading?
- What do I do when I arrive at university?
- How do I register or enrol?
- How do I pay my fees and accommodation costs?
- What funding can I get and what happens if I do not receive it before I start?
- What do I need to do in the first few weeks at university?
- What will academically be expected of me in the first few weeks?
- What support services do I have access to?
- What extra curricula activities can I engage in?
- What if I do not settle in and want to leave?

In Chapter 4, Christine Keenan from Bournemouth University provides advice and guidance on good practice and introduces four initiatives that have helped assist students, parents and other supporters make the transition from pre-arrival through to the arrival and orientation stage.

Stage 3 Arrival and orientation

For many students, arrival at university is a seminal moment in their lives, especially if it is the first time they have lived away from home, studied at a large institution or been exposed to a range of different cultures and life experiences. It can be an exciting yet nerve-racking time for the student. The experience can reinforce their belief that they have either made the right or wrong decision to go to university. Thus, the first two weeks can be a time of self-doubt or self-confidence.

Arrival and orientation is very different to 'induction' (Upcraft and Gardner, 1989). Arrival and orientation takes place over a very short period (e.g. two weeks) and relates to finding one's way around an institution, starting the process of making friends and settling into university life. Induction takes place over a longer period of time and relates to embedding students into university life and study (Upcraft and Gardner, 1989; Tinto, 2002; Morgan, 2008a). Induction will be discussed in Chapter 6.

Our role as practitioners during the arrival and orientation stage is to ensure that students adjust quickly to university life and that the university adjusts to the student. We must provide them with the chance and opportunities to make friends, to settle into their university life and study routine as soon as possible and provide the appropriate information and access to support. We know from the extensive research in the area (see the further reading section) that these key activities can help students successfully embed into university life. To do this, all of the key service providers involved need to work together with the home unit in managing this stage. Once the immediate arrival activities have been accomplished (e.g. registration or enrolment, moving into accommodation), the majority of activities undertaken will normally occur within or via the home unit (e.g. information about support services, starting to make friends, meeting personal tutors and lecturers, getting timetables and course information).

To help students settle into their studies as quickly as possible, it is critical that the academic imperative is at the heart of arrival and orientation. The primary focus should be on academic and not administrative activities. Expectations set during the first contact, admissions and pre-arrival stages need to be met and continually managed to ensure students have faith in the education in which they are investing. In Chapter 5, Professor Kerri-Lee Krause from Griffith University, Australia, looks at how the arrival and orientation period sets the tone of a university experience. The case studies she introduces look at initiatives addressing different aspects of the arrival and orientation stage.

Stage 4 Induction to study

Induction to study at university is a vital stage in the lifecycle of the student. If they do not embed quickly into their university studies, this can lead to disengagement and possible withdrawal. Ensuring a seamless transition between the stages of arrival and orientation and induction to study is particularly important. The process of induction to study at university takes place over a longer period than just a few weeks. This period of adjustment, once students have arrived and orientated themselves, is about coping with the demands of academia whilst also managing the pressures of life.

Today, students' lives are complex as they need to balance a range of demands. It is not realistic to expect the student to separate their personal and university life because the two are entwined and one can impact on the other. Conflicting life and study demands can mean less time on campus and thus fewer opportunities to become fully integrated into the university environment. Practitioners need take both of these factors into account when designing and developing academic, welfare and support initiatives.

Until a student goes through at least one academic cycle (e.g. studying for a module and submitting coursework and sitting exams), they have not been inducted into the process of study. Where a course is only one year long, students have only a term or semester in which to settle in and obtain the necessary academic skills. For longer courses, students have more time to achieve this. Direct-entry or transfer students going straight into academic Level 2 or above often lose out on this vital stage because it is not offered.

In Chapter 6, Mary Stuart Hunter and Kevin C. Clarke from the National Resource Center at the University of South Carolina look at the importance of this stage in the student lifecycle. The case studies they introduce are initiatives that support students in a range of ways across the induction to study stage.

Stage 5 Reorientation and reinduction

Returning students are often neglected in terms of being given advice, guidance and support which tends to be directed towards Level 1 students. A student can be returning to their studies having either successfully progressed from:

- their first academic level of study;
- a placement or study abroad;
- a different study mode;
- a period of intermission.

Institutions and practitioners should not make the assumption that a returning student will know what to expect because each academic level brings a different set of rules and regulations, skills and expectations. Institutional changes and developments, whether academic-, welfare- or support-based, commonly take place over the vacation period prior to the new academic year.

Normally, as a student progresses through the academic levels, demands on the student increase. It is short-sighted to assume that a returning student should be able to balance the stresses of study and everyday life with no extra help, support or advice. It is also unreasonable to think that their anxiety levels regarding their new academic level of study should be low because they have already navigated their way through the previous level. After the intense support of their first year at university, students can feel abandoned when they return to their studies. Support for returning students should be delivered via what I call the reorientation and reinduction stages in the Practitioner Model.

Reorientation is an activity that should take place at the start of each new academic level. Just as new students need to orientate themselves, so do returning students. Reorientation is an opportunity to remind students of the support they can access both academically and personally and what to expect in their specific level. (Note: if the course is limited to one year then this period would take place at the start of term 2 or semester 2.) It is also an opportunity for an institution to inform students of any changes that have occurred during the vacation period in relation to their course, support or institutional structure.

As with the induction to study stage, reinduction should take place over a longer period of time than just a few weeks. However, whereas induction can take place between a semester and a full academic year, reinduction takes place over the first term or semester of the new academic level (Level 2 and above). Students should review and reflect on the academic and personal skills gained in the previous year, look at how they can build on them in the coming year and determine what they need to achieve in order to successfully progress. The reinduction activities should be tailored to meet the needs of each academic level. Again, it is important that this stage is managed by the home unit.

In Chapter 7, I look at the importance of supporting all returning students in their studies. The case studies look at managing the expectations and needs of a diverse returning student body.

Stage 6 Outduction

Just as students are inducted to university, so they should be outducted. The term *outduction* was coined by Layer and Harle from the University of Bradford (Layer, 2005). Getting students through the student lifecycle involves more than simply getting them to complete their course. It is about supporting them in the transition from the world of study into the world of life. This is a much neglected area of support in the student lifecycle and research is limited. There are initiatives being undertaken which support students leaving university that come under the outduction stage but they tend to be local initiatives based on anecdotal or local research. For the practitioner, the challenge is to develop processes and initiatives that support students in preparation for leaving their studies and in deciding what to do next. Again, the home unit needs to manage this stage with input from other university key service providers, such as welfare and careers units.

The questions students may need answered include:

- How can skills learnt at university be transferred to life post-study?
- What are the different study, travel and work options available after graduation?
- How can these options impact on a student's career and life in general?
- How can the student make the adjustment from study to life after university?
- What if I do not get the qualifications I expected?

In preparing students for life after university, employment is not the only option. Further study, volunteering and travel are other routes students can consider, but they need advice on how these activities will affect or enhance their working and personal life. Students need to start thinking about life after university as soon as they start. However, I suggest that the practical activities, such as career advice and identifying transferable skills should start half-way through a qualification, and be part of the curriculum. By this stage, students should hopefully have an idea of what they wish to do post-study. It also provides time to identify and bridge any skill gaps. In Chapter 8, April L. Perry from the University of Canterbury in Christchurch, New Zealand, explains how this stage in the student lifecycle can aid both students and their institution. The case studies she introduces look at innovative ways in supporting this last transition and when.

What do students do in each stage?

Students need to have access to advice, support and guidance with each stage, and to be able to engage in a range of activities if they are to successfully complete their studies. All student experiences and activities, whether academic or personal, can be put into five broad interlinking themes. These are curriculum and assessment, pedagogy, support, finance and employment, as illustrated in Figure 2.3. Learning and teaching is central to the student experience and the key activity in the Practitioner Model. As throughout the different stages, again we need to manage student aspirations, expectations and social and academic integration throughout the different themes.

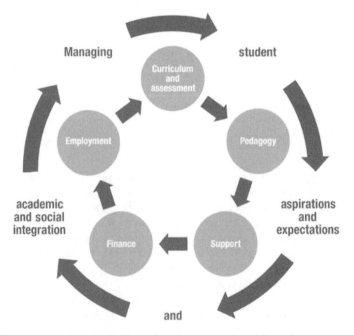

Figure 2.3 Themes in each stage of the Student Experience Practitioner Model

Source: developed from the HEFCE Student Lifecycle to demonstrate the Practitioner Model (Morgan, 2008b).

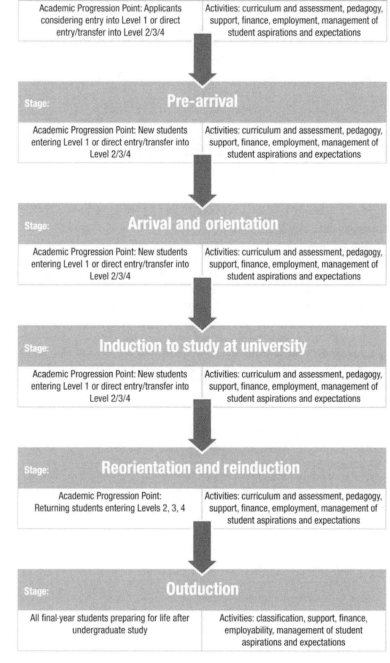

Stage: **First contact and admissions**

Academic Progression Point: Applicants considering entry into Level 1 or direct entry/transfer into Level 2/3/4

Activities: curriculum and assessment, pedagogy, support, finance, employment, management of student aspirations and expectations

Stage: **Pre-arrival**

Academic Progression Point: New students entering Level 1 or direct entry/transfer into Level 2/3/4

Activities: curriculum and assessment, pedagogy, support, finance, employment, management of student aspirations and expectations

Stage: **Arrival and orientation**

Academic Progression Point: New students entering Level 1 or direct entry/transfer into Level 2/3/4

Activities: curriculum and assessment, pedagogy, support, finance, employment, management of student aspirations and expectations

Stage: **Induction to study at university**

Academic Progression Point: New students entering Level 1 or direct entry/transfer into Level 2/3/4

Activities: curriculum and assessment, pedagogy, support, finance, employment, management of student aspirations and expectations

Stage: **Reorientation and reinduction**

Academic Progression Point: Returning students entering Levels 2, 3, 4

Activities: curriculum and assessment, pedagogy, support, finance, employment, management of student aspirations and expectations

Stage: **Outduction**

All final-year students preparing for life after undergraduate study

Activities: classification, support, finance, employability, management of student aspirations and expectations

Figure 2.4 Stages and themes in the Student Experience Practitioner Model

Figure 2.4 illustrates how the themes fit into each stage and academic level. Students need to engage in the same themes at every stage but the content and emphasis of each activity within each theme will vary on the stage and level. The stages should not be linked to specific levels and the practitioner needs to mould an activity to a particular group. For example, a reorientation session for a Level 2 student will have a different emphasis and content to that of a Level 3 student. Students need to be furnished with the knowledge, information, advice and support required for the level they are in so they can make a critical and seamless transition in, through and out of each academic level.

Table 2.1 illustrates how the emphasis in terms of information, advice and support in each theme alters throughout the stages of the Practitioner Model.

The themes are all interlinked so activities should be coordinated. For example, in Table 2.1 under the curriculum and assessment theme, one of the activities mentioned in the reorientation and reinduction stage is study abroad and placement options. This activity encompasses issues relating to other themes. Specific issues within these themes should be addressed, such as:

- finance – the cost of studying abroad for a year and the financial benefits of doing a work placement (summer or year-long);
- employment – how to apply for the placement and how it will help gain employment post-study;
- pedagogy – how to transfer academic skills from the learning environment to the work place (e.g. during placements and after study);
- support – how support can be accessed whilst studying or working away from the home institution.

Providing students with the information relating to study abroad and placement options requires the support of a whole range of key service providers across the activities.

For every initiative developed for an activity within a stage or theme, the following questions need to be addressed:

- What is the aim and objective of the initiative?
- Who needs to be involved in the development of the initiative?
- Who is the target group?
- What do they need to know?
- What information is going to be delivered?
- Who will deliver it?
- When is it going to be delivered?
- How will it be delivered?
- What is the cost/timeline?
- Is it financially viable?
- Can the initiative and information be adapted for another group?
- How will it be evaluated and monitored?

Table 2.1 Managing the themes against the stages in the Student Experience Practitioner Model

Stage	Curriculum and assessment	Pedagogy	Support	Finance	Employment
First contact and admissions	Information on subjects that make up a degree; specific subject study in each level of a degree; type of assessments undertaken in each year; using the degree post-study.	An outline of the different study and learning styles available.	An overview and promotion of support and facilities available.	Information on loans/ fees/bursaries; money management advice; accommodation costs.	Advice, support and guidance on part-time work during study; year placement options; internships; summer placements; voluntary work.
Pre-arrival	Specific information on subjects to be studied in the first year of academic study; pre-arrival preparation tests/ reading/coursework.	An outline of the different study and learning styles available; start engagement in learning the process.	Information on accessing services and support.	Applications for loans/bursaries; payment of fees/ accommodation costs; money management advice.	Advice, support and guidance on part-time work during study; year placement options; internships; summer placements; voluntary work.
Arrival and orientation	A reminder of subjects that make up a degree; specific subject study in each level of a degree; subjects to be studied in the first year of academic study; type of assessments undertaken in each year; using the degree post-study.	A reminder of the different study and learning styles available; start the main engagement in learning the process.	An explanation of the services and support available; learning when and how to access services and support.	Payment of fees/ accommodation costs; money management advice; accessing hardship funds.	Advice, support and guidance on part-time work during study; year placement options; internships; summer placements; voluntary work.

Continued

Table 2.1 Continued

Induction to study	An explanation of how different subjects and assessments are undertaken in the first year of study.	A review of learning how to study in a given year; understanding the different types of learning styles and approaches required.	Regular reminders of services and support available and how to access them.	Money management advice; accessing hardship funds; debt control.	Advice, support and guidance on part-time work during study; year placement options; internships; summer placements; voluntary work.
Reorientation and reinduction	A reminder of previous skills gap; making subject choices which count towards degree; learning and undertaking different assessments for the new level of study; study away/placement options.	A review of previous learning skills and styles in new academic level.	A reminder of services and support at relevant and appropriate times of the year.	Payment of fees/accommodation costs; money management advice; accessing hardship funds; debt control.	Advice, support and guidance on part-time work during study; year placement options; internships; summer placements; voluntary work; preparation to enter employment post-study.
Outduction	Explaining the classification structure; applying skills set post-study.	An explanation of how to transfer learning processes to future study and work.	A reminder of services and support available and how to access them in final level of study and post-study as alumni (career service, etc.).	Money management advice; preparation for repayment of loans/fees; debt control.	Advice, support and guidance to enter employment or further study as alumni.

Supporting the Practitioner Model

To enable key service providers to effectively engage with the stages and themes of the Practitioner Model requires the provision of, and their participation in, a range of other activities.

These are:

- developing academic student support whether it is student- or staff-led;
- the training and the support of staff to enable them to engage effectively in the student experience;
- supporting the learning and teaching process;
- understanding and engaging in student evaluation and feedback, which is a critical tool in enabling practitioners to identify the key issues and provide practical initiatives to improve the student experience.

Academic student support and development

Academic student support and development comprises of academic staff and trained student peers providing students with academic support. Both are essential support activities in helping students succeed in their studies. Peer support is a particularly powerful tool in helping students stay the course and succeed. In Chapter 9, Marcia Ody from the University of Manchester outlines why academic support in the student experience is so important. The case studies she introduces look at a range of different academic student support and development initiatives involving both academics and students.

Staff training

Staff at all levels, and across all areas, cannot properly support the student experience unless they understand the necessity for a high-quality student experience and undergo the relevant training. It is important for all staff to coordinate and collaborate on activities and initiatives and understand how their role contributes to the student experience. In Chapter 10, Glyn Jones from Kingston University will talk about the need for staff development and training in delivering a high-quality student experience. The case studies he introduces illustrate how institutions can inspire and support staff to be supporters of the student experience.

Supporting learning and teaching

Learning and teaching is at the heart of the student experience and students' experiences of learning and teaching environments (Tinto, 1993; Thomas, 2002) and curriculum design (Race, 2010) are critical to student success, especially where there is diversity in the student body. With a 'Google' and 'YouTube' generation of students, utilising new technologies can enhance innovative learning and teaching methods and processes. In Chapter 11, Liz Thomas from Edgehill University looks at how developing and supporting innovative teaching and learning activities can dramatically improve the student experience. The case studies demonstrate how various institutions have adopted creative approaches to learning and teaching.

Student evaluation and feedback

Evaluation and feedback by students is a critical activity in the tool box of the practitioner. It can provide an understanding of student expectations and their actual experience whether the feedback be immediate or via longitudinal studies. It is essential not to over-evaluate and important to close the loop by providing feedback to students on their thoughts, opinions and comments. Also, it is essential to demonstrate that change has occurred as a direct result of their input. In Chapter 12, Duncan Nulty from Griffith University discusses its importance and introduces a range of student evaluation and feedback case studies from across the student experience and lifecycle. As explained earlier, this chapter will not be looking at feedback from academics on assessment.

Conclusion

In conclusion, I hope that the Practitioner Model provides you with a more structured approach to supporting a diverse student body, that the case studies are useful templates for you to adapt and implement in your institution, and that the book has got you thinking about other ways you, as a practitioner, can improve the university experience not only for the students within your institution but for your colleagues as well.

References

Church, F. (2001) 'Students as consumers: the importance of student feedback in the quality assurance process', paper presented to the 3rd Annual Conference of the Learning in Law Initiative, January, Coventry: University of Warwick.

Eastwood, D. (2010) 'Higher Education Academy Pro-Vice-Chancellor Network', 22 April, verbatim quote.

Higher Education Funding Council for England (2001) *Strategies for Widening Participation in Higher Education: A Guide to Good Practice*, Stoke-on-Trent: HEFCE.

Layer, G. (2005) 'The final year experience', keynote address at the Course Directors' Conference, January, Kingston upon Thames: Kingston University.

Low, L. (2002) 'Best practices in student retention: best practices in recruitment and retention', paper presented to the 19th International Student Experience Conference, July, Bath: University of Bath.

Morgan, M. (2008a) The annual conference and exhibition of the Association of University Administrators (AUA), 'Induction and orientation: getting the balance right!', lecture, 31 March–2 April, York: University of York.

Morgan, M. (2008b) The importance of 'OUTduction' in the student lifecycle, paper presented at The Annual Conference and Exhibition of the Association of University Administrators (AUA), 31 March–2 April, University of York.

Race, P. (2010) *Making Learning Happen*, 2nd edn, London: Sage Publications.

Thomas, L. (2002) 'Student retention in higher education: the role of institutional habitus', *Journal of Education Policy*, 17 (4): 423–32.

Tinto, V. (1993) *Leaving College: Rethinking the Causes and Cures of Student Attrition*, 2nd edn, Chicago, IL: University of Chicago Press.

Tinto, V. (2002) 'Establishing conditions for student success', paper presented at the 11th Annual Conference of the European Access Network, June, Prato, Italy: Monash University.

Upcraft, M.L. and Gardner, J.N. (1989) *The Freshman Experience: Helping Students Survive and Succeed in College*, San Francisco, CA: Jossey-Bass.

Part 2

The stages in the Student Experience Practitioner Model

Chapter 3

First contact and admissions

Diane Nutt, Teesside University, UK

Introduction

The first contact and admission stage into higher education is a critical part of a student's learning journey. Decisions made during this transition stage can impact on their university success and career. It is important for institutions and practitioners to make sense of the first contact and admissions experience in order to develop effective processes to enhance all students' experiences at a challenging time in their learning careers. Supporting applicants who are our potential students through the first contact and admissions stage can take many forms, and encompass wider strategies at institutional or regional levels, as well as specific institution-based initiatives. These can be relevant for all applicants or for particular programmes or applicant groups.

This chapter considers what the first contact might be and how practitioners can plan to support them, as well as exploring strategies for supporting applicants through a positive first contact and admissions experience.

Much of the research on first contact and admissions has focused on exploring aspiration raising activities with 14–19 year olds and working on access issues more generally (Thomas and Cooper, 2000). This book does not deal with the 14–19 agenda as this is ably explored in other texts, some of which are listed in the suggested reading list.

It is easier to get the first contact and admissions process right if we know more about our applicants. Diversity within the HE student body has increased this challenge. When looking at the first contact and admissions transition into university, it is important for institutions and practitioners to understand:

- aspiration raising activities and the context;
- where new applicants are coming from;
- what they need to succeed when they join us.

Addressing these questions and developing initiatives to understand and support applicants enables us to provide the best conditions to help them succeed once they have made contact and begun the admissions process. For example, working with schools and colleges and knowing the access routes applicants are using to gain entry to your institution is a useful tool for providing the right kinds of support through this transition. It is important, where possible, to work with feeder institutions to understand what applicants learn in their earlier studies and to explore the differences in experience at each stage of their academic journey (Cox and Bidgood, 2003).

First contact: welcoming, engaging and embedding

For many students in a digital age, first contact is often made by visiting the university's website. It is important that university websites are well constructed and designed to effectively help applicants through this stage, where 'the key is to help make future students feel part of the student community long before freshers' week' (Fearn, 2010).

Aspects of university websites that applicants appreciate include:

- access to real student views on course and experiences;
- virtual access to parts of the university, such as virtual tours of residences or classrooms and access to the VLE;
- easily accessible information on course details;
- information on other aspects of the experience, such as teaching styles on the course;
- information on accommodation and nightlife;
- using language that students will understand.

There are other online first contacts to bear in mind when thinking about how best to support potential students, such as the range of social networking sites used actively by many applicants. This is a wide area for exploration, which needs to be handled carefully. A key way to ensure any developments you make in this area are successful is to involve current students in the development of this activity.

In the UK, UCAS (Universities and Colleges Admissions Service) uses its website to support UK applicants through the first contact and admissions processes. As part of this activity, UCAS have developed 'yougo' which, as the website says, 'yougofurther.co.uk – the social networking site that connects applicants just like you.'

Visiting a university can be the real first contact for many applicants, and hosting open days and events on your campus can be important ways of helping them make the transition. In some institutions, this visit may be as part of an interview for a place. It is important to remember that these activities are not just marketing tools or hoops for applicants to jump through, but rather are real opportunities for them to begin the journey involved in entering higher education. In general, applicants seem to particularly appreciate a chance to talk to the staff who will be teaching them and to see where they might be living and studying. Making their visit experience explicitly relevant to their future studies enables them to go away and begin thinking about what it will really be like.

For some applicants, first contact may be the material they are sent with their acceptance letter. It is important therefore for universities to make this material interesting and relevant to the applicant's future studies, and not to just send them the generic material that all students will receive.

And for other applicants first contact will be over the telephone during clearing. Can applicants at this stage talk with someone about the course and the teaching style, as well as get a small glimpse of what it might be like to study there? This could simply be a conversation with an enthusiastic member of staff who will answer their questions and suggest places they can find out more information. Some universities follow up the clearing process quickly with further contact, perhaps from a course leader or from a student mentor.

Involving current students in the first contact and admissions transition is an effective way of helping potential students connect with the community and begin to imagine what it might really be like to study there. For example, Bangor University provides a 'question-and-answer service … staffed by current students responding to applicants who have already made a bid for a place' (Fearn, 2010).

Admissions experiences: transparent, clear and applicant centred

Any admissions process needs to be transparent, possess clarity and have an applicant-centred approach. The diversity of applicants' experiences before first contact and admissions impacts on their confidence with these activities and can significantly impact on how they experience the process. The most efficient application process, for example, may be a centrally managed uniform approach. However, as has been highlighted in earlier chapters, in the Practitioner Model it is important for the home unit (department or subject area) to be involved: this ensures that each stage of the overall student experience is a positive one leading to a successful outcome. We also know that the most likely reason for students to withdraw is being on the wrong course or at the wrong institution (Bowl, 2003). And where the first contact and application processes are separated from the home unit, there is far greater risk of applicants making choices they may later regret.

Institutions and practitioners need to consider the admissions stage in the context of the wider student journey, so it is important to:

- understand where students come from, educationally and culturally, and ensure institutional and course fit is achieved for the applicant and university;
- join the dots between interested parties to ensure that first contact and admissions processes are smooth and consistent (marketing; admissions administrators; all faculty staff; central support services; learning developers);
- understand the role of new technologies for contemporary students and institutions.

The case studies in this chapter provide some examples of strategies focusing on aspects of the first contact and admissions stage. The case studies included here range from specific examples supporting particular student groups (mature students, international students) to wider national strategies designed to support all students in the UK through the first contact and admissions stage.

Case Study 1 by Trudi Woodhouse from the University Central Admissions Service (UCAS), UK, provides a wider context to the approaches institutions take in providing information to applicants, by telling the story of the development of the UCAS facility which coordinates all university applications in the UK. This wider strategic approach has both simplified applications and provided a route to information and support for applicants during the admissions process. Interesting developments at UCAS have led to the development of online applications and easily accessed support for potential students in the form of a friendly accessible website and the online social network mentioned above.

Case Study 2 by Katie Barnes from Kingston University, UK, describes an initiative designed to manage admissions processes for a non-standard group of students, those studying in partner institutions. This case study emphasises the importance of efficiency and clarity in the process, but also considers the importance of working together to provide the best experience for applicants. The case study provides a straightforward approach which is transferable to other conditions.

Case Study 3 from Jayne Tidd highlights the importance of integrating this stage with others in the Practitioner Model. Mature students at Teesside University have a supported first contact and admissions experience but this is integrated with pre-arrival support, arrival and orientation and the early stages of induction to study. This case study also identifies ways in which particular student groups can be supported through this key transition stage. Students coming from diverse backgrounds into HE can benefit from targeted strategies.

Case Study 4 is provided by Matthew Semple from Bristol University, UK. This case study offers a practical and clear example of how Bristol University enhanced its systems for dealing with international student applications and visa processes. International students represent a significant number of applicants for HE institutions in most Western countries. Continuing to provide a quality applicant experience (and therefore a first stage student experience), alongside government processes and expectations and institutional practices can be challenging. This example is designed to make it easier for both the student and the institution to manage this stage, and has also led to an improved and quick response to any queries and issues raised by applicants.

Case Study 1

Name and university
Trudi Woodhouse, University and Colleges Admissions Service (UCAS), UK.

Title of project/initiative
Developing a university and colleges admissions service.

Who was involved in the initiative
Committee of Vice-Chancellors and Principals (CVCP), Universities Central Council on Admissions (UCCA) and Polytechnics Central Admissions System (PCAS).

Reason for the project/initiative
A lack of standardisation in procedures used for university admissions and no central coordination.

Why it was developed
Most UK universities experienced a steady rise in applications for undergraduate courses from the 1950s onwards due to the increasing competition for places from service men and women retiring after the war, the availability of grants from public funds and the practice of students making multiple applications to universities.

There was a lack of sector-wide central admissions coordination. A variety of procedures were used by different institutions and there was no common terminology to describe offers and replies, thus making the process complicated for both applicants and institutions. Consequently, there was no reliable data or statistics about HE applications within the UK across the sector. The aim of the project was to provide a fair application process that was efficient to applicants as well as providing much needed statistical data to aid the planning and expansion of HE.

The target group
Applicants to full-time undergraduate courses in the UK and UK higher education institutions (HEIs).

How it was developed, what it included and how it was implemented

How it was developed
The admissions service in existence today has gone through many phases and developments.

In 1960 CVCP set up a working party, with a view to simplifying the university admissions process 'by co-operative action on the part of the universities' (Kay and Oakley, 1994). In 1961 UCCA was formed; the underlying principle of the scheme being that copies of an application would be simultaneously circulated to all the applicant's chosen HEIs.

In 1985, the polytechnics, which were a type of tertiary education teaching institution, established their own central admissions scheme, called PCAS. A contract was signed with UCCA to provide a computer and other technical and mailing facilities to PCAS for four operational years.

As a result of the government's 1991 White Paper, *Higher Education: A New Framework*, UCCA and PCAS built on their collaboration and came 'together as a central agency for admissions' creating the Universities and Colleges Admissions Service (UCAS) in 1994. UCAS is not a government body but a charity.

What it included

All member institutions adhere to the UCAS Application and Recruitment Policy to ensure that applications to courses are handled fairly and consistently. Each year all institutions are provided with the *UCAS Admissions Guide and Decision Processing Manual*, which describes UCAS' procedures and lays out 'the rules' and timetable.

Each member institution must recruit to all its full-time and sandwich first degrees, and any other undergraduate level courses through UCAS.

Applicants to any full-time undergraduate courses at UCAS institutions must apply through UCAS, unless specifically exempted, and each pay an application fee. There are a number of steps an applicant must go through in the application journey which UCAS supports. These are:

- choosing the course;
- applying;
- offers;
- results;
- next steps;
- starting university or college.

More information can be found at www.ucas.com.

Due to the education infrastructure in the UK, the majority of applicants who apply to UCAS need to apply and accept a place at an institution before the results of their entry qualifications are known.

How it was implemented

A key to the success of UCAS is good communication and the provision of sharing of data and information between UCAS, the institutions and the applicants (listed below).

Sharing of course data

Online UCAS-link products are used by institutions to view applicant data and update their course and institution data (courses are coded using the Joint Academic Coding System (JACS)). JACS is used by the Higher Education Statistics Agency (HESA) and other UK departments, such as the Department for Business, Innovation and Skills (BIS), the Home Office and the Higher Education Funding Council for England (HEFCE) for statistics.

Institutions provide entry profiles for most courses, which are also published on UCAS course search. They give potential applicants detailed information about each course, its entry requirements and the skills and qualities the university is looking for in their students. Entry profiles provide a way of communicating topical, accurate and up-to-date information directly to potential applicants.

Applicant data

With the exception of data used for statistical purposes, all information from the application is made available to institutions prior to them making their decisions. Operational statistics are supplied to institutions throughout the year and an annual report is produced at the end of each cycle.

Offers

There are six types of decision an institution can make that conform to a standard layout of fields or elements and use standard codes. The institution's official decision is sent to UCAS and subsequently made available to the applicant.

Each year we produce an operational calendar. This includes application deadlines and deadlines by which institutions need to make decisions on their applications, thus ensuring all institutions and applicants adhere to the same timelines and the communication channels are kept open. Automatic decline processes are in place for when a deadline is missed by either the institution or the applicant.

Confirmation and clearing

Once an applicant's examination results are known and the institution has all the necessary information, it can confirm or reject the application. We collect results of some examinations centrally and distribute them to institutions before the official publication date to enable UCAS to make timely confirmation decisions.

Clearing is a service available between July and September which helps people without a university or college place find suitable vacancies. Institutions inform us of the courses for which they are prepared to consider applications through clearing. We then publish clearing vacancy lists at www.ucas.com and supply this data for publication in the press.

Developments

Through UCAStv (www.ucas.tv), we offer video guides providing advice about applying to higher education to students, parents, advisers and HE staff, thereby utilising a different medium to communicate with our audiences.

We have also developed yougofurther.co.uk (or yougo as it is more commonly known), the UCAS student network. It allows UCAS applicants to meet people who will be doing the same course or attending the same institution before they start at university. HEIs can create profile pages, enabling them to engage with their potential students, and yougo also runs forums and online debates. A link to the Child Exploitation and Online Protection Centre (CEOP) is provided, thus creating a safe arena for communication between applicants, current students, HEIs and UCAS.

As students communicate through social media channels we have set up UCAS Twitter and Facebook accounts. Through these we can give advice on the application process at key times of the year, and from liaising with our customer service unit we know of any recurring queries they may be receiving. This allows us to quickly give advice to our followers and answer their questions; both are proving to be invaluable communication tools to help our applicants. We are also currently trialling social bookmarking from the UCAS website.

None of these are stand-alone social media ventures; they are all part of an integrated approach to UCAS communications as a whole. Attitudes to social media have changed a lot in the past few years and we are keen to take the initiative by responding to these changes and students' needs.

Analysis and feedback

A report based on discussions from the UCAS review meeting is presented at the December meeting of the UCAS board for members' consideration on all our activities.

The cost and timeline

UCAS applicants pay an application fee and institutions pay a capitation fee for each student who enrols with them.

How it is/was monitored

The UCAS admissions conference is held annually, providing advice and guidance to those involved in university admissions, recruitment and marketing.

The UCAS review meeting takes place six months after each admissions conference and provides an opportunity for UCAS institutions to review the previous application cycle and look forward to the future.

The outcome

Annually we help over 600,000 applicants apply to over 300 HEIs in the UK. Our application services are constantly reviewed to improve the applicant experience and the data quality.

Has or could the initiative be used for a different group?

We have acted as a consultant for a number of countries who are interested in adopting a similar centralised admissions system.

Advice and guidance

•   HEIs need to provide up-to-date and accurate information.
•   Collect applicant and HEI feedback to improve communications and services.

References

Kay, R. and Oakley, P. (1994) *UCCA: Its Origins and Development 1950–93*, Cheltenham: The Universities Central Council on Admissions.

Contact details

t.woodhouse@ucas.ac.uk

Case Study 2

Name and university
Katie Barnes, Admissions and International Liaison Officer, Faculty of Engineering, Kingston University, UK.

Title of project/initiative
Improving partner institutions (PIs) recruitment and admissions process.

Who was involved in the initiative
Faculty of Engineering (FoE) Admissions Officer, Course Field Leader and Liaison Officer for PIs, Learning and Teaching Coordinator and Student Experience Manager, Partner Liaison Officers in the PIs and their administrative team.

Reason for the project/initiative
Over the past five years, the FoE has accredited degrees at an increasing number of partner institutions. All but one of the PIs are industrial-based aircraft training providers. Although the students study at the PI, they are technically Kingston University students. Different PIs operated different recruitment and admissions processes for historical reasons and provided varying standards of information. Processes and information for activities, such as admissions and arrival had developed on an ad hoc basis without any real coordination of roles and responsibilities between the FoE, the university and the PI. We had received some complaints from students based at PIs relating to the lack of clear and accurate information and a disappointing student experience. Student withdrawal from the course at the PIs impacted on the university's retention figures.

We wanted to improve all aspects of the PI recruitment and admissions process and how it fed into the transition stages of pre-arrival and arrival and orientation in order to improve our retention rates and the student experience.

Why it was developed
We wanted to streamline, simplify and unify the recruitment and admissions process. We had to take into account the pro-activity of some PIs and the reticence of others to fully engage in the process. These PIs were not familiar with HE quality assurance standards, procedures, regulations and the HE culture and environment. Some of the PIs operated their own admissions process so we could not control the quality of the applicants coming through the system. We wanted a quality-based, consistent and standard recruitment and admissions process across the PIs.

The target group
The development of an efficient recruitment and admissions process for PI applications and to enhance the student experience in the early transition stages.

How it was developed, what it included and how it was implemented

How it was developed
We looked at the concerns, issues and problems listed by applicants, students and staff at our PIs. Students undertaking courses at PIs do not have the traditional university experience as they are often on two-year foundation degrees and are based with an industrial

trainer. Their mode of study means they do not fit neatly into the standard university systems and processes or student funding schedule.

We talked to applicants and students and looked at the information sent out from our central university departments to applicants to identify gaps or areas of confusion. Central units, such as marketing had a tendency to produce literature based on a 'one size fits all' approach with little input from the faculty. Discussions were also held with the field leader for the courses taught at PIs, who was the primary contact and responsible for overseeing the delivery of the courses.

The challenge was to develop processes and information for a variety of PIs whose pro-activity varied as a result of roles and responsibilities not being made clear from the point of validation and accreditation.

After much discussion, we developed a process which we refined and adapted year on year.

What it included

The key change was that we took control of the recruitment and admissions process. All applicants still had to apply through the University and Colleges Admissions System (UCAS) but all applications were managed by the FoE admissions team and not the PIs. This was a critical decision and proved to be key in targeting specific and dedicated information and ensuring the quality of incoming students. Any applicant who approached the PI directly would be referred to the FoE admissions team. Entry requirements were standardised so the FoE admissions officers could make conditional offers based on academic qualifications and subject to the successful completion of an entry test.

Information, advice and guidance about the recruitment and admissions process, the course and what to expect as a student studying at a PI was:

* simplified, unified and made clearer on our recruitment and admissions website, in our literature and on our student experience website;
* provided at open and admissions days.

Important entry test information was also supplied.

To help us and the PI track each applicant in the recruitment and admissions process, we developed:

* a schedule of activities and mailings;
* letters and email templates which were course-related;
* entry test and outcome guidance and advice (if the applicant failed, the offer would be changed to a lower level standard entry course and an explanatory letter and relevant information sent out);
* coordinated information and processes with central services (e.g. enrolment services, student support).

We worked with key players in the FoE to ensure that the recruitment and admissions stage continued through and linked up to the pre-arrival, arrival and orientation and induction stages. Dedicated information for these stages for PI applicants/students was developed alongside the information provided for Kingston University-based students. We wanted to ensure all students received a similar experience whether based at Kingston University or a PI.

How it was implemented

The procedure and information developed was agreed by all key stakeholders in the faculty, the university and with all PIs.

Analysis and feedback

We experienced a lot less calls and emails requesting information. There were no major complaints by applicants about the recruitment and admissions process.

The cost and timeline

The primary cost was time in developing new processes.

How it is/was monitored

It is monitored via the numbers of calls and complaints received. We regularly talk to partner liaison officers to monitor any complaints they receive. Complaints are also monitored through the student staff consultative committee at the PIs.

The outcome

Complaints have decreased and applicants are now fully aware of the experience to expect. The decision to centralise admissions in the faculty has increased transparency, consistency and quality standards both in terms of the processes and the quality of the applicants being offered places. As we receive requests for course information earlier we have brought the mailing dates forward.

The university has addressed the procedural problems we experienced via the course validation and accreditation process of the university which now requires all new courses taught at PIs to have a detailed contract outlining expectations, roles, standards and responsibilities and accrediting institution.

Has or could the initiative be used for a different group?

Any group that is non-standard and falls within or outside the normal university start dates.

Advice and guidance

- Retain control of the admissions process.
- Ensure PIs are aware of government, university and HE policies and regulations and the implications of not adhering to these.
- Communicate effectively with the PIs.
- Acknowledge and accommodate each other's culture and learning environment and requirements.
- Ensure admissions and other operational requirements are discussed and formally agreed at the validation and accreditation processes.
- Take into account UKBA rules relating to sponsorship of students at PIs when developing policies and procedures.

Contact details

k.barnes@kingston.ac.uk

Case Study 3

Name and university
Jayne Tidd, School of Social Sciences & Law, Teesside University, UK.

Title of project/initiative
Supporting mature students from first contact and admissions through arrival, orientation and beyond.

Who was involved in the initiative
Senior Lecturer and Assistant Director for Learning and Teaching from Central Learning Development Department. Cross-institution collaboration from Learning and Teaching Coordinators and Retention Support Officers plus support at the day event from academic and support staff across the university.

Reason for the project/initiative
Teesside University is one of the top UK universities for widening participation in higher education, with 40 per cent of full-time and 88 per cent of part-time undergraduate students aged 21 and over. The transition into higher education from first contact through arrival can be traumatic for some mature students, especially if they have not studied for some time. Research into the first-year experience at Teesside highlighted that many mature students found embarking on their academic careers a stressful and daunting experience; they also expressed feelings of isolation and disorientation and this impacted on mature student retention.

Why it was developed
We wanted to enhance the transition process for mature students by specifically designing pre-entry information and a mature students' programme as part of the arrival process which was advertised from first contact and through the admissions process. We wanted to emphasise that university was for them; we understood their concerns; reinforced that they had earned the right to be there; and that they were important to us. This message was reinforced through the admissions and pre-arrival stages.

The target group
Full-time undergraduate mature students who had been offered a place at Teesside University (approximately 800 students annually).

How it was developed, what it included and how it was implemented

How it was developed
The initiative developed and built on the Twenty One Plus Students (TOPS) event. TOPS was a pre-arrival event designed so that mature students could have the opportunity to meet other new students, current mature students and staff, and contribute to their academic and social integration and reduce first-day anxiety. The evaluation of the first event highlighted that students would prefer more pre-entry information so we developed the programme to incorporate three aspects.

What it included
The three aspects to the initiative designed to support mature students included pre-entry contact, the Mature Student Guide and the TOPS event.

Pre-entry contact
Mature applicants are made aware of the mature student support via the admissions process and open days. They also have access to online materials aiding support and providing advice. Mature students who are accepted onto a course at Teesside are told about the specific support available to them via pre-arrival contact which is initiated over the summer before enrolment.

The Mature Student Guide
The Mature Student Guide is available in hard copy and online. It contains a range of advice, support information and tips for studying in higher education. The material includes a brief 'welcome' by the current vice chancellor who was himself a mature student. It is available during the admissions process.

TOPS event
The TOPS event happens before the university's freshers' week. This is important because it is designed to get mature students on campus without their younger peers. Individual invites to the TOPS event are sent out to students well before they arrive. The event is run by staff and volunteer current mature students.

It is very important that:

- this event and the correspondence leading up to it are pitched relatively informally so the university is seen as welcoming and new students realise that they are allowed to seek further information from staff.
- the material is relevant for mature students who have life experience but often less academic experience.

The TOPS event includes talks from staff and current mature students about what it is like to be a student at Teesside interspersed with interactive games, campus tours, refreshments; all designed to encourage communication and allay fears. Opportunities to meet and talk to new people are built in wherever possible.

How it was implemented
During the pre-arrival period, students are sent an invitation to TOPS detailing the event's information. Registration for the TOPS event itself begins three-quarters of an hour before the main activities commence so that students can meet current students and staff. Badges are colour coded by school (discipline area) so that they can identify potential fellows and make their own introductions. A senior member of staff introduces the event (e.g. the vice chancellor or one of his deputies) helping the students realise they are valued by the institution. There are then presentations from staff who were themselves mature students and staff from different support departments. Presentations are informal and interactive.

There is also, importantly, a presentation by current mature students, who do their talk without staff present so new students can ask questions freely. Feedback suggests that students appreciate this and it helps allay some fears. The interactive elements have changed over the years and now incorporate team-building activities to encourage group work and further interaction. To ensure that participants are not overloaded by presentations, we have recently introduced 'stalls' for different departments to enable participants to browse services and talk to relevant staff during coffee/lunch breaks.

Analysis and feedback
The TOPS event has been running since 2000 with positive evaluations each year. Changes suggested by students are incorporated where possible, although the event and the pre-entry material always evaluate well. Three things that consistently evaluate highly are:

- getting information in advance specifically for them;
- meeting other students at the event;
- the campus tour at the event.

As one mature student commented:

> I really enjoyed the TOPS event – having the opportunity to meet other mature students before actually starting uni was invaluable … I met people that day who have since become good friends and just knowing that I knew someone else in the same boat definitely made me feel a lot more confident on my first day.

The cost and timeline

Printed invitations and student guides (although these are now electronic, so costs are reduced).

Refreshments for 200, prizes for games, name badges, evaluation forms.
Typical costs = £1,500 per event.

How it is/was monitored

A questionnaire is provided at the TOPS event.

The outcome

The event and early contact has proved to be very successful and popular. Around 150–200 students attend the event annually. Our evidence suggests that advertising TOPS during the application and admissions process and contacting them before they enrol in a targeted and supportive way helps them realise that they are valued by our institution. Since the introduction of this initiative we have seen a significant improvement in retention figures for mature students.

Has or could the initiative be used for a different group?

We piloted the event for students with disabilities and had some success with the programme.

Advice and guidance

- Identify what kind of information and guidance should go in the guide by involving your target group of students.
- Involve mature students who are already studying with you as much as possible in writing guidance material and in any event.
- Invite as many 'potential' students as possible to the event. We now advertise on our website as well as sending invites.
- We have found having a senior member of staff introducing the event, and providing a welcome in the pre-event material, makes students feel valued.
- Cross-institutional collaboration is important to ensure that there is someone from each school/faculty for students to talk to at the event, and in making sure the event is inclusive.
- Make the event informal, students really appreciate games and interactions with peers and staff.
- Replication of information that will be given in freshers' week is inevitable; try to make it different and emphasise the specialness of the mature student experience.

For a more detailed discussion of the event itself, please read Greer and Tidd (2006).

References

Greer, L. and Tidd, J. (2006) 'You need someone to share with: taking the fear out of the transition into higher education for mature students', *Widening Participation and Lifelong Learning*, 8 (1): 44–51.

Contact details

j.tidd@tees.ac.uk

Case Study 4

Name and university
Matthew Semple, Systems Development Manager, University of Bristol, UK.

Title of project/initiative
Processing international students' applications and visas: points-based immigration system (PBS).

Who was involved in the initiative
Director of Student Administration, University Secretary (Head of Legal Services), University Lawyer, Deputy Undergraduate Admissions Officer, Head of the International Office, Senior International Officer, Student Systems Officer.

Reason for the project/initiative
To improve the undergraduate application and visa process whilst adhering to government immigration policy.

Why it was developed
As an institution we were looking at the process of how we recruited and processed the application and visas of our international students. At the same time, UK government policy changed regarding the study of international students in the UK. As an institution we combined both activities to ensure that we were compliant with the new government legislation, and that we retained our UG international student market whilst still providing a quality student experience.

The target group
All undergraduate international students applying to the University of Bristol who required a visa to study in the UK.

How it was developed, what it included and how it was implemented

How it was developed
The working group wanted to improve the efficiency, timeliness and accuracy when processing international students' applications and visa. The process within the institution for producing visa requests was cumbersome and time consuming. The undergraduate application process via UCAS (see Case Study 1) provided the institution with the information required to produce the visa letter requests. All visa letters had to be produced with accurate details in hard copy format and posted to the overseas students who had accepted an unconditional offer. It is important to note that through the UCAS system in the UK, applicants are only allowed to accept one course at one institution in a given admissions cycle. For many of our students, confirmation of their results did not occur until six weeks before the anticipated start date which meant that the printing, checking and sending out of visa letters had to happen within a very narrow timescale. Also, all letters had to be sent by courier to enable the International Office to track lost or non-received letters reported by international students. This costly process took substantial time and put enormous pressure on staff to provide the accurate information whilst maintaining high standards of service.

What it included

After university-wide discussion, interpreting and understanding the government's United Kingdom Border Agency (UKBA) requirements, a new process was designed, implemented and disseminated.

We decided that as UKBA required the electronic transmission of data, that we would move the process managed by administrative staff for generating our visa requests from hard copy to fully electronic and web based. There were two critical elements to the success of the project. The first element was designing the software that would act as a bridge between the input of data from UCAS to the University of Bristol's student records system (SITS) and the output of data to the UKBA's Sponsor Management System (SMS). Although the supplier of SITS provided their university customers with a visa request screen, we decided to deliver this new functionality to our staff in a clearer web-based format. This reduced the need for complex staff training and increased accuracy.

The second element was creating an effective staff workflow model using management information reports to process the visa requests in a timely and efficient manner. We had to develop the software and workflow model in-line with time constraints placed on us by UKBA.

How it was implemented

The process of producing a visa request was as follows:

- Every day, staff run a report highlighting all international students whose data is ready to be processed for a visa.
- The student's data is checked for accuracy in terms of course, personal details, passport number, qualifications, etc. and changed if required.
- When students' data is ready and checked, it's approved by an experienced member of staff in the Undergraduate Admissions Team.
- The data is then exported into the UKBA system along with a payment of £10 per student.
- A Confirmation of Acceptance for Study (CAS) number is then generated for each student.
- A file containing the CAS number is then imported into our student record system.
- The import automatically generates an email to each student informing them of the CAS number.
- We designed the email template to include a range of information and advice to enable the student to successfully apply for a visa and access other forms of support within the university.

Students are invited to contact us via email if they have any queries or the information we hold on them has changed or is incorrect. We felt that this was a very important element in order to support our students at this potentially stressful and confusing stage in their experience of the application process.

Analysis and feedback

A major concern was that we would experience a decline in international students as a direct result of the changes in visa legislation. These fears were not realised because although there was buoyancy in the undergraduate international student market, we had made every provision to ensure that our visa process was efficient, accurate and fast. Electronic delivery of visa information direct to the student meant that inefficiencies associated with the paper-based process were removed. Students did contact us with queries and we managed to help and support them immediately.

The cost and timeline

The cost of developing the software and the training of staff had to be absorbed into our annual costs in order to ensure the continued recruitment of international students, who are important to our income stream, and who help create an international and diverse community. The revised systems and process took two months to develop.

How it is/was monitored

We regularly monitor and assess the effectiveness of our system.

The outcome

- We have an effective electronic and web-based process.
- The data from UKBA enabled us to monitor which students had actually applied for a UK visa. This helped us plan for expected numbers.
- We have maintained our international student body.
- We have an established dialogue with the student during the visa application process;

Has or could the initiative be used for a different group?

We have developed a similar process for our postgraduate students.

Advice and guidance

- If you have the luxury of time to plan your process, do so.
- Look for the positives in activities that are imposed upon you.
- Achieve compliance without adversely affecting the student experience by managing expectations.
- Liaise with all key players.
- Provide support and training for colleagues.
- Communicate the need for change to the wider university community so colleagues are not confused, nervous or feel left unsupported.

Contact details

matthew.semple@bristol.ac.uk

Conclusion

An open-door policy or a highly selective entry process will impact on what you want the first contact and the admissions process to achieve.

However, any process should:

- be considered in the wider context of the overall student experience and the student journey;
- be a positive experience for all potential applicants;
- recognise their previous experiences;
- help prepare them for studying and achieving their potential;
- enable applicants to understand what the course will be like: a positive relationship between what they expect and reality is vital to engaging students successfully.

References

Bowl, M. (2003) *Non-traditional Entrants to Higher Education: 'They Talk About People Like me'*, Stoke-on-Trent: Trentham.

Cox, B. and Bidgood, P. (2003) *Widening Participation in Mathematics, Statistics and Operational Research*, Birmingham: LTSN (Learning and Teaching Subject Network) Maths, Stats and OR Network.

Fearn, H. (2010) 'Deciphering the code', *Times Higher Education*, 19 August.

Universities and Colleges Admissions Service (n.d.) 'yougo'. Online. Available at: http://www.ucas.com/yougo (accessed 15 October 2010).

Thomas, L. and Cooper, M. (eds) (2000) *Changing the Culture of the Campus: Towards an Inclusive Higher Education*, Stoke-on-Trent: Staffordshire University Press.

Chapter 4

Pre-arrival

Bizarreness, collisions and adjustments

Christine Keenan, Bournemouth University, UK

Introduction

The relationship that a student develops with their institution during the pre-arrival phase will set the pattern for the future. The experiences that a new student has during the pre-arrival phase, including the first two or three weeks of term, can set engagement patterns and exert a strong influence on their ability to persevere and succeed. In my experience, those students who do not fully engage with university life during these early weeks are most at risk of early withdrawal or of failing their first year. Therefore, it is essential to step back and consider the impact that the pre-arrival phase has on the student experience. This chapter looks at the challenges and good practice of the pre-arrival transition.

How an individual student responds to change will be influenced by their personality traits and disposition sets. However, what is it about the interactions between the characteristics of the university (which often seem strange or bizarre at first to students) and the characteristics of the student, that impacts on their potential to persevere and succeed or give up and fail? What influences, or forces, are coming into play during the pre-arrival experience?

Institutions and practitioners need to acknowledge and understand this interesting, complex and multi-dimensional phase of student life. It is in the interests of everyone who works with students to ensure that university systems are put in place to provide a supportive pre-arrival environment that is welcoming, starts building a sense of belonging and seamlessly links into the other stages in the Practitioner Model outlined in Chapter 2 in order for new students to settle in and grow as learners.

It is useful to think of the pre-arrival stage in three phases:

1 first contact, confirmation of a university place and admissions;
2 getting used to the idea of actually going to university;
3 preparing for arrival.

It is critical that communication interlinks with the issues, challenges and support needs of new students during these phases.

Institutions are very good at supporting the practical information giving requirements of the new student as demonstrated in the previous chapter. However, as the start of term draws near, the new student's state of mind shifts from the functional to the more emotional and the emotional support can often be neglected. When starting to get used to the idea of going to university and preparing for arrival, their thoughts turn to:

- making friends;
- coping with independence, and living away from home, often for the first time;
- wanting to know what will happen when they first arrive: how will they find their way around, what will it be like;
- how to get started on their learning;
- knowing what will be expected of them;
- formulating more focused questions.

Communication requirements shift to being more personal and individualised. It is much more about identity, what sort of a learner they will be, will they fit in and what sort of people will they mix with. Placing the new student at the centre of things, opens the imagination to how adjustments can be made in the area of pre-arrival support that works with the student to meet the challenges of a stimulating first year. At an institutional level, the requirement of this pre-arrival phase is to provide new students with accessible, relevant and meaningful information that is contextualised to them and their learning. Activities such as online enrolment and registration increase their sense of belonging. The individual student is now the audience, and the purpose is to engage, enthuse and inspire the new student through the provision of an appropriate level of study advice, more in-depth information about the course, including some introductory learning activities and an outline of what is to be expected during orientation week (Keenan, 2010). Imaginative use of online mechanisms for information giving allows students to self-manage their engagement with it. For example, the availability of an orientation website provides a helpful reference point. It is also a useful time to find out more about the new student by offering an opportunity for dialogue between the student and their tutor. New students at this stage are also forming informal social groupings through social network sites.

When the arrival period finally comes, it is a time of accelerated experiences and almost a collision point between before and after. It is critical that new students are prepared for this exciting, difficult and possibly challenging period during the pre-arrival stage.

The case studies in this chapter provide illustrations of how some institutions have developed initiatives to effectively support the student through the pre-arrival period.

Case Study 5 by Tim May describes the development of an online system at the University of Sussex, UK, designed to simplify registration and enrolment for students which is particularly helpful for pre-arrival students. Shifting registration and enrolment to the pre-arrival phase can help the student feel a sense of belonging, as they can access a wide range of university support materials and resources.

Case Study 6 from Christine Keenan takes a student-centred approach to promoting academic engagement in the pre-arrival phase at Bournemouth University, UK. Stepping Stones 2HE promotes relationship development in three key ways: between the student and their learning; between the student and their tutor; and between the student and the wider institution. The aim is to improve confidence about starting at university by providing contextualised introductory learning activities as a starting point for collaborative work in induction week.

Case Study 7 by Becka Colley provides an example of the use of online social media and web 2.0 tools to provide students with information and a way of connecting with each other to form social interactions at the University of Bradford, UK. Develop Me!'s inclusive, flexible and pro-active approach is based on sound learning development and practitioner model principles. It encourages students to have ownership and control over their own development underpinned with social support that their networking provides.

Case Study 8 from Chris Ford demonstrates how a pre-arrival website provides much needed information for new students on the pre-arrival, arrival and orientation stages, but interestingly also provides information and advice for parents and other family members. This web resource provides advice and information from the first point of contact, through the application stage and on to the enrolment and registration phases for engineering students at Kingston University, UK.

Case Study 5

Name and university
Tim May, Head of Student Systems, University of Sussex, UK.

Title of project/initiative
Sussex direct online registration (SDOR): improving the registration (enrolment) process utilising the web.

Who was involved in the initiative?
Head of Student Systems, Business Information Systems (looks after and develops the student record database), IT Services (responsible for student IT accounts), University Student Experience Manager, Academic Registrar, Head of Financial Accounts.

Reason for the project/initiative
I arrived at Sussex University in 2001. In my previous university roles I had been heavily involved in the registration process and had seen in person the enormous burden that paper-based registration caused for students and staff in time, physical space and cost. With the support of the Academic Registrar and taking advantage of changes within the sector, I had the opportunity to develop a simple, robust and effective student self-enrolment process.

Why it was developed
It was developed to:

- reduce the administrative burden on students and staff;
- reduce costs and help improve the arrival and orientation experience of our new students.

Internal research had demonstrated that students did not enjoy queuing up for hours to complete a bureaucratic process that the university required students to undertake.

The target group
In the first year, we piloted the online registration process with all undergraduate students, both new and returning. The year after, the process included all postgraduate students.

How it was developed, what it included and how it was implemented

How it was developed
The University of Sussex Student Portal (Sussex Direct) was being developed at the same time. A portal is a way for students and staff to view data in a specific context. The Sussex Direct project put into place a mechanism for students to securely log onto the portal in order to see a range of personal and course data which was held on the student records database. Via this portal, we could deliver online registration. I had a clear idea of what student information we already held on the database, which would be displayed through the portal, and how that was collected. I knew what gaps existed if we were to put the whole registration process online. At the same time this development was taking place, the Student Loan Company (SLC) responsible for supporting student tuition fee arrangements, was bringing in a new process which would deliver information about a student's tuition fee liability to the university before registration. We wanted to take advantage of this new information to allow us to finalise the student tuition fee position for many of our undergraduate students well before arrival.

I pulled together a team to develop this process. It was intended that online registration would help the university:

- verify personal data;
- collect contact information;
- get students to sign up to our terms and conditions/regulations;
- collect tuition and housing fees in advance.

Online registration would help the student:

- confirm their tuition fee position;
- manage their university costs;
- access their IT/email accounts early;
- access other key university information (e.g. course information);
- remove an old fashioned, bureaucratic in-person activity.

What it included

The online process asks the student to work through a checklist of tasks. These tasks include:

- confirming personal details (e.g. name, date of birth, nationality, ethnicity, disability);
- recording next of kin;
- recording addresses (term time and permanent);
- making data protection choices;
- signing up to the regulations and terms and conditions;
- the payment of tuition and housing fees (choice of different modes of payment).

Most of these tasks only need to be completed once during the life of the student at university. So for the returning student, they typically only need to reconfirm their term-time address and make payment for tuition or housing fees. The system does not allow students who have any outstanding academic or financial issues to fully register online. Most students are able to fully register online before arrival at the university. For those who are unable to do so due to confirmation of academic conditions, or being unable to make credit card payments for tuition fees or housing costs, they can attend an in-person registration session within the first week they arrive.

How it was implemented

Once the system was built, the key was to get the information to students to enable them to start the process. In the UK, students typically start the academic year around the end of September. Throughout the summer, we are preparing each new student record by gathering data through various means (University and Colleges Admission Service, SLC and our own systems) in preparation for our online system to go live on 1 September each year. For returning students, we are allocating fees and flagging exam results for progression on their records.

In late August, new students receive a university pack of information which includes how they can register online. It provides them with a student candidate number which they combine with their surname and date of birth. This allows them to obtain their IT services username and password. Once they have this, they can log on to the university online registration system to start their registration by working through the tasks. Students are required to supply a passport photograph which is scanned onto their ID card containing their own unique barcode before being printed. We are looking at students being able to upload their own photograph but picture quality can be an issue. ID cards are given out during the first week at collection events. At this event, international students' ID is checked to comply with the United Kingdom Border Agency visa requirements. Collection also acts as an attendance record. Students who complete their registration in-person have their photograph taken at the time and are provided with an ID card immediately.

Returning students are sent an email and they are asked to log on and complete any outstanding tasks, such as payments and confirming their term-time address.

Analysis and feedback

Using the monitoring process below and also feedback gained via working with students who had gone through the process.

The cost and timeline

The software to deliver the online registration via the portal was developed and delivered over 6–8 weeks. This short timescale was only made possible by having a robust structure already in place on the database and a software development team able to develop in a rapid application development (RAD) mode. The main cost was the development of software. We have made savings in terms of the number of staff involved in the in-person registration process, space use, length of the registration operation and associated costs.

How it is/was monitored

Using database reporting tools, we are able to monitor the collection of username and passwords, the number of students who complete registration and those who have started the process. Some of this analysis coupled with user feedback (through the IT services help desk) enables us to detect and fix some generic problems before they impact on the service. We have a system that is robust and established. We still run regular reports though to monitor progress in order to detect any unforeseen issues.

The outcome

All our students at UG and PG level are asked to register online. Even those who cannot fully complete the process online must complete most of the online process. Approximately 80 per cent of the entire student body register fully online. New and returning student arrival and orientation reviews demonstrate much higher student satisfaction regarding the registration process.

Has or could the initiative be used for a different group?

This process can cover any student on any mode of course whether part-time, distance or work-based learner.

Advice and guidance

- Decide what you want to include in your process (e.g. does it include fee payment or housing costs).
- Map your current process.
- Fill the gaps.
- Pilot first but don't completely scale down the in-person process until you know online registration works.
- Expect more work upfront in the lead up to registration.
- Benefits are a more measured, calmer process for students and staff at the start of term.

Contact details

t.a.may@sussex.ac.uk

Case Study 6

Name and university
Christine Keenan, Learning and Teaching Fellow, Bournemouth University, UK.

Title of project/initiative
Stepping Stones 2HE: active transition into university.

Who was involved in the initiative
Christine Keenan, Programme Leaders, First-Year Tutors, Subject Librarians and Learning Technologists.

Reason for the project/initiative
The original aim was to address high withdrawal rates from an engineering programme at Bournemouth University by supporting the transition into university. The project aimed to:

- develop better understandings of student expectations;
- provide information for students in a more managed and phased way to avoid information overload;
- promote student engagement with their learning through contextualised pre-arrival learning activities;
- link the pre-learning activities with structured group working opportunities during the first week at university to facilitate social and academic integration;
- provide students with an opportunity through an 'About You' survey to reflect on their previous learning experiences and expectations, and ask any burning questions in a more private way.

Why it was developed
Initially, Stepping Stones 2HE was developed to reduce early withdrawal rates. This relied on a number of factors:

- finding a mechanism to phase information giving that would allow students to self-manage the process;
- developing a closer understanding of student expectations;
- developing a closer knowledge of students' previous curriculums in order to avoid false assumptions about starting points;
- providing structured learning activities (rather than a 'reading list') to give students some insight into their course;
- integrating this pre-arrival learning with collaborative learning during the first week to promote social and academic integration;
- being able to identify students early in the process who may be at risk of early withdrawal through monitoring engagement factors.

The key was to stimulate interest and engagement during the pre-arrival, arrival and orientation phases in three meaningful ways. To provide:

- an introduction to study at university;
- contextualised learning activities that would be developed collaboratively during induction week;
- the student with time to reflect on their previous learning experiences and their hopes and expectations of the university and themselves.

The target group
All first-year students arriving at university.

How it was developed, what it included and how it was implemented

How it was developed
In 2002, I identified a retention problem within my school at Bournemouth University which is broadly engineering based. Retention issues were problematic because it was not easy to recruit students to engineering courses and there was a high attrition rate. The financial implications to the school were clearly significant, but so were the social and financial implications for students who were leaving very early in the first term. After research was undertaken, I found that institutional practices played a large part in student withdrawal.

New first-year student focus groups suggested that they found their introductory week:

*   alienating, confusing and exhausting. One student said to me 'it felt like my head was opened up and my brains leaked out';
*   too long with some orientation activities like pub crawls not wanted;
*   did not contain enough 'getting down to work' activities;
*   did not explain habitual ways of doing things. 'Uni is OK once you get used to the bizarreness of it'.

University staff:

*   did not like the chaos of the first week;
*   did not feel that they really got to know their students very well;
*   felt that they had a lot of important information to get across but that it was not taken in.

Local A level teachers:

*   stated that our assumptions about the content of A levels did not always closely match the actual student experience;
*   felt that A level study developed strong independent learning skills.

Discussions with students and staff led me to develop the key principles outlined earlier.

What it included
Stepping Stones 2HE included:

*   information and structured guidance about study at university and how it would be different to previous learning experiences;
*   an 'About You' survey;
*   information about extra curricula activities with links to the Students' Union leadership and volunteering pages, clubs and societies, etc.;
*   guidance on registering for additional learning needs support;
*   news headlines from the wider university community;
*   course related information: what will happen during the first week, including learning activities.

How it was implemented
Stepping Stones 2HE was launched in 2003 on all courses within the School of Engineering. Programme leaders, subject librarians, study support staff, the Student Union and Additional Learning Needs Service staff all contributed to its development. Clear guidelines were given

to guide the level and amount of content. The Learning Technologist then consolidated all the information as a web-based resource. More recently we have experimented with locating the resource on the university virtual learning environment that students can fully access by registering online at confirmation time in August. Directing students to the resource via their confirmation letter ensures that no late applicants are missed (e.g. applicants through clearing).

Analysis and feedback

It had an immediate impact on retention during the first term so the approach was adopted by all schools within the university. This transition support is now articulated in university strategy documents. Attrition rates continued to decline in my school going from 24.7 per cent in 2005 to 19.5 cent cent in 2007. Enhancements have subsequently been made with more focus on first-year experience; the setting up of a university-wide first-year experience special interest group; a new position of a first-year experience Students' Union sabbatical officer; and a university-wide student experience committee that has a close focus on hearing the first-year students' voice.

Every year, new first-year students and staff are invited to provide feedback on the resource and this transition experience.

Students reported:

> It was great, made me feel part of the uni family.
> It helped me settle in quickly and know what was going on.

Staff reported:

> Group cohesion improves dramatically.
> It was great, there was a real buzz around the place.
> Second-year students were amazed at what the first years had achieved.

Staff development

Staff development sessions were undertaken to enhance Stepping Stones 2HE and related first-year experience issues. The 'About You' survey has enabled us to track and monitor the early engagement of students who struggle to settle in. Through understanding student and staff expectations, we have been able to manage both more effectively.

The cost and timeline

Stepping Stones 2HE was initially developed over a two-month period. The greatest resource is staff time and the way it is organised ensures that the workload of all staff is evenly spaced out.

How it is/was monitored

The 'About You' surveys are monitored and responses made to students. The effectiveness of the intervention is evaluated annually with both staff and students.

The outcome

Although originally conceived of as a retention tool, Stepping Stones 2HE is now seen as a fully rounded transition resource. It has had an influence on improving retention particularly into the first few weeks of term, and we know that as a confidence-building resource it certainly reduces anxiety about starting at university. There are plans to make the resource more visual by using video clips. The use of Facebook is being assessed.

Has or could the initiative be used for a different group?

Stepping Stones 2HE was devised to meet the needs of all new first-year students. It aims to be fully inclusive. Dissemination has shown the resource to be inclusive of students with disabilities and students from non-traditional backgrounds. Other institutions are adapting the approach to meet the needs of their students.

Advice and guidance

- Work with champions and devolve responsibility.
- Always involve students.
- In my view, web-based resources are preferable to VLE-based resources for transition materials.

Contact details

ckeenan@bournemouth.ac.uk

Case Study 7

Name and university
Becka Colley, Dean of Students, University of Bradford, UK.

Title of project/initiative
Develop Me!, Support Me, Engage and Retain Me: using online materials to support and enhance student transition.

Who was involved in the initiative
Dean of Students, Faculty Administrators, Associate Deans for Learning and Teaching, e-Learning Team.

Reason for the project/initiative
In our annual First-Year Student Experience Survey, student feedback strongly indicated that more support was needed to help with the pre-arrival through to the induction transitions in terms of:

- making friends and meeting other students;
- providing opportunities for different cohorts of students to interact with each other (e.g. locally-based students, international students, mature students, employer-based students);
- understanding levels of confidence in different skill areas (e.g. academic reading, academic writing, group working);
- becoming familiar with the campus and surrounding areas;
- engaging with academic and skills-based activities during August and early September once a place at university is confirmed.

Running alongside this was the explosion in the use of social media and web 2.0 tools as a way of people connecting with each other and sharing experiences and ideas which we wanted to utilise.

The key issues for us were to help students manage the transition into university level study more effectively right from the moment they applied for a place and to improve the retention of these students through academic and social engagement.

Why it was developed
Develop Me! was introduced to meet the needs outlined above and to also provide a framework for the development of other initiatives aimed at enhancing the student experience and ensuring student success. The primary objective was to enable students to do this through meeting other students and staff on the website and interacting with academic and skills development materials prior to arrival.

The target group
All students were targeted to become involved in the social network but especially those who were entering the University of Bradford for the first time. This included those on collaborative provision courses, distance learners, work-based learners and direct entrants.

How it was developed, what it included and how it was implemented

How it was developed
Develop Me! grew out of a number of different projects which all focused on increasing student engagement and providing the support learners needed at the time they wanted it and in a format they could effectively access. Most importantly, we wanted students to feel

like they belonged to a community and were given the opportunity to make friends before starting their course. The main concept of Develop Me! was to provide a space for students to develop themselves within a defined structure. It grew out of our Learner Development Unit (LDU) which is a central unit providing support to students in their academic, maths and interpersonal skills. Students would come to the LDU and ask for help in developing their skills and to get better marks. However, students were not really sure what they wanted to do or how they could do it.

For many, their contact with the LDU stemmed out of a need for motivation and direction with their studies. For many, university was a big, unfamiliar and complex environment where they did not feel that they could make contact with their lecturers directly and talk about issues to do with anxiety or nerves or lack of academic confidence/competence. The site aimed to address this.

In our expectations survey, students identified the following issues:

> Nobody has really even told us how to go about studying at the university. It's very different from A-Levels;
>
> New students need support and guidance so they don't feel dissatisfied with the university; and
>
> [I am] just feeling unsure of myself, as in am I capable of completing it [my programme] academically?

What it included

Develop Me! included:

- a social network (http://developme.ning.com) (such as Facebook);
- SaPRA (the University of Bradford's in-house Skills and Personal Development Activity);
- online skills development resources focusing on different skills (e.g. writing literature reviews, understanding what type of learner you are);
- mobile guides. Content which is available on mobile devices: skills materials, maps and university information;
- research into the student experience to ensure that what we develop and support meets student needs. The student voice has been crucial to the development of the approach.

How it was implemented

Develop Me! was rolled out across the university as a result of changes to our induction and retention policies and procedures. Schools were required to actively engage in the use of Develop Me! either as a whole or elements of the approach. A new induction framework was written and approved by the university senate which helped to ensure the approach was embedded effectively across the university.

The site was designed to be external facing so anyone landing on the home page could interact with the materials. Applicants were encouraged to use the site pre-enrolment. To post content and interact with students and staff, users had to register for a ning account. Enrolled students (August onwards) were directed to the site and had access to more online matierials.

Analysis and feedback

Our retention and progression rates have improved since Develop Me! was introduced. Students report that they feel more confident and positive about starting university and that they are more aware of what will happen. Staff and student expectations have been explicitly defined and where there is a mismatch between expectations and reality, this can be addressed and resolved.

The cost and timeline

Develop Me! has been under development since 2006. However the main components of the approach were all developed quite quickly within 2006.

- The social network took one staff member two weeks to establish and populate with content from start to finish.
- SaPRA took one staff member three weeks to write from scratch. Each year the tool is refined and enhanced following feedback from staff and students. About three weeks of development time is spent each year to achieve this. Delivering SaPRA to 3,000 new students takes about one week of one staff member's time, and we are working with faculties to ensure that they take more ownership and responsibility for delivering this in the future.
- The online skills development resources took one staff member about one month to create, develop, test and upload. We add more resources as and when we have time to increase the number of tools available. We also make use of other online materials, for example, those created by the LearnHigher CETL to enhance and supplement what we had been able to develop in-house.
- The mobile guides took one staff member about one week to produce. These are now being migrated into a new application which smart phone users can download straight onto their devices.
- The research takes one staff member about one month to complete. This time includes setting up the survey, publicising it, analysing the responses and writing a report for discussion internally.

The costs for developing this type of approach varies depending on staff expertise and workload. We obtained external funding from a number of different sources to develop and evaluate the materials.

How it is/was monitored

Our annual survey asks students and staff about their use of Develop Me! and how they feel the various elements could be enhanced/modified in the future. A recent QA audit highlighted Develop Me! as an example of good practice.

The outcome

Develop Me! has become embedded across the university leading to increased rates of retention and progressions. It has enabled us to support students from the moment of application as well as helping students increase their levels of confidence during their first year at university.

Has or could the initiative be used for a different group?

Develop Me! was developed for a large and diverse student cohort therefore it can easily be applied to other institutions.

Advice and guidance

- Don't be afraid to take risks.
- Involve students and staff in the process.
- Devolve responsibility to individual faculties rather than trying to do it all yourself.

Contact details

b.colley@bradford.ac.uk
Twitter: beckacolley

Case Study 8

Name and university
Chris Ford, Student Support and Liaison, Kingston University, UK.

Title of project/initiative
Pre-arrival, arrival and orientation website – managing student and family aspirations and expectations: a Faculty of Engineering initiative.

Who was involved in the initiative
Student Support Officer (SSO), Faculty Learning and Teaching Coordinator and Student Experience Manager, Faculty Web Team.

Reason for the project/initiative
The aim was to give both students and their families (parents, guardians, spouses, partners) the information they needed to effectively support the transition from first contact through to arrival and orientation. We knew through our Student Expectation Survey that students felt unprepared for their university experience because of the lack of advice, information and guidance they received from the faculty and university for this transition.

Why it was developed
We wanted to:

- manage the student experience from first contact;
- enable our students to succeed by providing targeted and concise information, advice and guidance;
- improve our retention and student satisfaction rates of our new students.

The target group
Undergraduate full-time students.

How it was developed, what it included and how it was implemented

How it was developed
The website developed from the internal research undertaken by the Faculty Learning and Teaching Coordinator and Student Experience Manager. From her experience of developing a similar website at another institution, it was evident that we had a gap in the support and information we were giving to students and their families during the application stage and after their place was confirmed at university.

The website was developed by looking at and utilising:

- internal research;
    - student expectation and orientation surveys;
    - parent feedback through the arrival faculty tea party;
    - student focus groups;
- national and international research on the first-year student experience;
- the knowledge and expertise of the Faculty Learning and Teaching Coordinator, Student Experience Manager and the SSO;
- user testing of the website for ease of use and navigation.

Once the gaps had been indentified, we adopted and adapted information used across the sector as well as developing our own information to create a comprehensive website for all new students and their families. A lot of time was spent on making sure the information was in the right place and structured in the best way to ensure ease of access.

Useful information for students already provided by the university was on the university's intranet which could only be accessed once the student had completed part of the enrolment process. Where this was the case, we copied the information and placed it on our external website.

What it included

The site included:

- information for parents and students about the different types of support services available to students before arrival and during their studies;
- a timeline of how the student may feel and what they may experience throughout the academic lifecycle and what support the university and the faculty had to offer;
- advice for family members on how to support the student in their studies;
- information on what to expect at university and what is expected of them;
- advice on how to study at university;
- information on the arrival, welcome and orientation processes;
- key contacts for students within the faculty and central support services;
- term and semester dates;
- frequently asked questions;
- links to other useful student advice websites.

How it was implemented

Once the information was collated, we worked closely with the faculty web team to design the pages. They advised us on the most appropriate design and on ease of use and access.

The pre-arrival, arrival and orientation site was situated within a section of the Faculty of Engineering website. Applicants and impending students could access it via a number of ways.

The URL address for the site was on all our faculty admissions and pre-arrival, arrival and orientation literature and letters. Applicants considering coming to the Faculty of Engineering at Kingston could access the site via the University and Colleges Admissions Service (UCAS) through which all undergraduate students in the UK must apply to university. Applicants looking at engineering courses at Kingston on the UCAS site could click on a link entitled 'what to expect at university' and it would take them straight to the pre-arrival, arrival and orientation site.

From August onwards, an 'arrival and orientation' button is put on the faculty's home page which takes users straight through to the site.

Analysis and feedback

The faculty regularly undertakes student focus groups to look at the site and whether it needs updating.

The cost and timeline

This initiative was developed within a small timescale but it happened as a result of knowledge, experience and research accrued over a number of years. The main cost was time by those involved in the initiative. They undertook the development as part of their job remit.

How it is/was monitored

As well as undertaking student focus groups, the site is monitored for the hit rate. The site is available all year round but as expected, the most hits occur when students are making university choices and just before they arrive. The family advice section receives a large number of hits.

The outcome

The benefits have been numerous for students in the Faculty of Engineering:

- the enrolment process is easier and there are fewer queues due to students being more prepared about what to bring to enrolment;
- there are fewer phone calls from parents about the support their son or daughter can access;
- there is better behaviour within lectures and fewer complaints from students as they know what to expect;
- the Faculty of Engineering regularly receives the best feedback in the university's arrival and orientation survey.

The site provides a holistic picture of support so it has also been a useful tool for staff in enabling them to understand the needs of the modern student and how all areas of the university support them. Personal tutors within the faculty are expected to interact with the site so they can update their knowledge on services.

As a result of this site, the university has undertaken two main initiatives for the benefit of all new students coming to the university which I have been heavily involved in.

The first was the introduction of the parents' website. In its first year of implementation, it had over 10,000 hits and was the most visited pages within the main Kingston University website.

The university has now established a 'Getting Ready' site which uses the same principles of ensuring that all information is clear and accessible. All faculties are expected to have a site like the Faculty of Engineering which can be accessed via the main university 'Getting Ready' site.

The main university sites can be accessed via www.kingston.ac.uk/gettingready or www.kingston.ac.uk/parents.

Has or could the initiative be used for a different group?

The Faculty of Engineering site has been extended to include postgraduate students and information for students studying at partner institutions.

Advice and guidance

- Don't reinvent the wheel in terms of information. Use what you have and use links to other sites.
- Involve all key players.
- Place it where and when students would want to see it.
- Design an accessible site that is easy to navigate around.
- Keep the information structured, targeted and concise.

Contact details

chris.ford@kingston.ac.uk

Conclusion

Students engage with their learning, their course and their institution in a variety of ways. The way they engage may be dependent on their personality and dispositions or it may be dictated by their goals and ambitions. It can also be fostered and nurtured by the way the institution welcomes and introduces them to university life (May and Thomas, 2010). However, what is abundantly clear is that if their engagement does not happen effectively they may make a decision to leave. It is important to 'hear' what students are asking for. For example, asking for a reading list may be a proxy for wanting to prepare for some contextualised learning. It is important to look at how pre-arrival resources can be designed to be inclusive and accessible to all. Students want to feel valued by the staff they are in contact with and they want to feel secure. How can they be made to feel valued and respected as individuals? They need to develop a sense of belonging and they want, and deserve, effective communications. Students also want to be proactive in their transition to university and to begin their learning journey quickly and smoothly. The interventions described in this chapter have emphasised the importance of:

- good organisation and management with clear and transparent communications;
- providing pre-arrival access to robust university systems;
- explaining the difference between school and university learning;
- helping students become confident, autonomous and independent through the provision of thoughtful introductory learning and skills resources;
- providing opportunities for students to engage in activities that promote social and academic integration;
- commitment of all staff involved with new students.

The examples of pre-arrival strategies and resources described in this chapter have all been developed by practitioners making an observation about the experience of their students and then providing a purposeful and deliberate intervention designed to improve that experience.

Provision of relevant information at the right time during the pre-arrival phase can help to address the information overload problem of orientation week but it must be remembered that students are still getting on with their pre-university lives and often responding in an emotional way to practical information. So, getting the relevance, timing, quantity and type of information right in the pre-arrival phase is really critical to help avoid the seeds of doubt that can often creep in due to a poor arrival, orientation and induction experience.

The advantages of addressing the multi-dimensional aspects of the pre-arrival phase is a direct positive impact on student engagement and sense of belonging. Sensitivity to student needs and discussion of mutual expectations will provide deeper understandings of student transitions through the pre-arrival phase and induction experience leading to a more transparent, inclusive and less bizarre environment for students and influence more effective student engagement.

References

Keenan, C. (2010) 'A personal development planning perspective on supporting students through transition into higher education', in P. Hartley, J. Hilsdon and C. Keenan (eds) *Learning Development in Higher Education*, Basingstoke: Palgrave.

May, H. and Thomas, L. (2010) *What Works: Student Retention and Success*, Leeds: Retention Convention.

Chapter 5

Arrival and orientation

Kerrie-Lee Krause, Griffith University, Australia

Introduction

As students prepare for their first year of university study, they often experience a combination of excitement, anticipation and apprehension. Some might even be quite fearful and uncertain, particularly if they are one of the 'pathfinders' or first in their family or community to attend university. One of the challenges for those involved in supporting new students during the arrival and orientation process is to retain a fresh outlook on the world of university study with each new cohort of students. It is easy to become so familiar with the 'way we do things around here' that we forget what it is like to encounter the challenges of the university environment for the very first time. As Tucker (Case Study 10) says, the key is to take the time to explicitly establish a 'common universe of meaning'. This applies no matter who the student cohort is, whether they be undergraduate or postgraduate students, part-time or full-time, local or international, mature aged or directly out of school.

This chapter explores the characteristics of effective arrival and orientation strategies for first-year students. 'Arrival' refers to students' earliest interactions with the institution once they have formally enrolled, though in some institutions, it may also include such elements as registration and enrolment. In particular, it refers to their first day or week on campus – or online if enrolled in external mode. What sorts of impressions do we want our students to have when they arrive? What knowledge and skills do we expect of them? How do we communicate those expectations and, in turn, give students an opportunity to ask questions and seek advice if they do not arrive with the requisite knowledge? These are the types of questions addressed when one considers the 'arrival' milestone.

To support students beyond the point of arrival, most institutions have some form of 'orientation' programme for their students. This may include: an introduction to the country, the city and the campus for international students; an academic orientation to their programme of study within a department; social activities and introductions to university clubs and societies; or a combination of these. Arrival and orientation milestones will be discussed in turn, though they are closely connected in many ways.

Managing diverse arrival needs and experiences

A defining characteristic of the student body in a mass higher education system is its diversity. As mentioned at the start, we cannot assume that all students will be positive and excited about starting university study; neither should we assume that all are nervous and uncertain. Some students may have had older siblings or friends to guide them prior to enrolment or they might arrive with a number of friends from their local high school or community. The arrival support strategy for these students would no doubt look quite different from the approach taken for international students, for example. Similarly, you may choose to adapt your strategy for mature age students as compared with school-aged students entering university for the first time.

While it is important to maintain consistency in terms of the types of information available to students about enrolment and course advice (see Case Study 9), it is equally important to adapt the ways in which you deliver this information in order to maximise the success with which you relate to diverse student cohorts. For instance, in Case Study 11, Ward refers to the use of social networking tools, such as Facebook, and a 3D virtual guide booklet to engage with international students as they arrive at university. These forms of engagement could be particularly appealing for some students but not for others. It is therefore essential to know who your students are, the nature of their support and information needs and the most effective means of communicating with them. In order to address these issues, you will need to gather feedback from students over time and evaluate your support strategies regularly.

In summary, when planning your arrival strategies for new students:

- know your students, their background characteristics and needs and adapt your arrival strategy accordingly;
- monitor and evaluate your initiatives on a regular basis with a view to continuously improving the effectiveness of your arrival and orientation strategies.

Characteristics of effective orientation programmes

This book adopts a lifecycle approach to the student experience. In other words, it highlights the fact that students move through a series of key milestones or defining moments in their transition to university study. As they move through these milestones, they need to be given the opportunity to revisit what has been learned along the way. One of the greatest mistakes made in planning orientation programmes is trying to do too much during students' early introductions to university study. The temptation is to cover as much ground as possible since there is so much to be done. If the communication of information is not managed wisely, students are likely to leave their orientation experiences frustrated, overwhelmed and confused. Keys to success in orientation include:

- Strike a healthy balance between academic and social orientation, making sure that students receive essential information about their programme of study while also having the opportunity to make friends and get to know academic and support staff who will be most important during their first few weeks of study.
- Prioritise information with great care so that students receive essential 'need to know' information that will be critical for survival during their first few weeks.
- Provide a roadmap and reference points to which students can refer after orientation. In other words, do not try to give them all the information at once, but show them how and where to find out more when they need it.
- Be explicit about expectations and provide evidence about what makes a successful first-year student. For instance, share with students your institutional data about how

best to balance full-time study with part-time paid work, use later-year students to highlight the characteristics of successful first-year study habits.

- Adapt the programme to suit diverse student needs and ensure that any social activities, such as the traditional 'pub night', are respectful of cultural, ethnic and religious diversity that so often characterises the first-year student cohort.
- Remember that students do not operate in isolation – it is important to take into account the value of providing information to parents, partners and communities so that they, too, can provide a support mechanism for students during their study (see Case Study 12).

While much of this chapter tends to focus on undergraduate first-year students, many of the strategies can be adapted to suit the needs of postgraduate students. It is equally important to support their arrival and orientation needs. Similarly, planning needs to take account of the fact that many undergraduate students follow non-traditional transition pathways. They may be credit transfer students entering university in their second year, yet they still require arrival and orientation support. Once again, the principle of knowing and catering for your student cohort and their distinctive needs applies.

Building on the arrival strategy tips mentioned earlier in this chapter, when planning orientation programmes for new students:

- remember, 'less is more' in orientation – it is a process that extends well beyond the first day or week so don't try to do too much;
- tailor orientation activities to the needs of diverse student cohorts while maintaining a core of consistent and accurate information available for all students;
- ensure that your orientation activities are inclusive and respectful of diverse cultural practices and beliefs.

The four case studies in this chapter provide practical strategies for addressing several of the arrival and orientation issues discussed.

Case Study 9 by Michelle Morgan describes a comprehensive, evidence-based approach to supporting new students during the arrival and orientation phase at Kingston and Sussex universities in the UK.

Case Study 10 by Chris Tucker looks at the role of later-year students as residential advisors for students in residence at the University of Sussex, UK.

Case Study 11 by Frances McNally and Margaret Ward highlights the activities of the orientation programme for international students at Glasgow Caledonian University, UK.

Case Study 12 by Richard Mullendore, University of South Carolina, USA, demonstrates an example of an orientation programme for parents of first-year students.

Case Study 9

Name and university
Michelle Morgan, Faculty Learning and Teaching Coordinator and Student Experience Manager, Faculty of Engineering, Kingston University, UK.

Title of project/initiative
The eight-strand approach to orientation for Level 1 and direct-entry students.

Who was involved in the initiative
The initiative was developed in two stages. Stage one was developed at the University of Sussex (US) and focused on students entering Level 1. It involved key players from each of the five schools and their departments and colleagues from all central university units. I then adapted it for direct-entry and transfer students into Levels 2 and 3 in the Faculty of Engineering at Kingston University (KU). It involved key players from across the faculty and institution. At both universities, the key players were members of the working group who supported and facilitated the changes.

Reason for the project/initiative
To improve the transition of students into university study and to aid retention.

Why it was developed
Stage one was developed due to external research and a major internal review at the US. We knew supporting the arrival and orientation (or 'induction' as it used to be called) of students was a critical activity in helping them settle into their studies and successfully progress through their degree. Internal statistics showed that a large percentage of students withdrew within the first eight weeks of starting university.

The review highlighted a number of poor experiences, including moving into accommodation, enrolment and lack of information. The primary failing was that the orientation activities in freshers' week varied greatly across the schools in terms of activities, quality and staff involvement. Apart from the enrolment process and students moving into accommodation, the rest of the programme was left to schools and departments to organise. This resulted in students across the schools getting a different experience within the first week of arriving at university. Students also complained that there was too much delay between moving in and the orientation programme starting.

Arrival and orientation needed to be friendly, not bureaucratic, appropriately pitched and with fully structured academic and social ice-breaking activities. We needed to move away from the traditionally administrative-led orientation that fitted around the needs of the university rather than our increasingly diverse student body.

The target group
At Sussex, the target group was all Level 1 students. The initiative was extended in the Faculty of Engineering at KU to include all new students entering Levels 1, 2, 3 or 4 and students at partner institutions (PIs).

How it was developed, what it included and how it was implemented

How it was developed
An extensive review was undertaken on the previous arrival and orientation event. Staff and students from across the institution were surveyed and interviewed. The findings were

published. This review contained quantitative and qualitative research and was critical in facilitating change and engaging staff across the university. The voice of the student was a very powerful change tool. All changes for the coming year were agreed by the working group made up of colleagues from across the university.

Improving the entire arrival and orientation processes was a huge undertaking and there were a number of new and improved interlinked initiatives. They included streamlining all the pre-arrival and arrival literature sent to new students, changing the activity of moving into university accommodation to a weekend and providing all staff with key information to engage them in the activity. International students were required to arrive, settle in and start their international orientation programme mid-week (just before the arrival weekend). However, the centre piece was the 'eight-strand approach to orientation' which started on the Monday after the arrival weekend and was a comprehensive orientation programme covering all activities a new student needed to undertake as well as including activities unique to each school.

It put the student's home academic unit (department) and the academic imperative at the heart of the orientation programme. There was some reticence from a number of academic colleagues about this but there was enough external and internal evidence to support this change in direction. Students stated that they needed specific activities and information in a specific order to help them settle in. These included getting key information, making friends and meeting academics.

What it included

Departmental welcome academic orientation – Monday morning
In this session, students would receive all academic related information, such as handbooks, timetables, course option literature, an overview of the academic year and the course and the chance to meet their course tutor.

Departmental social event – Monday afternoon
This event was designed to finish a hectic and potentially daunting day for new students in an informal and fun way. Many adopted a quiz-style approach. All departmental staff were required to participate.

University registration/enrolment – schools allocated time during week
For most students, this activity would be completed via online registration before arrival. This session was for those who were unable to complete the activity online. Students who had already completed the activity would be able to use the allotted time to sort out any queries or issues.

Library session – Tuesday
New students had a compulsory library talk and tour to help them orientate themselves with library services.

University, school welcome and introduction to university services – Wednesday
This was a general welcome by the university and school where students were given a range of support information and advice.

Introductory information technology sessions – Wednesday
All new students were introduced to the university IT systems. Free and useful software as well as information on IT services were given out during this session.

Study skills and fun lecture – Thursday
This session introduced students to study at university and the skills they would need to succeed in their studies.

Personal tutor meetings – Thursday

Personal tutoring meetings took place with students enabling them to make connections with their academic mentors.

There were gaps in the programme so students had time to reflect, relax with new friends and sort out an issues relating to their studies.

How it was implemented

All these events were centrally timetabled and rooms allocated based on size requirements in collaboration with the key players in order to avoid clashes. Once the departmental and school activities unique to them were added to the programme, it was passed to the Students' Union and other central services so they could schedule activities into the programme avoiding clashes to ensure maximum attendance (e.g. sessions on cooking and how to fix your bike).

Analysis and feedback

Another full review was undertaken after the arrival and orientation period to analyse our new programme and gain feedback on how we could improve it.

The cost and timeline

The review to implementation took one academic year. Increased funding was required to pay the costs of staff working over the arrival weekend when students moved into their accommodation. The major cost was staff time. The planning process starts in March.

How it is/was monitored

We monitored the event through questionnaires and focus groups with staff and students across the university.

The outcome

There was universal praise and support by students and staff for all the implemented changes especially the eight-strand approach. The most notable change was identified by academic colleagues who stated that students seemed more confident, were talking to fellow students and engaging with teaching staff in the first week of teaching. Each year the process was refined and developed resulting in a robust, fun and informed arrival and orientation process for students and their families and all members of staff. The eight-strand approach received a national award.

Has or could the initiative be used for a different group?

When I developed the eight-strand approach, I wanted to be able to adapt it to meet the needs of anyone studying at university. The programme could be undertaken over a period of two days instead of five. When I joined the Faculty of Engineering at KU, I developed the programme for our students studying on our part-time, direct-entry and postgraduate courses. I worked with central university services to implement the programme. This initiative can be implemented at university, faculty or school level.

Advice and guidance

- Listen to your students' needs.
- Win hearts and minds by using the student voice.
- Get everyone on board.

Contact details

michelle.morgan@kingston.ac.uk

Case Study 10

Name and university
Christopher Tucker, Residential and Student Support Manager, University of Sussex (US), UK.

Title of project/initiative
Residential advisors: supporting students in university accommodation starting with welcome and orientation.

Who was involved in the initiative
Residential Manager, seven Senior Residential Advisors (SRAs) and 74 Residential Advisors (RAs).

Reason for the project/initiative
To prepare new students for life in a shared university community.

Why it was developed
We had noticed that many disputes occurring in university accommodation (halls) over the course of the academic year had their origins in the first weeks or month of the autumn term. High expectations, lack of communication and planning during this period led to a high number of disputes.

The project aimed to integrate new students in the rigours of living and studying in a communal environment whether in on- or off-campus university accommodation using residential advisors. The RAs are existing students who live with new students and are specifically trained to support and advise them as well as acting as mediators in disputes between students.

The university accommodation arrival, welcome and orientation programme was developed to prepare and assist new students with the resources to help resolve conflict using communication and community development to form stronger bonds.

The target group
First-year undergraduate and postgraduate students who had not previously lived in a communal environment.

How it was developed, what it included and how it was implemented

How it was developed
Existing students who had experience of living in university accommodation were recruited and underwent extensive training to become residential advisors (RAs). There were 74 RAs who were managed by seven senior RAs. The senior RAs reported to the Residential and Student Support Manager. The RAs lived in halls with the new students. The RAs received a rebate for their accommodation costs and the SRAs received free accommodation for their role in the scheme.

I integrated the student development theory and the concepts behind transformative mediation theory when training the RAs. It was also used as the basis for initiating our students into using non-confrontational approaches to communal living.

What it included
After the RAs had been selected through a rigorous recruitment process, they underwent four days of training. Training included:

- peer mediation;
- health and safety;
- mental health awareness;
- disability;
- student welfare issues;
- fire safety;
- university policy;
- crisis intervention.

We explored the issues that students commonly experience when they attend university, such as loneliness, meeting new people and adapting to a new environment.

A key part of the training looked at the first day of arrival and the first meeting the RAs would have with the new students who would be meeting many of their flatmates for the first time. The first meeting within the flat, that we call a 'kitchen meeting', was the key point of contact and each RA would facilitate a kitchen meeting in every flat. This first kitchen meeting would be the key to laying the groundwork for all future interactions between the RAs and new students, the university and, more importantly, their interaction with each other.

How it was implemented

The RA to student ratio was one per 50 students. When the student arrived at their accommodation during the arrival period (weekend), they were greeted by their RA and shown to their accommodation. Once in the accommodation they were given a brief overview of the flat and then shown the sign on the communal noticeboard where they could find the time and date of their first kitchen meeting. This would occur on the Monday or Tuesday after they have arrived.

RAs were given an agenda to follow during this first kitchen meeting. The agenda allowed them to comprehensively explain the support and resources available to students from a range of staff members on campus.

The agenda included:

- residence staff
  - RAs
  - porters/cleaners
  - building manager/student support manager
- guidelines for behaviour (living with US)
  - anti-social behaviour/notice to quit
  - kitchens
  - safety/drugs
- flat rules
  - agree on flat rules early (cleaning, guests, noise)
  - confront issues early
  - seek help from your RAs
- health and safety
  - fire safety/evacuations
  - meningitis/swine flu
  - health centre/emergency numbers
- general information
  - shopping
  - night clubs
  - transportation.

A shared system of values and a university culture was developed so that a 'common universe of meaning' enabled bilateral negotiations to take place. This code of shared values was encapsulated in the university's guidelines, policy and structure. An example of the policies that we have developed are as follows;

Guidelines for behaviour – do:

- improve flatmate relations;
    - be honest, considerate, have mutual respect, discuss, compromise and understand which are fundamental in learning to live with your flatmates;
- talk to your flatmates;
- set ground rules;
- communicate;
    - discuss personal habits, sleeping schedules, musical tastes, needs, wants and expectations.

General guidelines – do:

- try to be accepting and understanding of alternate lifestyles;
- talk about your feelings – a flatmate cannot respond to unexpressed feelings;
- plan in advance for overnight guests, and be considerate;
- keep accurate records of all bills that you share;
- replace or return something broken or borrowed;
- make an effort to keep your living space clean, comfortable and pleasant.

The more liveable your space is, the happier and more productive you will be.

Do not:

- pretend that everything is fine if it is not;
- play practical jokes – the intent may be misunderstood;
- think problems are going to go away by themselves (e.g. address noise complaints from the beginning and do not wait until the problem is unbearable);
- leave nasty notes taped in the kitchen or in any other conspicuous location. They will be an embarrassment to both you and the addressee. When an issue arises, be honest. Communication is the best way of arriving at a solution.

Analysis and feedback
Since instigating this process in the autumn of 2003, we have had a significant drop in anti-social behaviour being reported across our university managed accommodation. Disciplinary cases have also been cut on a consistent, yearly basis and have continued to decrease as we have added more emphasis on this concept at the beginning of the first term.

The cost and timeline
The cost to the university is the reduction in accommodation fees for the RAs as payment and the resources for the four days of training for the RAs. The timeline for recruitment and training is about two months.

How it is/was monitored
We supervised this through the dedicated role of the Residential Student Support Manager and maintained all follow-up through incident reports and exit surveys.

The outcome

Consistently lowered the level of conflict between students on a yearly basis.

Has or could the initiative be used for a different group?

This could be easily integrated into their current student support structure.

Advice and guidance

- Decide a clear and concise message to communicate to students.
- Develop the resources through which to deliver this message and maintain clear lines of communication between students and staff.
- Identify the 'values' of your institution and place them in the context of your current policies.
- Provide continuous support to follow-up on any welfare issues that may arise.

Contact details

c.tucker@sussex.ac.uk

Case Study 11

Name and university
Frances McNally, International Student Support Service Team Leader, and Margaret Ward, Student Advice and Wellbeing Services Manager, Glasgow Caledonian University (GCU), UK.

Title of project/initiative
An international welcome programme.

Who was involved in the initiative
Hosted and coordinated by GCU International Student Support Service (ISSS). Invited to participate: Support Services, Accommodation Office, International Office, Academic Departments, Students' Association and external links/businesses.

Reason for the project/initiative
A recognised platform to:

* officially welcome international students (and families) to university for each intake of the year;
* orientate students to campus and city;
* provide a support network;
* create integration opportunities between international and home students;
* encourage self-orientation (to enhance/develop independent learning within student's academic career);
* encourage students to become a part of our international community;
* establish a lasting relationship between the student and team/university;
* support student transition and aid retention;
* begin an enjoyable and unforgettable international student experience at GCU.

Why it was developed
As a result of student feedback, a longer, more comprehensive programme was developed to enhance and improve the international student experience.

The target group
It is primarily targeted at all new international (European and overseas) students joining GCU each term. We invite home students to support those who are new to the city of Glasgow and to enhance integration opportunities within our diverse student population.

How it was developed, what it included and how it was implemented

How it was developed
The programme was initially set up to welcome international students and give them a general introduction to the university. This was coordinated by the International Student Advisor. As the team grew and a dedicated member of the team was able to focus on this area of the student experience, this was developed to a four-week programme. Continual development is essential to keep the programme fresh and welcoming as well as informative and valuable to students.

What it included
The programme includes various stages and elements:

Relationship (pre-arrival)
As students are given an offer from GCU admissions, we begin communication over email to provide information to students about the experience they can expect at GCU. Thus helping to establish our relationship with the student as an individual and a group. This also alerts them to the activities, events and support in place at GCU.

We work very closely with the International Office to aid the recruitment of international students through this online communication and also attend conversion events involving FE institutes and 'INTO Scotland'.

Social networking
An important element of communication throughout the welcome programme, and whole experience at the university, is our online presence. We have various online social networking groups for international students, including Facebook, LinkedIn, Orkut and Twitter.

The welcome to GCU group on Facebook includes:

* key information;
* volunteers who engage with new students offering advice and welcome messages;
* opportunities for new students to communicate with fellow new-starts before they arrive;
* a link to the main international students @ GCU group which includes events, photographs and student comments.

Dedicated communication
A publication is produced as a guide for students and staff detailing the programme. We have a dedicated email inbox for all students (orientation@gcu.ac.uk) and a quick-link web address so it is easy to find information: www.gcu.ac.uk/orientation. This opens activities to all students to aid integration within the student population.

Multimedia
Through the use of the website and social networking groups, we have developed:

* podcasts for students with practical advice;
* a 3D virtual booklet available on our website, through social groups and included in email communication;
* videos created by students.

Meet and greet at airport
As part of a joint programme with other Glasgow universities, we operate a free meet and greet service to students arriving at Glasgow International Airport (domestic and international arrivals). The Glasgow International Student Welcome Programme (GISWP) is operated by student volunteers in branded t-shirts. They are easily identifiable on arrival, providing support, answering questions and guiding students towards transport.

GISWP benefits from its own website jointly maintained by the universities, allowing students to register and upload arrival details: www.giswp.org.uk.

Welcome on campus
We coordinate a welcome desk in the Saltire Centre Building manned by volunteer students on a daily basis for a three to four week period. Answering questions, escorting students around campus, providing literature and promoting our events, the welcome desk is the first stop for students on arrival to the university.

Our welcome lounge operates during our welcome weekend in our student residences, welcoming all students and families, assisting them in moving into accommodation, answering enquiries and searching for alternative accommodation.

Welcome weekend

Alongside GCU students' association freshers' timetable, a range of activities are organised in the weekend prior to term start. This includes our City Rally Challenge (a self-orientating Glasgow city tour with prizes) and a welcome BBQ. International student support, accommodation and registry services are available during this weekend.

Activities

All activities across the university are designed to complement each other and address student needs and interests with diverse cultures; to offer a full programme to all students. Careful attention is taken to avoid event duplication or overlapping activities.

Our key events include the:

- welcome buffet and ceilidh;
- orientation information sessions;
- university student support services fair;
- international fair;
- day-trips to explore Scotland;
- regular social activities.

Refresher programme

We have identified that, after a six-week period of their new university life, students can become frustrated, unsettled or homesick. We have devised a refresher programme to support students at this time. Events include settling-in buffet, culture event, money wise session and a Glasgow city open day.

Welcome team

The welcome team consists of student volunteers who are the most important element of our programme and its success. They offer a vital support network at peer level and aid student integration. Students volunteer without pay and are happy to support their fellow students and be a part of the university community. We recognise their efforts and participation with a service certificate and thank you celebration. They are also invited to participate in the GCUSA student leader programme.

How it was implemented

The programme is coordinated by the GCU ISSS team with close involvement from induction groups across the university and within the city. The programme is embedded in university activities across the whole student population. Key players implement the programme utilising excellent communication and organisational skills as well as a passion from all involved.

Analysis and feedback

We have been awarded the *Times Higher Education* award 2008 for outstanding support for overseas students (reigning winner) and ranked first for international student support service within the ISB.

Our open-door policy and extended hours help maintain a high level of service for all students.

As our student participation levels increase with each year, we strive to create a fresh and interactive programme that represents the ethos and culture at GCU.

Student feedback is positive, examples are:

> Thank you for the last email! That website [Orientation Programme] ... was very informative and helped me out a lot on the living arrangements that I must have for the next couple of years.

The staff and students here are all friendly and welcoming and there is always a positive and happy learning and social environment.

The university support service for international students is magnificent. The staff are also accommodating and friendly, they don't discriminate.

The cost and timeline

Due to continual development, dedicated planning and project review, time is essential. As one programme ends, planning begins for the next intake. The majority of implementation takes place three months prior to the programme start date; project work is carried out while balancing with other service provision and project work commitments. The programme costs cover the booklet, catering and GISWP project.

How it is/was monitored

The events are monitored by creating a log for student enquiries, attendance at events and participation on Facebook. A record is kept of all activities and tasks carried out during the planning and implementation of the programme.

Student feedback is collected:

- informally while meeting students;
- on printed feedback cards;
- by comments and participation on Facebook;
- from volunteers;
- from team reviews.

The outcome

The orientation programme has:

- established a key role in communicating with students early (pre-arrival) to initiate and enhance their student experience;
- enabled students to develop a lasting relationship with the ISSS team;
- encouraged students to 'give something back' to the university to enhance their fellow students' experiences;
- established the ISSS team as a key stakeholder in induction/welcome activities across the university.

Has or could the initiative be used for a different group?

This programme has been developed for the inclusion of students' families. There has also been a focus to create activities that encourage integration in our student residences on campus.

Advice and guidance

- Communication is key to beginning the student journey – a range of methods to appeal to a greater audience through various channels.
- Plan early.
- Devise a schedule plan for each task/stage to ensure a high standard throughout and for future project development to enhance the programme.
- Use your current students – peer support is one of the most valuable sources of support for students and the university.
- Monitor, gather and review feedback.
- Continually develop services.
- Look after yourself and your fellow team members.

Contact details

frances.mcnally@gcu.ac.uk
margaret.ward@gcu.ac.uk

Case Study 12

Name and university

Richard Mullendore, Professor of College Student Affairs Administration, University of Georgia, USA.

Title of project/initiative

Planning parent orientation programmes using Maslow's hierarchy of needs (Maslow, 1970).

Who was involved in the initiative

A range of key colleagues across several institutions that implement the model based on their programme priorities.

Reason for the project/initiative

To improve the quality of parent orientation programmes.

Why it was developed

Parents today are more involved in every aspect of the lives of their children than previous generations. Technology has made it very easy for parents and children to stay constantly in touch. (I have often referred to the mobile phone as the world's longest umbilical cord.) Media broadcasts of missing children, violence, etc. have made parents afraid to let their children out of their sight, unless they know where the child is and who the child is with.

Throughout the pre-college years, parents are encouraged by school systems to be visible and involved in the educational process. Parents do not see their involvement ending when their son or daughter enrols in college. Many of today's students have been sheltered from conflict as their parents have sought to resolve issues for their children, and these parents believe that they should continue to advocate on their student's behalf in college. Because parents are going to continue to be actively involved in their student's life, it is important for colleges and universities to develop orientation programs for parents that help them understand how the institution functions, what parameters may exist regarding their involvement and how they can best support their student.

Who was the target group

Parents of all first-year students at any college or university.

How it was developed, what it included and how it was implemented

How it was developed

After running two-day orientation programmes for parents for several years, it became apparent that many of today's parents are more anxious than previous generations, and they have a lot more questions and concerns. All parents appreciate that a programme exists just for them, but some parents struggle with their anxiety about their student's college experience. In responding to the concerns, we learned that the issues of most immediate importance were the basic human needs (housing, food, safety, etc.). As a result, it seemed that developing a parental orientation model programme based on Maslow's hierarchy of needs might reduce the level of parental anxiety.

What it included

Maslow's hierarchy depicts human needs in a specific order. For example, it is difficult to think about career counselling if you don't have food or shelter. It is difficult to think about joining a service organisation if you don't feel safe where you live. The hierarchy consists of five levels of needs: physiological, safety, belonging, esteem and self-actualisation. Once one level of needs is met, it is easier to consider needs at the next level.

This model of parent orientation uses the hierarchy in determining the content and order of events of the programme. It is important that the college/university offer a simultaneous, yet separate orientation programme for parents.

How it was implemented

In a parent orientation programme, these five levels have significance regarding the order of events because of the issues, concerns and anxieties that parents have. On a residential campus, parents want to know about the living arrangements. Is my student going to have a roommate? Is the facility kept clean? What are the rules and regulations? Where does the student eat meals? How good is the food? What are the hours of operation? These are basic (physiological) needs. In addition, because of the high cost of higher education, billing and financial aid information are also often considered basic needs. Since the basic needs are the areas of most concern to parents, it is imperative that these issues be addressed early in the programme in order to reduce parent anxiety.

Too often, orientation programmes are designed to be convenient for the presenters without consideration of the audience. So, if residential and dining issues are of primary importance to parents, then the presenters for these areas should be among the first to present. If the housing director says she wants to present on the afternoon of the second day, the orientation director should explain the value of an early presentation and schedule accordingly.

Once housing, food and money concerns have been addressed, the programme should move on to the next level of needs (safety). Is it safe to walk on this campus alone at night? What crimes have been committed here? How does my student contact someone if there is a problem? Alcohol and drug issues are also considered safety issues as so many problems occur as a result of use/abuse. In addition, many of today's students have never been to see a doctor without a parent, so what arrangements are made for medical concerns? These issues should be addressed early in the orientation programme as well.

Addressing primary parental concerns early and satisfactorily in the orientation programme will lower anxieties and they will be more willing to hear and understand what is appropriate regarding their involvement in their student's college experience. It is helpful to make the parents comfortable before addressing the areas where they should not be involved.

The third level of needs are the belonging needs. In many orientation programmes, this level includes academic advising, registration, career counselling and student organisation involvement opportunities. Most colleges want parents to be aware of these processes and opportunities, but believe the student should learn how to navigate the institution and choose what level of out-of-class involvement he/she desires. If parents have developed a comfort level with the institution based on the early components of the orientation, then they will be less likely to demand to be present during academic advising and registration.

At the fourth level (esteem), parents can learn about personal counselling availability, as well as recreational and leadership opportunities for their students.

The fifth level is self-actualisation. At this level of the orientation programme, parents can learn about appropriate ways to stay involved in the life of their college student and ways to renegotiate the relationship they have with their 'child' as he/she becomes an adult college student.

Analysis and feedback

Colleges that consider this model in their programme planning have indicated that they are pleased with how it works for parents and the institution. It empowers the orientation director to schedule sessions in a way that makes sense for his/her institution.

The cost and timeline

There is no additional cost to implementation of this model, unless the institution has no separate parent orientation programme. If this is a new endeavour, parents can be charged an orientation fee to cover all costs.

How it is/was monitored

Monitoring is dependent on each orientation director.

The outcome

Virtually all orientation programmes in the USA are evaluated and/or assessed by participants. The results are institution specific.

Has or could the initiative be used for a different group?

It could be extended to guardians.

Advice and guidance

The most important piece of advice is for the Orientation Director to put together an advisory committee consisting of the primary programme stakeholders and talk through the model based on the needs of that institution in order to get the necessary support.

References

Maslow, A.H. (1970) *Motivation and Personality*, New York: HarperCollins.

Contact details

richardm@uga.edu

Conclusion

The case studies in this chapter provide practical strategies for developing, implementing and reviewing programmes designed to support students during the early arrival and orientation phases of their university experience. Together with the five tips outlined in this chapter, these case studies illustrate a number of good practices, including:

- make use of a range of media and technologies to communicate with and engage your first-year students as they make the transition into university;
- encourage students to self-regulate and to progressively become more independent learners as they build on the information you provide during the orientation process;
- the first six weeks are critical as students decide whether the university experience is for them – be particularly vigilant during this time with orientation and on-going induction support;
- parents and partners are key support mechanisms for enhancing student retention in the first year – include them in your orientation planning where possible;
- work towards a shared value system among students, particularly when they are living in residential accommodation (though this also applies in classroom settings), and take the time to induct students into the culture and expectations of the university;
- develop a sense of belonging among first-year students by ensuring that they receive orientation support in their home academic unit, including making connections with academic staff.

Effectively supporting new students through the arrival and orientation stage can enable a seamless transition through to induction which is the focus of the next chapter.

Chapter 6

Induction

Mary Stuart Hunter and Kevin C. Clarke,
University of South Carolina, USA

Introduction

Following arrival and orientation, students settle in and begin the real "business" of their education. We know that students quickly find that the freedoms and responsibilities for managing their lives and the consequences of their choices become an on-going balancing act. They need institutional support to help them maintain a healthy equilibrium to succeed at the university level. Many higher educators, psychologists, researchers and scholars have addressed the factors that influence university student success, and we, as educators, can turn to that scholarship to guide our efforts to help students make successful transitions to university level study and life. Kift (2010) asserts:

> The first year of university study is arguably the most crucial time for engaging students in their learning community and equipping them with the requisite sills, not only to persist, but to be successful and independent in their new learning throughout their undergraduate years and for a lifetime of professional practice in which they will be continually required to learn and to engage with new ideas that go beyond the content of their university course. All members of the university, students and both professional and academic staff, have a responsibility in this regard to ensure that the first-year curriculum is engaging, supportive, intentional, relevant and social.

This chapter explores this assertion and identifies good practice to enable students to succeed in their first year of study. In addition, the induction experience must be a process, not a single event as outlined in the Practitioner Model, which helps students reevaluate their expectations of their university experience to ensure that our students are academically, emotionally and socially prepared to manage the rigors of university life. We believe that the first-year experience must be a holistic one that integrates classroom experiences with co-curricular and extra-curricular activities to fully engage students in learning.

We cannot begin to develop an intentional student induction experience without first referring to Sanford (1967), who found that institutional efforts towards college student development must be a two-pronged effort that both challenges and supports students as they grow, learn and develop. If students do not have enough challenge, they likely to become bored and complacent. However, students cannot succeed without the appropriate counter support. Challenge with little or no support may cause students to feel overwhelmed, give up and potentially drop out. Therefore, the importance of students finding a niche – a community – and becoming engaged at an institution is a vitally important element in student induction.

There is a direct relationship between the quality and quantity of student involvement in campus activities and their academic performance and satisfaction (Astin, 1993). Also, positive interaction with peers brings about a sense of belonging, increased student satisfaction and a sense of responsibility. Finally, we know that students are more likely to invest greater effort to their learning when they become involved as members of the university community.

Relevance in the undergraduate experience is also important in student induction. The concept of social and academic integration, coined by Tinto (1987) asserts that undergraduate students will have a more valuable learning experience when what they learn outside the classroom is incorporated and related to what they learn inside the classroom. When students are able to integrate their in-class and outside-of-class experiences, they will reap greater educational and developmental benefits.

Chickering and Gamson's *Seven Principles for Good Practice in Undergraduate Education* (1987) put forward broad standards for improving teaching and learning that are applicable in a wide variety of curricular, co-curricular and extra-curricular settings. They suggest that good practice encourages contact between students and faculty, develops reciprocity and cooperation among students, encourages active learning, gives prompt feedback, emphasises time on task, communicates high expectations and respects diverse talents and ways of learning. More recently, the Association of American Colleges and Universities' Liberal Education and America's Promise project found that high impact activities encourage and support deep learning (Kuh, 2008). The 'good practices' applicable to induction and beneficial to a diverse student body include first-year seminars and experiences, common intellectual experiences, learning communities, writing-intensive courses, collaborative assignments and projects, undergraduate research, diversity/global learning and service-learning and community-based learning.

As higher educators, it is our responsibility to use the available research and theories to help inform and guide the development of programs and services to best meet the needs of our diverse students. It is vital that our initiatives are engaging, supportive, challenging, intentional and relevant. The following case studies illustrate much of the research described above, by including the broad tenants of good practice in undergraduate education and illustrating high impact learning activities.

Case Study 13 by Diana Pace, Wendy J. Wenner and Nancy Giardina utilises research and theory on the developmental and transitional needs of college students to inform staff and faculty on how to best challenge, support and engage students at Grand Valley State University (GVSU), USA. The blueprint tool provides staff and faculty a common understanding of the university experience, which promotes connected and intentional advising for students and allows adjustment for individual needs and learning styles. The blueprint provides faculty and staff with a structure and process to set high expectations and provide students valuable resources for success. For students, the instrument outlines the opportunities and resources available to them, as well as creating a visual understanding of the connection between curricular and co-curricular activities. This program provides common ground for faculty, staff and students, within a context of challenge and support, to develop community and to discuss opportunities for engagement and success.

Case Study 14 by Laurie Witucki exemplifies the High-Impact Educational Practice of learning communities at GVSU, USA. The Women in Science and Engineering programme (WISE) develops an integrated learning experience by linking courses, co-curricular activities, students and faculty. The aim of WISE is to provide a supportive space, for a typically underserved population, to develop their levels of competence, to develop a sense of belonging and to increase their engagement with their academics, peers and campus life. This induction programme provides students an integrated learning experience that encourages students to explore, connect and find success in their academic interests. The living–learning community model encourages active learning in a highly cooperative environment, which further promotes student learning and academic success.

Case Study 15 by Deborah Anderson and Georgy Petrov from Kingston University, UK, illustrates an active learning environment in which students can connect their classroom experiences to the development of necessary skills for success. Similar to the High-Impact Educational Practice of a first-year seminar, KU brings together small groups of students with personal tutors to develop intellectual and practical skills. It utilises active learning strategies to engage students in meaningful and relevant learning experiences. To enhance the induction process and to help students understand the value of the module, KU double weighted the module and extended it for the entire first year. By connecting small groups of students to peer mentors and faculty, the module provides students opportunities for individual consultations to support their diverse learning styles.

Case Study 16 from Juliette Stephenson and Elisabeth Dunne was developed to create a seamless induction process providing personalised support for student transition at the University of Exeter, UK. A module was created to connect students to personal tutors who guide their personal development through induction. The module provides students opportunities to connect and collaborate with peers and faculty as a means of support and engagement, considered a best practice for student success. Student reports improved feelings of competence and the development of skills for current and future success. The module is effective in establishing itself among students as relevant and useful.

Case Study 13

Name and university
Diana Pace, Wendy J. Wenner and Nancy Giardina, Grand Valley State University (GVSU), USA.

Title of project/initiative
Mapping transitions: a four-year blueprint for student success.

Who was involved in the initiative
Administrators, faculty and student services personnel.

Reason for the project/initiative
The Campus Wide Student Success Planning Team was convened in December 2005. The charge to the committee from the Provost and President of the university was to review the current graduation rate and retention data and make recommendations to improve them.

Why it was developed
The aim behind the four-year blueprint for student success was to record and map the most important activities and transitions a student should undergo during their four-year full-time degree (four academic levels) that would enable them to succeed in their studies. The aims in order to achieve this were:

- to provide an inventory of current curricular and co-curricular programmes designed to support student success;
- to allow staff and faculty to identify gaps in support services and identify groups of students who were not being served;
- to develop programmes that would provide an appropriate range of academic challenge, support and engagement over the four plus years of student enrolment at the university;
- to create a visual curricular and co-curricular road map that would provide students, staff, faculty and advisors with the tools to encourage personal and educational accountability and success.

The target group
The original target group was faculty and staff (university-wide) who support students' academic and co-curricular success. We wanted the advisors to be able to encourage students to set goals and markers for themselves and to share information about the wide range of resources available on campus for student success. During the process, we realised that students could also be a target group for the information. We wanted students to stop thinking of their education as a list of check boxes that needed to be filled and think of their educational path as a process of development with broader markers of success and achievement. We also wanted students to understand that there is an important connection between curricular and co-curricular engagement in their educational journey. This blueprint would help them do this.

How it was developed, what it included and how it was implemented

How it was developed
We used the university's Student Success Model, which incorporated the concepts of challenge, engagement and support, as a framework for task force and planning team

discussions. The Student Success Planning Team drew upon a variety of internal resources including research and committee reports for the basis for their work. External data looking at current best practices in retention was also analysed. It included the National Survey of Student Engagement data on other institutions and Documenting Effective Educational Practice (DEEP) as described in *Student Success in College* by Kuh *et al.* (2005).

A subcommittee of the larger retention committee interviewed students about their experience at Grand Valley and reviewed exit interview data. We reviewed best practices and our own retention data to find out what markers were most important for student success. We contacted departments around the university and asked for information about existing support programs as well as activities designed to engage and challenge students. We compiled lists and circulated them to units around the university for feedback and additions. After we had a reasonably comprehensive list, we experimented with several different formats until we developed the current timeline format for the blueprint. The Institutional Marketing Office redesigned and enhanced the basic format for publication. At this point the committee also selected milestones of participation, academic accomplishment, co-curricular involvement and utilisation of student support programmes to be assessed by the university.

What it included

The four-year blueprint for student success includes a timeline for each of the four years a student is studying at university. On the timeline are the key markers and milestones that support student success. Below the timeline is a list of programmes that challenge students, provide opportunities for engagement outside the classroom and support for their success. Each year is focused on the most important developmental task that faces the student that year. For example, the task of the first year is the 'personal transition to college'. The task of the second year is 'exploration of the college community'. Tasks for the third and fourth years are 'integration and involvement in the larger community' and 'transition to career'. The markers and challenge, support and engagement activities change with each year.

How it was implemented

We sent the plan to departments and deans across the university. We also sent the plan to the dean's council and the faculty senate, who endorsed it. Implementation was not centralised, but units across the university were encouraged to use the blueprint in advising students and continue to develop activities that would support the goal of increased retention. Grand Valley is an unusually entrepreneurial university and once the community endorsed the idea, units felt free to pick up pieces of the plan as appropriate.

Analysis and feedback

The Retention and Time to Graduation Committee meets twice a year to review the progress of the timeline. The Director of Institutional Analysis reports to the committee on achievement of the assessment benchmarks, and the committee makes suggestions for additional programming and assessment measures.

The cost and timeline

The only cost apart from staff time that we have incurred has been for the publication and dissemination of the blueprint.

How it is/was monitored

It is monitored annually.

The outcome

The blueprint is being used by the offices of Academic Advising, Career Planning Services, Student Life and Residence Life. The blueprint is also published in a poster format and hung in the residence living centres.

Has or could the initiative be used for a different group?

This model could be adapted by another institution of higher education but it would require identification of services and the points of assessment appropriate to the individual institution.

GVSU is going to use it with parents to give them an idea of markers that the students should be achieving as they move through their time at the university.

Advice and guidance

- Get a range of staff across the university on board at the beginning of the development process.
- Seek the input of faculty academic advisors and student services personnel as well as students.
- Provide structure for on-going review, and support for revision and new initiatives.

References

Kuh, G. D., Kinzie, J. and Whitt, E. J. (2005) *Student Success in College: Creating Conditions that Matter*, San Francisco: Jossey-Bass.

Contact details

paced@gvsu.edu
wennerw@gvsu.edu
giardinn@gvsu.edu

Case Study 14

Name and university
Laurie Witucki, Faculty Director, WISE Programme, Grand Valley State University (GVSU), USA.

Title of project/initiative
The WISE living and learning community: a first-year residential experience for women in science and engineering.

Who was involved in the initiative
Faculty Director for WISE, Director of Housing, Dean of Students, Associate Dean of Students, Dean of the College of Liberal Arts and Sciences (CLAS), Dean of the College of Engineering and Computer Science, Head of Admissions and Housing Staff.

Reason for the project/initiative
We wanted to increase the number of female students undertaking and persisting in the science, mathematics and engineering fields at GVSU by establishing subject-themed student residential communities on campus.

Why it was developed
In traditional male-dominated subjects such as the sciences, there is still a higher drop-out rate of female majors at every level (Bachelor, Master, PhD) than their male counterparts. The aim of the project was to create a learning environment where women could study in a supportive, conducive and relaxed atmosphere with fellow female students and female role models in the sciences. This would lead to an increased confidence in their abilities, interest in science, a sense of belonging and increased involvement in their science and lab courses as well as the university community as a whole.

The target group
Female first-year students with an expressed interest in a variety of science-based majors including biomedical science, biology, mathematics, chemistry, computer science or engineering.

How it was developed, what it included and how it was implemented

How it was developed
A planning and working group made up of key players from across the university who would be involved in delivering the programme looked at issues, such as:

- Could the programme be justified in terms of cost and the target group?
- Which campus would the community be located on?
- What number of students would be accommodated?
- How would those students be selected?
- Were there particular majors to target over others?
- Should the programme include some senior students (final year)? If so, how should they be selected?

Funding by the Housing Department and Dean of Students Office were pledged to support the programme in its development and on a yearly basis. The Provost Office provided funds for the initial start-up costs. No external funds were obtained and the programme was developed and implemented with 100 per cent financial backing from the university. Support for the programme was obtained at the highest levels of the university at the start. We described in detailed presentations what we felt the community would need and how we envisioned the programme to run.

The planning and working group toured another WISE programme at a university in the state and talked to its Faculty Director and WISE students to get a feel of what was most important to the students, what worked and what did not.

During the initial planning stage, the Faculty Programme Director for WISE (me) had their teaching load slightly reduced. Faculty and administrators involved in the initiative equipped the computer lab in the residential area with 15 PC computers loaded with specific science and mathematical software, one laser printer, a scanner and other printers.

What it included
The residential hall selected was on the main campus close to dining facilities and could house 47 students. It contained suite-style bedrooms, communal social spaces, a computer lab, study rooms and a room for a faculty advising office. It was the closest residential building to the main science laboratories and mathematics classrooms on campus so was popular with first-year students.

A strategy was developed to help support the WISE community create and develop learning groups. It included recruiting a senior high grade science student to be a residential assistant (RA). In subsequent years, the WISE programme recruited between two and eight returning WISE students (Level 2) to remain in the programme and live in the building as peer mentors (PMs) in addition to the RA. PMs and the RA were recruited via an application process.

PMs contacted the new first-year students by mail or email during the summer prior to college. They:

- advised students on arrival and orientation procedures;
- helped new students move in and showed them around campus;
- participated in the WISE events and programmes;
- helped the RA set up and run events and programmes;
- maintained information and bulletin boards in the building;
- served as a resource about classes, labs and majors and sometimes served as tutors and study group leaders (dependent on schedules and academic fields).

The peer mentors got to work closely with the faculty involved in WISE, which often led to research projects in the faculty labs, letters of recommendation or support for scholarships, internships, graduate schools and jobs. In addition, the peer mentors were paid a small stipend each semester that they were involved with the programme.

WISE events, activities and programmes included:

- on- and off-campus team-building science-related field trips;
- two or three residential building events per month (e.g. social activities to meet the faculty, panel discussions about study abroad, research, careers advice, academic study sessions, information on wellness and health, etc.);
- the Faculty Director and at least two other science faculty holding weekly advising sessions (two hours each) in the building.

The Housing Department provided food for events, prizes for participation and the end of year formal banquet for WISE. Faculty were very willing to attend the events.

How it was implemented
Information on the initiative was given out at open and admissions days, was put on the university housing website and tours of the building were given to prospective students and their parents.

Analysis and feedback

WISE students' results were monitored each semester and we continued to monitor them as they progressed through their university programme. At the end of each academic year we also surveyed the students to look at their participation experience, increased confidence, enjoyment of the programme, satisfaction with GVSU housing and their involvement with the faculty. These surveys helped improve the programme.

The cost and timeline

The planning and working group met (monthly) for approximately 14 months prior to implementation.

The initial costs for building renovations and computers was around $50,000 the first year. Costs for field trips, in-house events and peer mentor support totalled $3,500.

How it is/was monitored

The WISE committee meets monthly throughout the academic year to assess programme success, plan events, discuss the budget, particular student issues, building issues, events on campus, etc.

The Faculty Director meets with the RA and peer mentors twice a month to check the programme events and with the two other faculty fellows in the programme to establish office hours and plan programmes.

We have published on the process of establishing this community and given several talks at external conferences as well as numerous in-house presentations to other faculties and administrations.

We continue to keep open communication with the invested parties and key players (e.g. deans, provost, president) via email updates about the success of events and student involvement not only in the WISE community but also in the greater university community.

The outcome

The programmee has been successful. It has recruited more female students in science year on year and retention rates have improved. The outcome was a major university investment to build a dedicated accommodation and study block for women studying science and engineering. WISE now houses non-first-year students (sophomores Level 2, juniors Level 3 and seniors Level 4) who have selected a major subject in the sciences. The accommodation houses 74 students. This has led to increased interaction between WISE students and more discussions about research, graduate studies, involvement with the faculty and futures careers. The university is supporting and investing in living and learning communities in other fields. In addition, the WISE programme was awarded a prestigious external grant called a CAP (Campus Action Grant) to support its programmes and activities in the winter 2011 semester by the American Association of University Women (AAUW).

Has or could the initiative be used for a different group?

Mature or postgraduate students living on campus.

Advice and guidance

- Get support from senior managers.
- Be bold.
- Advertise the benefit of an all-female science living and study space in university literature.

Contact details

wituckil@gvsu.edu

Case Study 15

Name and university
Deborah Anderson and Georgy Petrov, Kingston Business School in the Faculty of Business and Law, Kingston University, UK.

Title of project/initiative
Integrating skills into the curriculum: a case study in business.

Who was involved in the initiative
Faculty Learning and Teaching Coordinator, Module Leader, Faculty Director of Undergraduate Programmes, Head of Department, Faculty Employability Coordinator, Network College staff and students.

Reason for the project/initiative
It has always been apparent that students need to develop academic and employability skills to be able to perform well on the business programmes offered in the Faculty of Business and Law at KU and in the subsequent workplace. Previous modules covering these skills had been a regular feature on business programmes, although they were not always well received by the students who often failed to see the connection with other modules. In an attempt to clarify and confirm the importance of the link between skills development and the programme, we decided to develop a double-weighted, year-long module in which academic and employability skills would be integrated with the academic content of a core module. The logical module for this development was Organisational Behaviour (OB), already a core first-year module for all business degrees at Kingston University. The idea was that this module would provide a hands-on experiential approach to learning with regular class contact and a truly interactive online environment for independent learning. The OB subject area would provide the material through which to develop and apply the relevant skills. Assessment would be carefully planned to encourage attendance and engagement throughout the module. By double weighting the module, it was hoped that students would understand the importance of the module to their first-year studies. The new module was named 'Managing Yourself and Others' (MYO).

Why it was developed
We wanted to ensure that students were equipped with the academic and employability skills crucial for studying and working in business. Previous stand-alone skills modules had not worked and we wanted students to see the benefit of acquiring the skills and applying them immediately. We also wanted students to have experience of working in one subject area for a whole year. While all other modules on their programme lasted just one semester, we wanted them to experience some continuity from one semester to the next whilst inducting them to skills over a longer period of time.

The target group
A very diverse group of first-year business students were our target group. We wanted to ensure that all of them had an opportunity to acquire academic and employability skills in a meaningful and relevant way (i.e. in a way in which they could be applied immediately). An additional consideration was the fact that this module would be delivered at partner network further education colleges. In total, 900 students would take this module across five sites.

How it was developed

Initial discussions were held between the Learning and Teaching Coordinator and Module Leader, the Head of Department of HRM, Leadership and Organisation, the Director of Undergraduate Programmes and academic staff.

A particularly useful feature during the planning cycle was a 'creative development' event to which staff from several areas were invited to discuss the learning and teaching and assessment aspects of the module. Representatives from the module team (including network college staff), Learning Resources Centre staff, Academic Development Centre skills support staff, students and educational technology experts met to discuss and agree possible approaches to the new module. From there on, the module leader took leadership on the actual development of the module liaising and working with various parties across the faculty and university.

What the new module includes

Two hours per week of seminar-based work is delivered to groups of 60 students by a member of the teaching team. In addition, students receive five academic and employability skills workshops in which skills are explained by staff from support and other departments. For example, information search and referencing are delivered by library staff and CV writing is delivered by the faculty employability coordinator. The skills from the workshops are then applied in the weekly seminar-based classes as students work through the module syllabus.

In addition to class delivery of OB material and integrated academic and employability skills, this module also makes use of educational technologies and peer mentors (second- and third-year students). Regular online activities are important to ensure consistency across the network of colleges, providing all students with exercises and activities to supplement classroom learning. The use of peer mentors is also considered important as a way of convincing the first-year students of the importance of skills development; hearing about this from peers would be far more effective than from staff.

How it was implemented

During the summer before the module started, extensive development of teaching materials and online resources was undertaken. Working with the university's e-developers, the module leader produced materials which are accessed by students via the university's virtual learning environment 'StudySpace'. These resources include online reading guides, tests, skills guides and questionnaires, videos, case studies and reflective exercises. The module leader also developed all material to be used in class, including a book of in-class exercises and activities that all lecturers could use.

Analysis and feedback

Students are asked to give written feedback on various aspects of the module twice a year (at mid-point and at the end of the module). Analysis shows that the great majority of students evaluate the module overall as consistently or generally good. The module leader also organised a focus group with students to yield more detailed feedback. A second focus group was organised with peer mentors and they had found the experience of helping on the module very beneficial. There were also regular meetings with the teaching team and skills tutors where any issue about the module could be raised.

The cost and timeline

Costs were mainly staff time in developing the interactive support materials, including the services of a university e-developer.

Initial development discussions took place in November 2008 and the module started in September 2009.

How it is/was monitored

The module is monitored through normal university procedures (e.g. mid-module and end of module feedback, annual module review). Feedback on the module is also provided by student representatives via various faculty committees and attendance at classes and completion of online activities is monitored.

The outcome

The module is core on all business programmes in the Faculty of Business and Law at Kingston University. The module will continue to evolve in response to student, peer mentor and teaching team feedback, but mostly it will remain in the same format.

Has or could the initiative be used for a different group?

The integration of academic and employability skills is particularly suited to OB as there is an overlap between academic content of OB and the skills (e.g. communication, working in teams, leadership, etc.). However, other subject areas could use the principle of delivering skills through content (e.g. presentation skills, note-taking skills, group work) by working with experts from other areas of an institution, such as library staff, employability experts and learning support staff. The module could also be developed to deliver advanced skills in Levels 2 and 3.

Advice and guidance
- Gather the whole team at the early stages of the module's development.
- Ask for expert advice and help for specialist aspects of the module (e.g. e-resources).
- Be prepared for time-consuming planning and actual development of the module.
- Be prepared to listen to student, peer mentor and teaching team feedback and adjust if appropriate.

Contact details
d.anderson@kingston.ac.uk
g.petrov@kingston.ac.uk

Case Study 16

Name and university

Juliette Stephenson, Head of Student Learning, Business School, and Elisabeth Dunne, Head of Project Development: Education Enhancement, University of Exeter, UK.

Title of project/initiative

Leading on from orientation: a personal and professional development module.

Who was involved in the initiative

From the Business School: Head of Student Learning (Senior Teaching Fellow), Teaching Fellow for Leadership, Teaching Fellow team (of 14), Employability Officer and Undergraduate Student Services (admin support), staff from Education Enhancement and the library.

Reason for the project/initiative

We wanted:

*   to improve personal tutoring (PT) in order to support a seamless move from orientation to induction and the transition of academic ways of working;
*   to ensure that all students receive personalised support and feel known within an increasingly large and diverse undergraduate cohort;
*   to encourage students to engage with their own personal and professional development.

Why it was developed

The Business School has been going through a 'step change' in terms of increased student numbers and internationalised intake. As a result, the school has been working in numerous ways to provide and improve orientation and induction for this diverse range of students, including close contact between first years and their personal tutors. From research, we knew the role of PT can be critical in enabling students to succeed in their studies through encouraging engagement and personal development.

The 'step change' expanded the number of academics, in particular the position of the teaching fellow (TF), across all departments with part of their role to support students pastorally and with their development of all academic skills.

At school and institutional level, we felt that our students' personal tutoring experiences had been piecemeal and variable. We wanted to develop and formalise PT via a compulsory module.

Who was the target group

The initial group targeted has been all undergraduate first years (approximately 700) in the University of Exeter Business School (economics, accounting, management, leadership and finance).

How it was developed, what it included and how it was implemented

How it was developed

A pilot was undertaken with the new TFs and 500 undergraduate students. Each TF had a maximum of 96 personal tutees and met with their tutees in smaller groups on five occasions over the year and covered a programme of suggested topics and activities. In addition, students could access:

- an introduction to an electronic tool for personal development planning;
- a schedule of voluntary skills workshops from which to choose;
- employability sessions run by the Business School's Employability Officer;
- English language workshops provided by specialists.

A review demonstrated that we had made many changes for the better. We decided that a new programme should be devised in the form of a non-credit rated but timetabled module that coherently 'rolled' together all of the above strands. We built on the success of our pilot and made some key improvements.

What it included

There was a clear module programme across both semesters for pastoral meetings. In addition, students could:

- participate in a team development programme during week one;
- attend face-to-face skills workshops with parallel online provision for each skill area;
- access a variety of language support tutorials;
- attend employability sessions.

Activities were designed to support the transition between the orientation and induction of students throughout this important first year.

How it was implemented

Our entire first-year undergraduate intake (approximately 700 students) were assigned a personal tutor. Although a non-credit rated module, there were explicit expectations for attendance, completion and recognition with students required to engage with all the different activities either individually or in small groups, face-to-face or online.

Analysis and feedback

A detailed online survey providing student feedback on the module indicated that we had hugely improved our personal tutoring system. Overall total satisfaction of first-year students was 93 per cent with only 7 per cent not satisfied.

Figure 6.1 demonstrates a broad range of satisfaction in relation to tutor availability and support, listening and responding to questions and giving advice.

While there were advantages to meeting in groups, we continued to be available to personal tutees on an individual needs basis. The new first-year module showed that satisfaction was significantly higher than for second- and third-year personal tutoring which was not provided via a compulsory module. Such figures suggest that the module, with the inclusion of personal tutoring as a major component, has been highly successful in providing a coherent and personalised experience for students, where students feel known and well supported.

Although there was some constructive criticism in the qualitative feedback relating to some of the online materials, overall student feedback for skills support was very positive across the broad range of support.

For many students, the module has been about:

- 'encouragement' and developing self-confidence;
- enabling them to become 'effective learners';
- the opportunity to develop 'transferable skills good for university modules and later on in working life'.

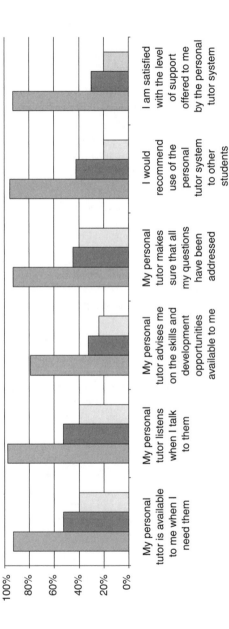

Figure 6.1 A comparison of student feedback on personal tutoring across years one to three

This reinforced one of our aims which was to help students begin to prepare for their career management.

We were delighted with the feedback, especially as no part of the module was formally assessed. We intend to further contextualise the module and take note of the very different backgrounds and prior experiences of the student group. We believe we have a firm foundation on which to build in coming years.

The cost and timeline

The module was devised over a relatively short period of time, but meant considerable effort in terms of drawing up a coherent timetable that covered all required elements. There was no additional cost in implementing this module as TFs were already expected to run personal tutorials and skills support. Online materials were already available through education enhancement as well as additional face-to-face support for academic skills and advice on employability.

How it is/was monitored

Student attendance or engagement was carefully monitored by individual tutors (with administrative support) and added to a single, central spreadsheet.

The outcome

Since the module has been extremely successful, there is a real commitment from TFs and the school for its continued use. We regularly review and update the module and incorporate further changes. We intend to restructure and formalise our second- and third-year provision. The success has also led to the planning of a different version of the module for masters' students in the school.

Has or could the initiative be used for a different group?

A similar module could be developed in a variety of contexts and for differing levels of student, with any content that enables students to develop personal and professional skills rather than focusing on subject knowledge.

Advice and guidance

*   Ensure that both students and staff understand the purpose and expectations of the module.
*   Be clear with students that their attendance and engagement is being carefully monitored and that mandatory attendance really does mean mandatory.
*   Where possible, available or appropriate, make use of expertise external to the subject area, for example, centralised support for academic and library skills or online resources.
*   Engage students in on-going evaluation to promote focused review and development of each aspect of the module, so that the student voice is heard and that staff develop practice that is evidence-led and constantly evolving.

Contact details

j.stephenson@exeter.ac.uk
e.j.dunne@exeter.ac.uk

Conclusion

It is obvious to those of us who have toiled in the higher education vineyards that the induction year is not an isolated experience for students or for the educators who assist students in their transition to university. The outcomes of what occurs through programmatic approaches and curricular innovations will remain with students well beyond induction. Attitudes and behavior patterns that students set during induction are difficult to reverse or change. It is, therefore, critical that we:

- learn from each other, psychologists, researchers and scholars who have addressed post-secondary student success in the past and who are presenting cutting-edge research and initiatives today;
- base our work on proven best practices and valid research;
- frontload our efforts and institutional resources to the induction period so that the student experience begins well;
- work together in a collaborative, integrative, comprehensive and intentional manner as opposed to a competitive way;
- constantly work to improve the induction experience. There will always be opportunities for improvement as students, our institutions and cultures change.

The first-year experience for students depends on our efforts, and the future of our institutions and our societies will reflect our students' experiences. There is no more important work before us than the need to bolster our efforts to provide students with an outstanding induction experience.

References

Astin, A.W. (1993) *What Matters in College? Four Critical Years Revisited*, San Francisco: Jossey-Bass.

Chickering, A.W. and Gamsom, Z. (1987) *Seven Principles for Good Practice in Undergraduate Education*, AAHE Bulletin, 39: 3–7.

Kift, S. (2010) Presented at the 3+3+4 Symposium, City University of Hong Kong, Kowloon, Hong Kong.

Kuh, G.D. (2008) *High Impact Educational Practices: What They Are, Who has Access to Them, and Why They Matter*, Association of American Colleges and Universities. Online. Available at: http://www.aacu.org/leap/hip.cfm (accessed August 26, 2010).

Sanford, N. (1967) *Where Colleges Fail: A Study of the Student as a Person*, San Francisco: Jossey-Bass.

Tinto, V. (1987) *Leaving College: Rethinking the Causes and Cures of Student Attrition*, Chicago: University of Chicago Press.

Chapter 7

Reorientation and reinduction to study

Michelle Morgan, Kingston University, UK

Introduction

Although research has shown that students are traditionally more at risk of dropping out in their first year of study (McGiveny, 2003; Crosling *et al.*, 2008), the experience of the returning student (returners) and the barriers that can impact on their ability to succeed on a course have been neglected in terms of research and policy. I believe that the levels of study following the first year of study are just as important in the lifecycle of the student as their initial year at university. Support to help facilitate the transition of students from one level of study to the next can be provided via stages I call reorientation and reinduction. Reorientation is for returning students to enable them to orientate themselves into their new level of study and it takes place over a short period of time. Reinduction for returning students introduces a range of skills and support required for their new level of study and it takes place over a longer period of time. This chapter explores the importance and characteristics of the reorientation and reinduction stages as highlighted in the Practitioner Model.

Hunter *et al.*'s (2010) book entitled *Helping Sophomores Succeed: Understanding and Improving the Second Year Experience* is the first real attempt at offering an in-depth and comprehensive understanding of the common challenges that arise in a returning student's life at university or college.

Schaller (2010) argues that, although initiatives to support returning students do exist across the sector in the United States, 'more comprehensive programmes, across academic divisions or beyond single offices, are few and far between'. The picture is similar across the international higher education (HE) sector.

Settling back into study can be a troublesome and difficult period for returning students. The problems and difficulties a student can experience are often categorised under the 'sophomore slump' or 'mid-term blues' heading and is perceived to occur midway through a course.

The term the 'sophomore slump' is used to describe students who:

> lack motivation, are indecisive about selecting a major, feel disconnected socially and academically, engage in behaviour that interferes with their academic success (e.g. excessive drinking), flounder academically, absenteeism, lack of extracurricular involvement and are disappointed and frustrated with the academic experience.
>
> (Maggitti, 2003:1)

There are three common misnomers that reinforce the sophomore slump experience. First, there seems to be an acceptance across the sector that students must experience the sophomore slump or mid-term blues as a rite of passage when at university. Second, it is assumed that the characteristics of the sophomore slump are just restricted to a student being halfway through their degree rather than them occurring at anytime during their studies. It is also important to recognise that the description of the sophomore slump relates to the symptoms of stresses and problems a student can face and not the causes. Third, the approach of many institutions is that once a student has gone through their first year of study, whether as a part-time or full-time student, they should automatically know what to expect both in terms of academic requirements and support available in the upcoming levels of study. To effectively support students through the transition process across the different levels requires these misnomers to be discarded and a new approach adopted.

The problems a returning student can experience

There are general personal/academic problems and issues that can happen to a student at any time during their studies but there are also specific ones for returners. These problems can act as major barriers to the successful completion of their course. It is important for practitioners to recognise that many of a returning student's issues will be different to that of a student in their first year of study (especially academic ones) so applying the same initiatives must be avoided.

The problems a returning student can experience will vary and may include personal, social and academic issues. Some of these are listed below.

Personal and social issues: general

- Having to balance studies with paid work.
- Coping with distance or work-based study.
- Relationship break-ups and illness.
- Bereavement.
- Childcare problems.
- Financial problems (debt is likely to increase as duration of course increases).

Personal and social issues: specific to returners

- Coping with moving from university to non-university accommodation.
- Losing an academic or social network of friends due to accommodation or course changes.
- Concern or inability to balance the demands of study and life outside of university as the level of study increases.
- Giving up paid work to concentrate on study.

Academic issues: general

- Change in study mode.
- Identify learning support needs.

Academic issues: specific to returners

- Returning after a long vacation between academic levels of study.
- Returning after a gap year or period of intermission.
- Returning after a placement.
- Carrying failures or poor performance from a previous level into the next level.
- Engaging in a full academic year that counts towards classification.
- Uncertainty about course and career options.
- Weak academic skills base.
- Not integrating into the new academic level of study or feeling supported.

These factors can all impact on a returning student being able to effectively settle back into their studies. For students from non-traditional groups considered to be at risk (e.g. lower social classes, mature) the pressure can be even greater. It is not unusual to see an increase in students utilising welfare and support services while their academic support decreases as they progress through their degree.

Each academic level brings different requirements and pressures. Students will not automatically know what to expect and what is required of them in the new academic level of study unless explicitly told. Returning students can experience feelings of confusion, anxiety and bewilderment just as they did when they entered university as a new student. Anxiety levels may even be greater as the course progresses as more of their work counts towards their final degree, and they have more to lose as their investment in their education increases. It is important to recognise that not all students can successfully make the progression from one level to another without any major academic or personal mishaps and without support, guidance and advice.

Kennedy and Upcraft (2010) argue that the academic, personal and social problems can result in students experiencing one or more of the following:

- academic deficiencies (e.g. not making significant academic progress);
- academic disengagement (e.g. lack of motivation, non-participation);
- dissatisfaction with the university/college experience (e.g. unhappy with the process and support provided);
- course and career indecision (failing to meet requirements, anxiety about the future);
- developmental confusion (e.g. identity, spiritual beliefs, life purpose).

(Kennedy and Upcraft, 2010:39)

An increase in the problems is likely to result in withdrawal by the student from their course. If students are effectively supported throughout the reorientation and reinduction stages, then the misery of the sophomore slump or mid-term blues for returning students could be reduced if not avoided.

Reorientation

Through the reorientation stage, we can start to support returning students in a number of ways so they do not experience the barriers identified by Kennedy and Upcraft (2010). We can help re-engage students in their academic studies by:

- providing targeted information and support;
- identifying reasons for disengagement;
- identifying barriers for preventing success in the next level.

We can improve student satisfaction in the student experience by:

- listening to and acting on their concerns and needs;
- engaging them in improving their own experience.

Reinduction

Through the reinduction stage, we can support returning students through each academic level to achieve success. We can support students attempts to correct academic deficiencies by:

- helping them build on their academic achievements to date through the curriculum or extra academic support;
- identifying any issues impacting on their academic learning (e.g. weak key skills, falling behind in their studies) and helping them to bridge the gap.

By providing clarity on course and career direction we can:

- help students properly evaluate their ability or chance for success in their academic studies;
- help them develop employability skills through the curriculum or extra curricula activities.

We can assist students in improving their sense of self by:

- encouraging them to engage in reflection and personal development to support them in their studies, enhance their employability profile and improve their self-identity;
- helping them increase their confidence and ability in all areas of student life.

The four case studies in this chapter are initiatives aimed to support returning students by managing their expectations and experience in their new academic level of study; to provide clarity on their new level of study; to help them develop their academic and employability skills; and encourage reflection and personal development.

Case Study 17 from Michelle Morgan from Kingston University, UK, looks at why she developed the reorientation and reinduction stages, and the programme that she designed and implemented in the Faculty of Engineering for returning students.

Case Study 18 by Erica Arthur looks at how returning students at Keel University, UK, are supported in the decision-making process to undertake study abroad and how the university assists them in the process.

Case Study 19 by Emma Weber from Millersville University, USA, explains how her institution supports outgoing home students and incoming international students on their study abroad programme.

Case Study 20 from Patricia Willer demonstrates how returning students from study abroad or placements at the University of South Carolina, USA, are encouraged to reflect and continue their personal development by supporting other students through a range of voluntary and paid activities.

Case Study 17

Name and university
Michelle Morgan, Faculty Learning and Teaching Coordinator and Student Experience Manager, Faculty of Engineering, Kingston University, UK.

Title of project/initiative
Reorientation and reinduction for all returning students in the Faculty of Engineering.

Who was involved in the initiative
Faculty Learning and Teaching Coordinator and Student Experience Manager (LTCSE), Faculty Student Support Officer, Heads of Schools, Faculty Placement and Employability Coordinator, Course Module Leaders, Student Office Administrator and Director of Student Affairs.

Reason for the project/initiative
The Faculty of Engineering has grown substantially in the past five years. An average Level 1 intake has grown from 80 to over 200 students. Levels 2, 3 and 4 each have around 300 students per level. Our progression rates are good but engineering is a hard subject so we expect relatively high repeat or resit module rates. From internal research and faculty student feedback processes, we discovered that many returning students reported feeling lost when they entered a new academic level of study and their stress levels were quite high. Students felt let down because the support they had received in their first level of study in terms of academic support and advice had fallen away when they entered their next level of study. They were expected to 'just get on with it'. They did not know what support they could get and were worried about asking for help and clarification on many issues because they were returning students. They said that this resulted in them disengaging and the moment that happened, they struggled to cope. We were good at managing the Level 1 student experience but poor at managing subsequent levels.

Why it was developed
We wanted to improve the student experience for all returning students whether in our faculty or those based at partner institutions (PIs) by delivering a reorientation session that:
*   provided targeted support, advice and guidance appropriate for each level of study;
*   gave students the opportunity to reflect on what they had achieved in their previous level of study;
*   started the academic skills induction process for their level of study (reinduction).

Who was the target group
We wanted to provide targeted support to all returning students whether they had successfully progressed, were repeating/resitting, returning after a placement/study aboard session or a long non-academic intermission. This totalled around 800 students across Levels 2, 3 and 4. Each academic level had its own reorientation session. At these sessions, information for reinduction support was collected (see 'what it included' section below).

Those who were returning after a long non-academic intermission were required to attend a separate orientation programme with direct-entry/transfer students first (see Case Study 9). The first year of implementation concentrated on students returning to KU and not PIs.

How it was developed, what it included and how it was implemented

How it was developed

The Learning and Teaching (L&T) Coordinator developed a draft reorientation programme which was agreed on by academic and support colleagues at the end of year Faculty of Engineering away day.

What it included

Reorientation session

The aims and objectives of the session was to let students know about:

- what to expect in their new level of academic study;
- the academic differences between the level they had just left and the level they were entering;
- the academic rules for their new level of study;
- things to think about in their new level of study and what skills to build on.

We delivered these aims and objectives and a range of information through the various speakers listed below:

- Welcome back by the Head of School. Returning students were congratulated on their success for progressing onto the next level. They were encouraged to keep up the hard work and ask for help if they needed it. This was an important message for a male-dominated student body who often do not like asking for help.
- What to expect in this academic level by the L&T Coordinator. Academic expectations and the differences between the previous level and new level of academic study were explained.
- Academic rules and regulations by the Head of School. Students were reminded and guided through the rules and regulations for their new level of study.
- Accessing support in the faculty by the Student Support Officer. A reminder of the faculty support available was provided.
- Accessing central service support by the Director of Student Support. Information about central services appropriate for returners such as health and counselling, dyslexia support, finance advice and Student Union support was provided.
- Personal Development Planning (PDP) by the L&T Coordinator. Students were reminded about the importance of reflection and personal development and given advice on how they could engage in this activity.
- Placements and careers by the Employability Coordinator. Information on the benefits of undertaking placements and study abroad opportunities were covered for Level 2 students and advice was provided on how to access career support and advice.
- Reflection on previous year and extra support for the coming year survey. This activity required returning students to think about what they achieved in their previous level and to identify what extra academic help and support they felt they may need in the coming year. These extra activities would be delivered over the coming months as reinduction activities. The survey also asked for feedback about the reorientation session.

Returning students were given detailed information in a reorientation handbook produced by the LTCSE. It contained practical advice and up-to-date contact numbers. A hard copy handbook was provided as well as an electronic version on StudySpace (Blackboard) because students had stated that they preferred to have a hard copy handbook for reference.

How it was implemented

Returning students start their teaching timetable as soon as they come back at the start of the academic year, unlike new students who spend their first week undertaking orientation activities. Colleagues who ran core modules were asked to give up their first teaching slot for the reorientation session. A number of modules had to be identified to ensure all students were accessed.

Analysis and feedback

The reflection surveys were analysed and the results published for students to see. Many of the extra support activities students asked for related to extra study skill and career oriented sessions. As engineering students timetables are so full, extra activities could not be fitted into their timetable. However, extra support was delivered on an extra curricula basis throughout the academic year.

The cost and timeline

It was developed quite quickly but thought; knowledge, experience, consideration and consultation had taken place. Internal research had informed the activity. Colleagues who participated undertook the activity as part of their remit. The photocopied reorientation handbooks that were provided to all returners cost around £500.

How it is/was monitored

Feedback on the initiative was provided by course representatives via various faculty committees and attendance at extra curricula activities were monitored. The cohort pass rate per level has improved.

The outcome

It is now part of the faculty's diet of activities delivered at the start of the new academic year.

Has or could the initiative be used for a different group?

This initiative is being adapted for our partner institutions. It could be adapted for work-based or distance learners and delivered via email or a virtual learning environment.

Advice and guidance

- Get colleagues on board.
- Listen to your returning students issues and concerns.
- Be positive when describing what to expect in the new academic level of study to students.
- Make all your information explicit and clear. Don't always rely on electronic forms of distributing information.
- Feedback your findings to your students on the reflection survey.

Contact details

michelle.morgan@kingston.ac.uk

Case Study 18

Name and university

Erica Arthur, International Development Manager (North America), University of Birmingham, UK. Former Study Abroad Manager, Keele University, UK and former Chair, British Universities Transatlantic Exchange Association (BUTEX).

Title of project/initiative

Tick Off to Take Off: the study abroad pre-departure guide (TOTTO) at Keele University.

Who was involved in the initiative

Study Abroad Manager, MSc student, IT intern, freelance illustrator, student focus groups.

Reason for the project/initiative

We recognised that study abroad students have to negotiate a complex administrative journey before they set off on their study abroad experience. Expected to juggle planning their time abroad with degree study, students can neglect crucial elements of the application process or become de-motivated. While it was tempting to see this process as a litmus test for a student's suitability for study abroad (evidencing the organisational drive, time management and initiative needed to cope in another educational environment), it also meant that only those who were already competent would be able to take advantage of the opportunity. We wanted to ensure that students who needed more support at the outset to access the personal development potential of study abroad did not miss the boat. To better support outgoing students, we needed to think creatively about the application and pre-departure process.

Why it was developed

We developed TOTTO to better prepare students making a formal application to an overseas university, to guide them through each step of the pre-departure process and to maintain their enthusiasm for study abroad.

Who was the target group

We wanted to develop an accessible, centralised resource which would benefit others besides the cohort of students preparing to travel. Thirty subject-specific academic advisers would have access to TOTTO to assist them in their advising roles. TOTTO would be a valuable training resource for new study abroad staff, and parents would be given access to the site, thus providing much needed reassurance and answers to queries that might otherwise take up staff time.

How it was developed, what it included and how it was implemented

How it was developed

While it fulfilled wider strategic purposes, this project began as a bottom-up initiative in response to issues arising from my day-to-day interaction with students. TOTTO was partly inspired by electronic resources, such as Bachnik's *At Home in Japan* (2004) and *What's Up With Culture?* (La Brack, 2003), that tackle cultural preparation for study abroad. While the subject matter of these tutorials keeps users interested, it was much harder to make potentially boring, bureaucratic tasks fun. Developing creative strategies for packaging web-based information in a clear, inventive manner enabled us to overcome this inherent difficulty.

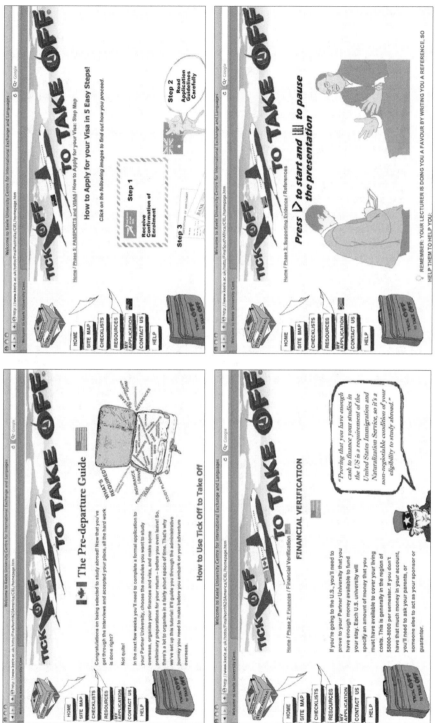

Figure 7.1 Interactive guidance and step-by-step formulas

What it included

Through a series of interactive modules (see Figure 7.1), TOTTO provides practical guidance on everything from selecting courses overseas, applying for visas, writing CVs and keeping tutors happy. A comprehensive 'resources' page links to useful external resources, including embassies and travel-booking services. Print-friendly versions exist for students who prefer hard copies, and 'checklists' allow students to 'tick off' their progress and ensure that they have met all the necessary requirements (see Figure 7.2). Students found this 'immensely helpful', as it helped alleviate doubt and worry:

> I found it easy to navigate and the checklists helped me immensely to get my head round all that needed to be done.

TOTTO has also revolutionised a major element of the administrative process, cutting out large amounts of paperwork with an efficient IT solution. The 'my application' feature produces a customised information page for individual partner universities, from which official application documents, course catalogues and web-pages can be accessed (see Figure 7.3). This has transferred responsibility onto the student to manage their own application and conserves office time and photocopying costs. Keele students responded very positively:

> It was innovative and easy to use. The fact that you could access forms electronically was particularly useful.

How it was implemented

The passive format of the application meeting has become more interactive. Relocated to a PC lab, students log on to TOTTO and review partner-specific requirements while I navigate through the tutorial and relay general guidance. Rather than covering all the requirements in minute detail, I raise the main points and guide students toward the online resources. This interactive mode of logistical preparation has aided students' retention because they are now required to find information themselves. Instead of relying on staff to answer questions during office hours, students have access to a comprehensive resource 24/7 and, importantly, can work through the application process at their own pace in their own time.

Analysis and feedback

A multiple-choice test and evaluative questionnaire enabled me to assess whether students were using the tutorial and to obtain qualitative feedback:

- 92 per cent of students found TOTTO easy to navigate.
- 94 per cent found the layout clear and forms easy to download.
- Students assessed how prepared they felt for study abroad having completed TOTTO. 23 per cent ranked themselves excellent, 67 per cent good, 9 per cent fair and just 1 per cent poor; encouraging evidence that TOTTO has instilled confidence four or five months prior to departure.
- In an overall rating of TOTTO, 39 per cent rated the site excellent, 53 per cent good and 8 per cent fair.

The cost and timeline

The project evolved over a year and a half from 'The Study Abroad Web Tutorial', targeted only at Keele students going to North America, to 'Tick Off to Take Off', a package comprising four distinct tutorials for North America, Europe, Australia and South Africa, which would eventually be licensed to other universities. Producing TOTTO with a professional IT consultant would have been very expensive. Working with student interns made the

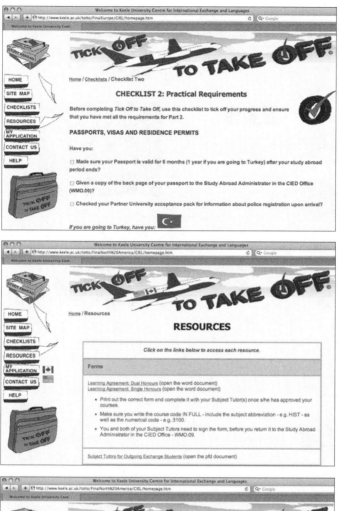

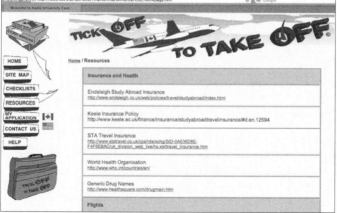

Figure 7.2 Checklists and resources

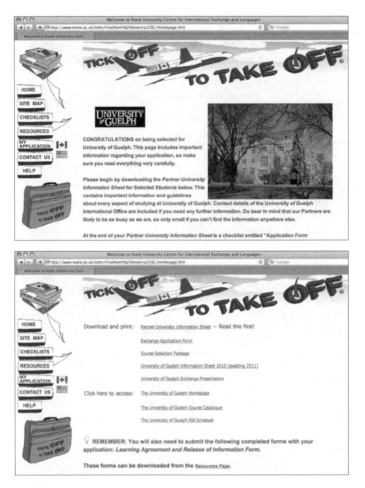

Figure 7.3 My application

project affordable on a HE budget and enabled us to produce a professional product with limited financial resources.

How it is/was monitored

I introduced an annual feedback survey and implement changes and update pages in response to student suggestions and new procedures.

The outcome

Without committing additional staff time, TOTTO prevents students from losing direction and improves retention rates. In 2007, I won the Association of University Administrator's (AUA) Award for Excellence in Higher Education Management and Administration, and TOTTO was highlighted as an example of best practice in Fielden *et al.*'s (2007) *Global Horizons for UK Students: A Guide for Universities*. The wholesale changes that TOTTO has brought to study abroad administration have amassed national significance, as seven UK and two overseas institutions have purchased the licence and are now able to provide a more integrated and innovative service. The overall impact of TOTTO has therefore exceeded my original objectives, enabling Keele to set a new benchmark in best practice for study abroad.

Has or could the initiative be used for a different group?

Three generic versions of TOTTO were developed for licence as a result of interest generated at conferences. By making TOTTO available externally we have saved other institutions the time and effort involved in developing similar resources. Licensing institutions are able to customise TOTTO to address their procedures and requirements directly which has recently led to the exciting development of a Taiwanese TOTTO. The development process and design objectives offer a template for creating similar resources for incoming students and, indeed, for other areas of HE administration. If staff resources are limited, supplementing a meeting with an online pre-departure aid that simplifies the application process, centralises information and increases efficiency provides an ideal solution.

Advice and guidance

- Simplify complex bureaucratic requirements using step-by-step formulas.
- Use student queries to inform the development of guidelines.
- Use an array of presentation styles, e.g. image-driven text, checklists and narrative examples, to maintain interest in procedures.

References

Bachnik, J. (2004) *At Home in Japan*. Online. Available at: http://athome.nealrc.org/index.html (accessed 9 September 2010).

Fielden, J. (2007) *Global Horizons for UK Students: A Guide for Universities*, London: The Council for Industry and Higher Education.

La Brack, B. (2003) *What's Up With Culture?* Online. Available at: http://www2.pacific.edu/sis/culture (accessed 9 September 2010).

Contact details

e.d.arthur@bham.ac.uk

Case Study 19

Name and university
Emma Weber, Program Coordinator, Office of Global Education and Partnerships, Millersville University, Pennsylvania, USA.

Title of project/initiative
Supporting study abroad students at Millersville and partner institutions (PIs).

Who was involved in the initiative
Director of Global Education and Partnerships, fellow coordinators and other stakeholders at Millersville, directors and other key stakeholders at eight international partner institutions.

Reason for the project/initiative
The project was multi-faceted. After operating on an informal basis, the university decided that globalising the campus would be one its top goals.

It wanted to globalise the campus by:

*   sending students out to other international institutions;
*   bringing international students to Millersville;
*   delivering a quality experience for both students and staff at institutions;
*   providing students with an extended skills base due to study abroad opportunities;
*   giving students who could not undertake the study abroad option, whether for financial or academic reasons, the chance to mix with international students on their home campus;
*   better preparing them for a global market through exposure and experience.

Millersville is part of the Pennsylvania state system of higher education which encompasses 14 institutions.

Why it was developed
The development of the office has occurred over a period of 20 years but most importantly over the past ten years.

As the scheme grew, we needed a structured framework on which to effectively deliver a quality student experience for all key stakeholders. This became especially important when we started to increase our PIs. Many had different educational systems and cultural environments. We had learned that the better prepared our students were (whether incoming or outgoing), the better the experience they would have. The scheme operates across 17 institutions worldwide (Spain, Australia, Germany, France, UK, Chile, South America, Africa, Japan). The most significant growth in PIs and students studying abroad has been within the past 5–7 years. Our office would collect student opinions and experiences of our students going out and international students coming in during their study abroad period. Students reported:

*   cultural differences;
*   academic differences;
*   lack of support, advice and help not always being available at the other PIs.

We discovered that the management of student expectations of our outgoing and incoming students was not effective. We wanted to improve on these areas and minimise the stress and negative experience which impacted on the overall study abroad experience as the start can often set the tone for the entire experience.

The target group

A student should be at least a Level 2 student wishing to study between a week and 18 months abroad with a minimum of 24 credits from Millersville. The average credits per level is 30.

How it was developed, what it included and how it was implemented

How it was developed

We wanted to develop a framework which would improve all areas of the students' experience so we looked at the internal management processes at Millersville and most PIs. We also talked to past participants and students currently engaged in the scheme to understand their expectations and experiences.

Once we did this, we then broke the process down in two stages; students going to a PI and students coming from a PI to Millersville.

After we developed a framework of good practice for students leaving and coming to us, it was shared with PIs who were encouraged to adapt a similar international study aboard process. This would help manage the expectation and experience of the student.

What it included

For students going from Millersville to a PI:

- The recruitment process was developed to give students a good overview of the experience they could expect (activities include: information session, one-on-one advising session, extensive literature).
- They would undergo a rigorous application process to demonstrate commitment to the programme, their ability to succeed both academically and personally, and to determine whether they would be a good ambassador for Millersville.
- They were given pre-departure information (financial, immigration, health, flight, accommodation), would undertake a course approval process for study when aboard (to make credits transfer, etc.) and complete the international paperwork.
- Previous year study abroad students talked to outgoing students so they could understand what to expect academically, socially, culturally, how to behave, and the emotional impact of the experience. These students were invaluable and are a key part to preparing outgoing students for success.

Whilst abroad, there is regular contact with the university and their experience is monitored. When it is time for our students to return, we start re-entry activities. We help:

- The students prepare to return to studies by completing pre-registration and providing academic advisors who help them make course choices and ensure the courses undertaken aboard are transferable.
- With culture shock re-entry issues by addressing re-assimilation issues relating to family, friends, the Millersville academic structure, and the wider community. A range of support is provided including one-to-one and information.
- Returning students by encouraging them to become global education ambassadors for Millersville. Students receive a certificate and letter from the director to put on their CV for raising the profile of the programme and supporting students. They are also provided with an opportunity to share their experiences abroad in an on-going way.

Supporting students coming in from PIs

We expect our PIs to prepare their students in a similar way to how we prepare our students for study abroad. We provide PIs with all the information their students need to know about Millersville and what to expect. The PIs manage the pre-arrival process in conjunction with us. We:

- liaise with the individual students regarding course selection, registration, accommodation, costs if relevant, health, immigration, arrival requirements, and orientation schedule;
- include academic orientation (academic skills, course structure differences), cultural and social orientation, immigration orientation (travel restrictions and regulations) and support orientation (health, safety, etc.) in our schedule;
- assign returning students to act as an information and buddy support network;
- check in with them throughout their stay and are available when needed;
- encourage them to attend cultural and social experiences so they can meet Millersville and other international students. This helps us touch base with them and encourages the globalisation experience.

Supporting students going back to their PI

We:

- work closely with the PIs in ensuring that their students' return journey is problem free;
- ensure all the necessary paperwork is completed for both parties including the issuance of transcripts;
- expect the PI to provide their student with the appropriate re-entry information;
- have a pre-departure social gathering for all returning PI students so they can talk about their experiences.

There is an annual study abroad/global ambassador award ceremony which recognises all ambassadors, study abroad students and the work of the faculty and administration.

Analysis and feedback

Our analysis and feedback comes from our monitoring processes.

The cost and timeline

Most of the activities are time intensive rather than cost intensive.

How it is/was monitored

- Evaluation surveys.
- Focus groups with students.
- Evaluating experience of students and staff at PIs.
- Annual report produced.
- Annual monitoring and review exercise.

The outcome

The wide choice of study abroad options has attracted students to Millersville over other higher educational state institutions.

Our framework is constantly evolving and we adapt good practices from across the sector. We have strengthened the programme, the quality and the overall students' experience of all students studying at Millersville. It has improved student employability and increased student satisfaction.

Has or could the initiative be used for a different group?
The framework covers all aspects of study abroad so another institution could adapt it.

Advice and guidance
- Listen to the needs of your students and the specific support they require whilst preparing to study abroad, whilst aboard and upon re-entry.
- Communicate on a regular basis with PIs and students.
- Recognise differences between PIs and students and help facilitate transitions into your processes.
- Utilise the experience and knowledge obtained by students studying abroad for the good of the home institution's academic community.
- Make sure that it is real globalisation by making connections and having the opportunities available.

Contact details
emma.weber@millersville.edu

Case Study 20

Name and university

Patricia Willer, Associate Vice President for International Programs, and Gabriela Peschiera-Carl, Assistant Director for Study Abroad, University of South Carolina (USC), USA.

Title of project/initiative

Sustaining global perspective: a peer advisor programme for students who have studied abroad.

Who was involved in the initiative

Associate Vice President for International Programs, Director for Study Abroad and two Assistant Directors for Study Abroad.

Reason for the project/initiative

The programme was developed at the University of South Carolina to strengthen advisement services for university students interested in studying abroad.

Undergraduate students who had studied abroad were recruited as peer advisors. These students would manage the advisement and recruitment load in an expanding Study Abroad office as well as using their voices to guide students in the study abroad process. In addition, their perspectives would guide staff about the effective service delivery in response to current student needs.

Why it was developed

We developed the peer advisor (PA) programme to incorporate highly motivated and internationally experienced undergraduate students as paid workers. It was founded on the belief that these students could effectively engage their peers in advising capacities by providing fresh, firsthand and invaluable perspectives. These students would support the professional staff in the university's Study Abroad office allowing us to focus on more complex tasks. The programme provided these students with the opportunity to extend and integrate their international education learning experiences into their studies and those of others as well as acting as a pathway for internationally focused careers or graduate study. Professional staff members in the Study Abroad office served as mentors and role models to undergraduate students in a collegial manner.

The target group

The target group comprised of eligible students who had completed the equivalent of at least one academic term in a credit-bearing international study programme and who were interested in student employment.

How it was developed, what it included and how it was implemented

How it was developed

We adapted the practice of hiring part-time student workers for office work into a more organised, intentional student intern programme. A set of duties that could be performed by PAs was developed as well as new protocols for the delivery of advising services. These positions were advertised through the internet, and a job announcement was e-mailed to those who were returning to campus from study abroad.

What it included

The application and interview processes were critical components in developing a success-ful PA programme. Applicants underwent a formal application process, including a letter of application and an interview that required them to prepare a five-minute oral presentation. Based on the interviews, between three and five students were chosen for PA positions for the upcoming academic year.

How it was implemented

A PA's time was divided equally among three components: advising and marketing, admin-istrative tasks and specialised projects. Their job duties included:

- delivering general information sessions and guiding prospective students researching study abroad options;
- presenting study abroad information and sharing their experiences abroad at university venues;
- assisting with study abroad events;
- maintaining the listserv and e-mail account and responding to student inquiries;
- performing reception and general office duties;
- completing special projects related to study abroad.

Analysis and feedback

In order to acquire accurate feedback on the effectiveness of the PA programme, we sur-veyed former PAs. The feedback was very positive, and the following quotes illustrate the sentiment felt by those surveyed:

> I had such a rewarding experience abroad that I wanted to help make that happen for other people. [The PA programme] was a great way to help advisees by sharing my excitement and calming their fears.

> Working in the Study Abroad office confirmed my opinions on the importance of promoting understanding between people from different cultures. This is something that I do want to be a big part of a future career.

> I think studying abroad was what really prepared me [for pursuing international activi-ties postgraduation] … but being a peer advisor added time, relationships, and depth to my experience at home, not just abroad.

> I was excited and proud to have an on-campus job that wasn't just for earning money but rather was an enjoyable experience that taught me valuable skills and allowed me to promote something that is very important to me.

> Many students come to the office with just an idea of what studying abroad is and leave the office with a well thought out plan to make it happen. PAs are an integral part of making this process as they are the first point of contact for meeting with students and assisting in choosing the right programme for them.

The cost and timeline

The programme was implemented during the 2004–5 academic year. At that time, there were three PAs working a combined total of 30 hours a week. To address staffing needs in the office, their hours were increased to a combined total of 45 hours a week. The cost of three PAs is approximately equivalent to one-third the salary of a full-time, professional study abroad advisor.

How it is/was monitored

The PAs met with their supervisor individually on a regular basis and participated in group meetings once a month. The individual meetings allowed the supervisor to provide on-going feedback on each PA's performance. In addition, the supervisor reviewed the PAs at the end of each semester. If the review was satisfactory, the PA continued working the next semester.

The outcome

The programme is evaluated annually to determine its effectiveness and modifications are made on an on-going basis. It has proved to be a highly cost-effective programme in providing guidance to prospective study abroad participants seeking assistance in a busy office. Equally important has been the level of engagement and professionalism that PAs are challenged to develop and demonstrate as they learn life and work skills that will serve them in the future.

A number of PAs have chosen professional pathways informed by their international experience. One former PA obtained employment with the United States Department of State; two chose to work in the field of international education; one served in the Peace Corps in Cameroon; two received Rotary scholarships to study in Northern Ireland and Peru; and several taught English overseas, including two who were awarded the Fulbright scholarship awards to teach English in China and South Korea.

Has or could the initiative be used for a different group?

Due to the programme's success, USC introduced new internationalisation intern positions in international programmes. These positions provide additional opportunities for students to engage in pre-professional work related to international education and their chosen academic fields. Two interns were selected, one majoring in international business and one in public relations. The public relations intern worked in the Study Abroad office to promote international education opportunities and developed a significant portfolio based upon her work. The other intern worked on intercultural programming that augmented his résumé for work in international business. Both internationalisation interns made significant contributions. In a further modification, the Study Abroad office created another internship, employing a marketing major who has studied abroad to promote international study opportunities at the university.

Student workers have traditionally been used in a number of ways on college campuses. Peer advisor positions provide substantive work experiences. These positions are challenging opportunities and they create professional pathways for students.

Advice and guidance

- Use student workers to perform pre-professional duties.
- Ensure they receive good training and supervision.
- Develop a staff culture of collaboration to create a programme that is intellectually stimulating and professionally challenging for these students.

Contact details

pwiller@sc.edu
gpcarl@sc.edu

Conclusion

The case studies in this chapter provide advice and guidance on support for both students and staff. The advice provided by the case study authors includes:

- listen to the needs of your students;
- communicate with all the key players;
- utilise the experience and knowledge of university units, colleagues and students;
- create and develop a staff culture of collaboration;
- reduce bureaucracy.

References

Crosling, G., Thomas, L. and Heaney, M. (2008) *Improving Student Retention in Higher Education: The Role of Teaching and Learning*, London: Routledge.

Hunter, M.S., Tobolowsky, B.F. and Gardner, J.N. (2010) *Helping Sophomores Succeed: Understanding and Improving the Second Year Experience*, San Francisco, CA: Jossey-Bass.

Kennedy, K. and Upcraft, M.L. (2010) 'Keys to student success: a look at the literature', in M.S. Hunter, B.F. Tobolowsky and J.N. Gardner (eds) *Helping Sophomores Succeed: Understanding and Improving the Second Year Experience*, San Francisco, CA: Jossey-Bass.

Maggitti, S.T. (2003) 'Sophomores: the struggles of the "middle children" of college'. Online. Available at: http://www.cabrini.edu/Student-Life/Health-and-Wellness/Counseling-and-Psychological-Services/Helpful-Links (accessed 25 November 2009).

McGiveny, V. (2003) *Staying or Leaving the Course: Non-Completion and Retention of Mature Students in Further and Higher Education*, Leicester: NIACE.

Schaller, M. (2010) 'Understanding the impact of the second year of college', in M.S. Hunter, B.F. Tobolowsky and J.N. Gardner (eds) *Helping Sophomores Succeed: Understanding and Improving the Second Year Experience*, San Francisco, CA: Jossey-Bass.

Chapter 8

Outduction

Preparing to leave, graduation and beyond

April L. Perry, University of Canterbury, New Zealand

Introduction

If you went to university, take a moment to think back to your undergraduate degree, whether that was two or 20 years ago. If you work with students soon to complete a course, think about their concerns and worries. When students come to the end of a course, especially a degree course, do they know exactly what they want to do with their life? How quickly will they make the transition from university to everyday life? Their university experience is likely to have changed their values, beliefs and outlook on life, so how easily will they make the transition post-university? Do they immediately land a job in their chosen career field? Do they land a job that is even degree required? Does that job meet all their expectations of what the working world would be?

Alternatively, do they have some feelings of uncertainty, ambiguity and lack of direction? Do they pursue further study because they do not know what else to do, or because they do not want to work in the field of their undergraduate degree? These are just a few questions to gain a perspective into the kind of thought process that university graduates have. But, with today's generation of young graduates, we also have to consider these questions and emotions coupled with the international economic climate, the large pool of graduates and the massive changes in technology that create and omit jobs fluidly.

As someone who personally struggled with the post-undergraduate transition and who is now a higher education practitioner and researcher in this area, I have devoted my efforts to better understanding this transition and how that knowledge can help others. In this chapter, I will discuss general information about the post-university transition, also referred to as outduction, post-undergraduate transition and re-entry, which is a critical stage in the Practitioner Model. I will briefly highlight the research in this area, and then introduce four case studies developed to support students in their transition from university.

Framing the post-undergraduate transition

Throughout the last decade, increasing attention has been drawn toward students in transition, as they move into and through university, but much less attention has been paid to the transition beyond university. As practitioners, I am sure we can all identify numerous anecdotal experiences we have had with students facing this transition and can agree that this is an area needing support. Additionally, as higher education personnel, we pride ourselves on understanding the students whom we serve, and we excel in a variety of support efforts for our students. But, how can we provide effective support for our final-year students and recent graduates if we do not fully know and understand their experiences, perspectives and needs? Often, approval and funding for institutional initiatives requires empirical evidence and not merely our anecdotal experiences with students and graduates. Furthermore, initiatives that are based on local research and developed in a bottom-up way are often not shared within the institution or across the sector.

To fully understand the needs of our students and graduates and the role institutions can play in the last transition of the student lifecycle, we need to ask them, research them and dive into their lives. Before support initiatives can be implemented to better prepare students for employment and other transition issues, we should first research, listen and understand what our applicants, students, and future employers need.

Students, practitioners and researchers have identified that the move from study to life after-study is a complex and difficult transition (Schlossberg *et al.*, 1995). This is also demonstrated in my research.

> Transition is when you leave one thing, and you're not there anymore ... and you're on your way to another thing, but you're not there yet either.
>
> (Justin, research participant)

> I'm in a transition into adulthood ... and not to just know who I am and what I want, but really finding it ... and having it ... and working towards it.
>
> (Lisa, research participant)

> Going from comfortable to not comfortable ... that's what the definition of transition should be ... From old to new ... from old experiences that you're good at to new experiences that are up in the air.
>
> (Talon, research participant)

The importance of the post-undergraduate transition

Students undertake a degree as part of preparing for the next step of life. Most students are not enrolled simply to be educated, but to gain skills for future life which encompasses far more than what is just taught in the classroom. Common reasons given by students for attending university include improving their chances of getting a job (UNITE, 2007); to further their career (Gedye *et al.*, 2004; UNITE, 2007); or to increase their earning potential (Wood, 2004). Therefore, 'it appears that reasons given for students going to university are becoming more "outcome" focused with university being seen as a worthwhile investment' (Morgan, 2008).

Of all the emergent themes and implications that have surfaced throughout my research on this topic, two have become dominant. First, the research has shown that recent graduates' expectations of what their degree can deliver is quite different from their actual experiences (reality) after graduation, specifically in terms of job obtained, position level, salary and other career related issues. Second, recent graduates are experiencing high levels of uncertainty in many aspects of their lives, such as career direction and choices, relationships, personal identity, living situation, self-image and finances (Perry, 2010).

Implications for institutions, based on the research available and my findings, indicate an opportunity to guide students in mentally and emotionally preparing for life after university, as their primary identity shifts from student to graduate. If students are prepared and understand these concepts, their transition into post-university life may not be much different, but their approach, mindset and emotional state may be more adaptable.

Based on the findings of my research, as well as the advice offered from my research participants, some of the implications for practice include:

- final-year/postgraduation seminars;
- support groups for students postgraduation;
- holistic career services offered to recent alumni;
- enhanced internships and mentorship programs with professionals in their career field;
- continued university staff mentorship/counselling postgraduation;
- community service/volunteer efforts for recent graduates and young professionals.

These implications lead us to look at four case studies where initiatives have been utilised to help support students in outduction or the post-university transition.

Case Study 21 from Ginny DeWitt at Westminster College, USA, looks at a new course developed to help Level 2 students choose a 'major' subject that utilises their strengths and values for life after university, while also increasing retention rates between Levels 2 and 3.

Case Study 22 by Marion Webb, based at Kingston University, UK, discusses a collaborative project between the universities of Bradford and Kingston, UK, that facilitated a research questionnaire aimed at gathering ideas for implementing support and transition programs for final-year students and beyond.

Case Study 23 from Michelle Morgan reviews an implemented campus initiative of creating a handbook aimed at supporting and preparing final-year students for post-university life at Kingston University, UK.

Case Study 24 by Pam Fearnley discusses how Leeds Metropolitan University, UK, changed its style and approach to graduation services and rituals to support and celebrate the achievements of their graduates.

Case Study 21

Name and university
Ginny DeWitt, Associate Director of the START Centre, and Beverly Christy, Director of the Career Resource Center, Westminster College, Salt Lake City, USA.

Title of project/initiative
A new course: sophomore solutions – major to career.

Who was involved in the initiative
Associate Director of the START Center, Director of the Career Resource Centre and Associate Provost for Student Development.

Reason for the project/initiative
To help Level 2 students (sophomores) who have not chosen a major subject (undeclared) explore major choices and careers and encourage them to examine their strengths, skills, values and career paths as they make this important decision. This course aimed to provide another way to increase the retention of our students from their Level 2 to Level 3 (junior year) as well as developing and supporting the college-wide learning goals listed below:

- critical, analytical and integrative thinking;
- creative and reflective capacities;
- writing and other communication skills.

Why it was developed
Often, there is a disconnect between academic activities, advising and career planning. Students in their second level are pressured to select a major subject by the end of the level without enough information about the implications of their choice. This course was developed to provide this connection and broaden students' perspective on the many options available if they took into consideration their strengths, skills and values when making their 'major' decision. Students who chose to leave college at the end of Level 1 (freshman year) or into Level 2 typically did not find personal meaning and goals during their college experience. The aim of this course was to meet students' needs and greatly enhance the personal journey of discovery to find their bliss which 'is that deep sense of being present, of doing what you must absolutely do to be yourself' (Campbell and Kudler, 2004).

We wanted our work to be informed by our students telling us why they were in college and what they hoped to accomplish. Our aim was to get meaningful and goal-driven answers by students.

The target group
Undeclared Level 2 students.

How it was developed, what it included and how it was implemented

How it was developed
After reading current literature on retention, looking at our Level 1 and 2 populations, informally collecting data on students' needs and discussing how an academic course would benefit these students, we submitted a proposal and sample syllabus to the Associate Provost for Student Development for a pilot course. The course was designed as an interdisciplinary department course and therefore did not require approval from the formal curriculum committee.

What it included

Self-exploration

Assignments focused on critical thinking about challenges and pressures/stresses students may face in terms of having to declare majors, meeting personal and parental expectations, and knowing what they wanted to do with their lives. The students completed several personal and career assessments to determine interests, skills, positive work environments, and academic potential. We also discussed what various career paths demanded in terms of graduate school and beyond. Decision making, critical thinking, goal setting and dealing with stress were discussed using case studies and current articles from the literature.

Career exploration/major exploration and advising

Faculty members from all schools on campus were invited to share with students their process of selecting a profession and reflections on their experiences during Level 2. They also marketed their programmes, discussed expectations and options in their professional field and answered questions. Students conducted an information career interview with an employer about a profession of interest in order to gain in-depth knowledge and understanding about the world of work, and learn how networking with employers could benefit them. Important class time was spent getting students to discuss what got them excited about the future, what they needed to know and how to ask the right questions to find a fulfilling profession (their 'bliss'). Students attended individual advising sessions to discuss their comprehensive academic plan in their proposed major, elect a faculty advisor and register for the next semester.

Career planning/major declaration and student portfolios

Throughout the semester, students compiled a portfolio which included all their class work. It was designed to provide support, information and samples of their work for future reflection and use. It was a portfolio of their personal development. It included all career development pieces, such as networking lists; cover and thank you letters; résumé; personal assessment results; written assignments; reflective writing; faculty interview reports; and a reflective assignment summarising the outcome of the employer interview. Also included were the major declaration assignments, reflective writing and their personal comprehensive academic plan leading to graduation in their newly chosen major.

How it was implemented

This course was developed, approved by the Provost and Associate Provost, and implemented in 2006–7. The interdisciplinary course team was made up of two professional staff members with advanced degrees. It carried two semester hours of upper division elective credit and one section was taught every fall (autumn) semester. The course was advertised to the general campus community through targeted emails, by distributing flyers, through faculty, discussed by academic advisors in the Start Centre and by word of mouth. We met throughout the year to develop new curriculum and assignments based upon professional experience, current literature and student suggestions from course evaluations and discussion groups.

Analysis and feedback

The course was formally evaluated by students through the college's academic system at the end of the semester along with all other courses they take. Our evaluations averaged 4.5 (scale 1–5). The mandatory 'final exam' consisted of an open-ended questionnaire in which students shared their opinions about specific parts of the curriculum. Students were encouraged to stay and participate in a voluntary open discussion where they talked about what they had learnt and how they would use information/resources from the course in the future.

The cost and timeline

The course proposal was submitted in the summer of 2006 and was first taught in the spring semester 2007. The proposal was very well received because it fulfilled the college's student learning goals, provided new services to students, and cost the college nothing initially. The Provost/Vice President for Academic Affairs approved associate faculty pay in fall 2009, but prior to that we were not paid to teach the course. No other costs were incurred by the college.

How it is/was monitored

Student feedback and evaluations helped us modify our pedagogy and curriculum.

The outcome

- The course is now an annual interdisciplinary offering with on-going institutional support.
- The combined retention rate (students continuing into their next year) for all students who have taken this course is 90.4 per cent (N = 63).
- Students have consistently indicated that the class helped them research and select majors of interest given their strengths, skills, and values. Of those students who graduated by spring 2010, 100 per cent graduated in the major they chose during the course.
- Here are quotes from students that we hear repeatedly:

  > I believe that this time of your life can be one of the most difficult and trying time periods and having a course such as this available is the key.

  > I found everything to be beneficial – especially meeting with faculty and a potential employer in my field.

  > It's great to finally BE a major. It is part of who I am – finding something I'm passionate about.

  > This class should be mandatory – even for freshmen!

Has or could the initiative be used for a different group?

This course could be adapted to meet the needs of any student needing to make major subject or career choices.

Advice and guidance

- Get faculty on board as supporters.
- Publicise to students and the advising/registration office.
- Track progress and communicate success to administration.

References

Campbell, J. and Kudler, D. (eds) (2004) *Pathways to Bliss: Mythology and Personal Transformation*, California: New World Library.

Contact details

gdewitt@westminstercollege.edu
bevchristy@comcast.net

Case Study 22

Name and university
Marion Webb, Academic Development Centre, Kingston University, UK.

Title of project/initiative
Outduction: improving the final-year experience.

Who was involved in the initiative
The Academic Development Centres, the Project Manager and key university players at the universities of Bradford and Kingston.

Reason for the project/initiative
This case study outlines the outduction project by the universities of Bradford and Kingston and gives an account of one of the events organised as one of the outcomes of this project. The varied challenges and issues of the final year of undergraduate study have not been subject to the same level of holistic investigation, analysis and discussion as the first-year experience (see http://www.sc.edu/fye and Higher Education Academy, 2007). The universities of Bradford and Kingston jointly applied for a National Teaching Fellowship project seeking to address 'the common neglect of the final year experience' (Eckel, 1994), with the overall purposes of improving the experience of final year students, to reframe the final-year experience to broaden graduate horizons, and to prepare final-year students to be successful, ethical and empowered citizens in a complex world.

Why it was developed
The National Student Survey in 2005 (http://www.hefce.ac.uk/pubs/rdreports/2006/rd22_06) first alerted us to the fact that, although evaluation of individual modules had yielded positive results, there was some disquiet among final-year undergraduates particularly in terms of their experience of assessment and feedback. KU's annual learning and teaching conference in 2007 was based on the theme of enhancing the final-year experience and, in his keynote speech at this event, Professor Geoff Layer of the University of Bradford spoke about the importance of supporting final-year students in their transition into the world beyond university: 'outduction'. Following this conference, a National Teaching Fellowship project on outduction was awarded to a team from Kingston and Bradford in the summer of 2007.

The target group
The project sought to enhance the experience of:

- those on a conventional three- or four-year undergraduate programme;
- part-time students who have studied for five or six years;
- students returning from a sandwich or international year;
- students on top-up degrees (HND/foundation degree to honours).

How it was developed, what it included and how it was implemented

How it was developed
The outduction project was in fact a series of mini-projects at the universities of Kingston and Bradford. One of the key features was the use of student interns to undertake some of the research and to assist the project team in both conducting the research and organising events.

The first stage of the project at Kingston University involved the distribution of a questionnaire to final-year students in the Faculty of Business and Law.

What it included

The aims of the questionnaire were to discover the students' perceptions of themselves in terms of academic preparedness for final-year study and to discover students' views on the transition beyond the final year. The questionnaire was followed by a series of focus groups and other events. At the University of Bradford student interns invited final-year students to capture their thoughts on the final year by identifying key words and memories.

How it was implemented

Questionnaires were distributed in lectures.

Analysis and feedback

The questionnaire revealed a high level of anxiety about the next phase of life in terms of progression to postgraduate study or employment.

The responses analysed totalled 189. When asked to volunteer key words about the final year, 155 words were used. The most commonly used words were connected with difficulty (e.g. 'tough', 'hard', 'demanding') or stress or fear. Of the words, 24 were positive (e.g. 'enjoyable', 'exciting'). Ten students used the word 'interesting'.

Students asked for more access to information about opportunities in the next stage, whether it be postgraduate study or preparation for employment.

In response to this request the Kingston interns arranged a 'big event' for final-year students which was held in October 2009. This took the form of a 'freshers' fair with conversation'. The interns took complete responsibility for the event and invited, among others, employability coordinators, the Students' Union volunteering organisers, directors of postgraduate study, representatives from student travel companies and entrepreneurship organisations and a number of others. They arranged competitions and evaluation forms and publicised the event to all final-year students.

The cost and timeline

The interns were given responsibility for the budget and spent £1,500 on the event. This included refreshments, a photographer and prizes for various competitions and for filling in the evaluation form. The first event took place in October and the interns spent approximately two months organising it but worked part-time and did not necessarily work the same number of hours each week.

How it is/was monitored

The project team attended the event and the project officer oversaw the budget but mostly the interns were in full control. The events were evaluated by a short questionnaire.

The outcome

The evaluations were overwhelmingly positive with requests for more events of this nature. There have since been two more events.

Has or could the initiative be used for a different group?

A key feature of the outduction project was the use of student interns. Our interns initially supported us by inputting data from the questionnaire. This role then developed into organising the 'big events' which has led to the interns using a wide range of skills: project management, budgeting, booking speakers, liaising with estates and other university departments and the Students' Union as well as with the project team.

Features from this project that could be used elsewhere are the 'freshers' fair' event for returning final-year students and the employment of student interns who make life easier for us all round.

Advice and guidance

The members of the project team were concerned that students were facing an uncertain future with a sense of gloom. By asking students to organise an event of this type gave them the opportunity to identify what for them may be realistic steps for the future, such as volunteering or travel.

References

Eckel, P. (1994) *Building Community in the Freshman and Senior Year Experience: Completing the Cycle of Student-Institution Involvement*, paper presented at the First-Year Experience Conference, Dublin, Ireland.

Higher Education Academy (2007). Online. Available at: http://www.heacademy.ac.uk/assets/documents/resources/publications/FYEFinalReport.pdf (accessed 9 July 2010).

Contact details

m.webb@kingston.ac.uk

Case Study 23

Name and university
Michelle Morgan, Faculty Learning and Teaching Coordinator and Student Experience Manager, Faculty of Engineering, Kingston University, UK.

Title of project/initiative
What next? A guide for engineering students preparing to leave university.

Who was involved in the initiative
Faculty Learning and Teaching Coordinator and Student Experience Manager, Faculty Employability Coordinator, Faculty Placements Coordinator, International Office, Alumni Office, Student Support Office and Student Course Representatives (SCRs).

Reason for the project/initiative
To support students in their preparation for leaving university.

Why it was developed
There was limited guidance and support for students in the faculty and those at partner institutions in preparing them for the challenges of leaving university.

The target group
Any student in their final year of study.

How it was developed, what it included and how it was implemented

How it was developed
The idea for the handbook came out of a visit to the International Student Centre at the University of Adelaide. While visiting the centre I was given a handbook entitled 'Finishing your studies at university: what now? A guide and workbook for international students'. The handbook, which was given to all international students just before they were about to leave, included practical advice and guidance on preparing to go home, information on visa requirements and career planning support. The handbook was informal, easy to read and not a glossy, corporate document. It was a great way of giving international students advice on making the transition from study to life after university. I was told that the handbook had been developed as a result of international students asking for advice and support.

I decided to implement the idea in my own faculty but I wanted to take the handbook a step further. First, I wanted it to be given to all students leaving university and second, it would be given to them as part of their outduction activities the faculty operated. These activities started just over half way through a student's course and were designed to get students thinking about what they wanted to do after university and to start preparing them for that eventuality. Outduction activities included employability advice and developing and improving key skills. The handbook would be given to students about six months before they were due to leave.

What it included
The aim of the handbook was two-fold. First, it was to compliment the outduction activities aimed at supporting, advising, guiding and preparing students for life after university so it would include a précis of the employability and key skills information and advice students had already been taught. Second, how to make a successful transition from university and

deal with potential cultural, social, professional and political adjustments. This was one of the many facets of the University of Adelaide handbook that I incorporated into our faculty handbook. I considered this to be a vital part of the handbook and felt that it was insightful of the International Office at the University of Adelaide to address this.

Life at university can be a protected environment. The faculty has a very diverse student body and it is easy to forget that students may be returning to environments which are fraught with difficulties which they have not had to deal with for a while and may have forgotten how to do so. For example, it could be returning to a country where there is political unrest or a country/home life where cultural behaviour is stricter. University is also a place where questions and issues can be explored in a safe environment. Returning to a non-democratic environment after a student is used to freedom of expression and debate can be problematic.

The handbook included a farewell message from the dean and information on:

- the re-entry experience;
- further study or a year out;
- career planning (employer's perspectives, career planning, job websites);
- international student information (staying in the UK, leaving the UK);
- checklists of things to do (personal and university);
- how to keep in touch (your graduation, useful graduate contact details, being an alumnus).

Certain sections, such as the further study and career advice section were more detailed and focused towards engineering students and their specific needs. For example, engineering specific job websites were listed along with the general job website addresses. Information and web addresses were supplied for professional bodies.

How it was implemented

Once the draft handbook was written, I circulated it to faculty and university colleagues and to student course representatives for comment. Their feedback fine tuned the handbook. It was a useful exercise having a variety of colleagues from across the institution commenting on their own information as well as others. The final version was sent electronically via email to all final-year students six months before they were due to leave. I do not believe that all information for students should be electronic. Over the years, students have often complained to me that some information is just easier to read and absorb if it is in hard copy. However, in this case providing the information electronically was the most efficient and effective way to target the handbook. The reasons were:

- it meant that the students did not 'lose' a hard copy;
- it was easy for the student to store and keep;
- they had access to the information post-study. If we had put it on Blackboard, which is our internal information site for students, once they stopped being a student, they would not be able to access the document;
- the handbook could be accessed by students in partner institutions overseas.

And it would be churlish not to admit that it made the initiative extremely affordable.

Analysis and feedback

The first year I circulated the handbook to the final-year cohort, I asked for their comments on how they thought it could be improved. The students who provided feedback stated that it was a very useful book.

The cost and timeline

The initiative was developed very quickly because the concept had already been established by the University of Adelaide. I got a copy of the handbook in March and by the end of April, I had the final Faculty of Engineering version completed. In the first year of the initiative due to its late development in the academic year, students got the handbook almost near the end of their studies. They were circulated in May ready for their departure in June. The following year, the handbook was circulated in January. We still circulate it at this time. Apart from staff time involved in compiling and checking the handbook, the cost of the initiative was negligible.

How it is/was monitored

I annually review the handbook to ensure that it is up to date, and talk to student course representatives to see if the handbook needs more information.

The outcome

The handbook is a very useful tool in helping students make the transition from study to life after university.

Has or could the initiative be used for a different group?

The handbook has been developed for students in partner institutions and for our postgraduate student body. It will be developed for work-based learning students.

Advice and guidance

- Just do it!
- Make sure that the handbook encompasses any special requirements for your chosen body of students.

Contact details

michelle.morgan@kingston.ac.uk

Case Study 24

Name and university
Pam Fearnley, Project Manager for Improving the Graduation Experience, Awards and Examinations Office, Leeds Metropolitan University, UK.

Title of project
Improving the graduation experience.

Who was involved in the project
The Registrar and Secretary (overall responsibility for graduation), the Awards, Examinations and Graduations Office (the office which managed the activity) and the Project Manager for managing the graduation and its stakeholders.

Reason for the project
Leeds Town Hall closed for refurbishment in 2004 and it was discovered that there was no venue large enough in Leeds to accommodate the numbers of graduating students. Therefore the decision was taken to construct a temporary, purpose-built venue on Headingley campus.

Why it was developed
Leeds Metropolitan graduation ceremony was primarily redesigned to improve, and make memorable, one of the last activities in the student lifecycle. Graduations had previously been held in a city centre venue during November when the weather was poor. Finding a venue large enough in the city in which to hold the entire event along with the provision to accommodate an ever-increasing number of graduates was impossible. This meant that gowning and photography services were provided in a building some distance from the main venue and the postgraduation reception for families and graduates was held in the unprepossessing university refectory at a similar distance from the main venue. This resulted in students and their families trailing from one area of the city to another often in the rain. A large number of students would also leave immediately after their ceremonies to celebrate elsewhere in the city. As a result, it was decided that we would create a temporary venue on our Headingley campus to hold the event. This would not only provide us with sufficient space but would provide an opportunity to show off the beautiful and historic Headingley campus and market the university to a larger audience.

The target group
All graduating and returning students, family, friends, staff and the wider student community.

How it was developed, what it included and how it was implemented

How it was developed
The style of ceremonies previously held in the Town Hall could not be replicated on Headingley campus but it was redefined into a different event which was more like a garden party, enabling the university to hold fewer but larger ceremonies over more days than had been held in the past. A very large marquee with two main areas, the graduation hall and the reception hall, was constructed on the centrally grassed area called the Acre on our Headingley campus.

What it included

Gowning and photography services were held in the sports halls and a car park was provided adjacent to the campus. The marquee, which was designed specifically for the event, included a foyer, an auditorium and a reception area as well as toilet facilities. This new site enabled students to collect their gowns, have their photographs taken and attend a formal ceremony and reception on campus. Students were also presented with their certificates on the day.

Prior to 2004, honorary degrees were conferred at a separate ceremony and venue. The changes to graduation enabled the university to bring the conferment of both award ceremonies together and to recognise the achievement of those significant figures who could serve as a role model to graduating students. These have included a number of internationally recognised sporting, cultural and academic figures as well as those linked to the institution or from the local area including civic dignitaries.

How it was implemented

A project plan was implemented covering all tasks needed to enable graduation to take place, for example, traffic management, crèche, health and safety, gowning and photography. Working with the various departments in the university including cleaning staff, hospitality staff, communications and marketing, estates and academic staff as well as administrative staff and the event management company, plans were developed and preparations commenced. Faculty coordinators liaised with students regarding their expectation and input, an important element of the project.

Analysis and feedback

Throughout the planning and execution of the event, regular meetings were held to evaluate progress and make adjustments where necessary until objectives were achieved. After the event, a post-project review was undertaken. This involved collecting feedback from staff and inviting students to complete an online survey regarding the event. Feedback was analysed and incorporated into the review. Action points were written and formed the starting point for the planning of subsequent graduations.

The cost and timeline

Planning of the event in 2004 commenced in March and the dates for graduation were mid-July. The marquee had to be constructed and in place one week before the first event took place to enable any problems to be dealt with in plenty of time, to enable health and safety checks to be completed and rehearsals to take place.

The cost of graduation to students was kept to £15 per guest and free for students, despite the increased cost of building the marquee. Although the cost of the event was not recovered through the ticket price, this was a great opportunity to market our university to a massive audience. A survey done to measure expectation showed that most students' and guests' expectations were exceeded in 2004 and each subsequent year as the event has developed.

How it was monitored

Regular meetings with the registrar and secretary were held to monitor and review the project as well as meetings with the events management company, faculty event coordinators and other university staff. Throughout the days of graduation, a number of meetings were held prior to the start of each ceremony to ensure collaborative working and to monitor the event as it happened and make appropriate adjustments accordingly.

The outcome

Between 2004–9, summer graduations were held on the Acre at Headingley in a purpose-built marquee. Year-on-year, more students attended graduation and brought an increasing number of family and friends to share in the celebrations. In excess of 100,000 students and visitors have attended graduation at Headingley over the six years. The need to provide a good student experience became the focus of all graduations. It soon became apparent that this also had a positive affect on staff as departments worked together collaboratively to achieve the university vision. The strategy of our university turned the ceremony into a festival to be enjoyed and embraced by every stakeholder involved from students, staff, to our university partners and to those living and working in the local community. Improvements to the event included:

- a hard-sided marquee;
- online graduation registration;
- merchandising stands;
- a paid-for champagne bar;
- a variety of food outlets;
- outside entertainment.

As a result of the project, the staff development and freshers' festival have taken place on campus in the new venue.

The project also led to the development of the new site which was advertised to the city of Leeds and surrounding region as a major conference venue. Operational models developed specifically for the project have been used for other events at the university. For example, the traffic management plan was used during the 'Great Student Run' in 2006 and 2007.

Has or could the initiative be used for a different group?

The project has provided a model for overseas collaborative partner's graduation events.

Although the model described is unique to Leeds Metropolitan University, the strategy of holding graduations or indeed any project to suit individual institutes can and has been used to improve the student experience and market the university to a wide range of stakeholders.

Advice and guidance

- Plan early.
- Get all staff on board.
- Communicate expectations to students, colleagues and all other stakeholders.
- Practise continuous monitoring, evaluation and feedback.
- Share best practice with colleagues, other organisations and institutes.
- Keep updated of changes in the external environment you are working in.
- Pay attention to detail.
- Expect the unexpected (proactive working).
- Leave nothing to chance.

Contact details

p.fearnley@leeds.ac.uk

Conclusion

This chapter discusses some basic ideas behind the final-year experience, research that has been done on this topic and four case studies that offer ideas for supporting students through the outduction or postgraduate transition.

The four case studies discussed in this chapter demonstrate that:

- It is good to start early. We do not have to wait until our students are in their final year before we start facilitating career development.
- Students not only need support within this transition, but they are calling out for it. By utilising a questionnaire, programmes, events and ideas, we can help bridge the transition gap for students leaving university.
- A small, fairly easy initiative can go a long way. By simply providing a handbook for final-year students, a giant step in supporting and aiding them through the outduction process was taken.
- A positive graduation ceremony can leave a lasting impression. Shifting the focus of graduation to providing a good student experience can help foster closure and integration for students.

To continue the better understanding of our students in this transition and our support of them, we must research this area whether formally or informally and share that research with stakeholders across the sector.

References

Gedye, S., Fender, E. and Chalkley, B. (2004) 'Students' undergraduate expectations and post-graduation experiences of the value of a degree', *Journal of Geography in Higher Education*, 28(3): 381–96.

Morgan, M. (2008) 'The importance of "OUTduction" in the student lifecycle', paper presented at the Annual Conference and Exhibition of the Association of University Administrators (AUA), 31 March–2 April, York: University of York.

Perry, A.L. (2010) 'Real graduates, real transitions, real stories: a real insight to life after university', unpublished manuscript, Christchurch: University of Canterbury.

Schlossberg, N.K., Waters, E.B. and Goodman, J. (1995) *Counseling Adults in Transition: Linking Practice with Theory*, 2nd edN, New York: Springer.

UNITE (2007) *UNITE Student Living Survey*, Bristol: UNITE.

Wood, F. (2004) 'Preventing post-parchment depression: a model of career counselling for seniors', *Journal of Employment Counselling*, 41(2): 71–9.

Part 3

Core activities in the Student Experience Practitioner Model

Chapter 9

Academic student support and development

Marcia Ody, University of Manchester, UK

Introduction

The student learning experience in modern higher education settings has changed significantly and continues to alter at an ever-increasing pace, as described elsewhere in this book. The increasingly diverse student community and their high level of expectations mean that we can no longer adopt a linear approach to education. As McCaffery argues:

> The increasing heterogeneity of the student body (in terms of entry level qualifications, prior learning and prior working experience, age and ethnic mix, etc.) along with the heightened expectations of students as fee-payers, has generated and will continue to do so, a concomitant demand for customised and personalised service, not one that is or has been based on, a standardised 'one size fits all' approach.
>
> (McCaffery, 2010:275)

The need for us to ensure effective structures of academic support and development with personalised delivery has never been greater. This chapter will look at this challenge and discuss how practitioners can provide students with the foundation blocks, an intellectual map and the tools and techniques to understand and use the different approaches to study and higher level learning.

A holistic approach to academic development

Academic support and development is commonly thought of as an additional, specialised, often centralised (sometimes peripheral) learning support service provision provided to students either with specific needs or who are proactive in accessing provision. For the purpose of this chapter we are referring to the integrated support offered to all students with an emphasis on a 'holistic' as opposed to a 'silo' approach. The holistic approach supports the 'whole picture' in which partnerships are developed, recognising the interdependence of services, academic units and individuals.

Academic support and development should be seen as an on-going activity available and accessible by all students which is not time bound but instead relates to all stages of the student lifecycle, from entry to exit. Staff (academic and professional support) and students all need to play an essential role at every stage of the Practitioner Model with the greatest emphasis being during induction, reinduction and the subsequent transitional periods throughout all levels of study.

As practitioners, we need to be proactive and strategic in developing and ensuring the delivery of support is student-centred and less provider-centred.

There are a number of elements/providers that make up a holistic academic support structure including:

- students, academic home unit (teaching staff, personal tutors/academic advisers, personal development planning, course units);
- peers (formally, informally, within year group, from higher levels);
- central services (academic advisory services, learner support, academic skills, library, careers, Students' Union);
- specialised/targeted services (international students, mature students, students with disabilities, mathematics provision, writing support);
- external support (families, friends).

As practitioners we need to be proactive in bringing together services. Cuseo (2002) identifies the importance of collaboration among organisation units and members of the college/ university community and argues that integration is essential to effectively address issues that affect students' academic success. He identifies four forms of collaboration as indispensable elements of comprehensive academic support. These are:

- collaboration between students (peer collaboration);
- collaboration between classroom instructors and academic support services;
- collaboration between the divisions of academic and student affairs;
- collaboration between higher education and further education (college and school).

(Cuseo, 2002:8)

There is a need to create stronger partnerships between central services and local support. Most institutions adopt a model that is primarily based on local, front-line provision of guidance by the academic home unit, extended and supported by the central, professional support services. In broad terms, the support and guidance provided locally is academic in nature with central support tending to be more generic and geared towards study skills and welfare. The two providers need to integrate to maximise the complementary provision benefits.

Academic advising

At the local home unit level, personal tutoring/academic advising typically provides the basis for the front-line academic support for students. The role of the academic adviser varies considerably between and within institutions: as a minimum the role should explicitly act as a gateway to wider academic support provision within the institution.

Academic advising provides a framework for support and development as students encounter the various transition points inherent in their programme of study including:

- induction to programme/level of study;
- expectations setting;
- skills audits;

- understanding how to handle problems;
- making the transition to independent learning;
- understanding assessment criteria;
- receiving results/feedback;
- course/module choices;
- avoiding academic malpractice;
- preparing for placement/study abroad;
- undertaking research.

Good practice should entail a student being allocated an academic adviser at the start of their period of study and, where possible, he/she should remain with the same adviser throughout in order to develop a meaningful relationship. Students should have regularly scheduled meetings with their adviser and reasonable provision should be made to enable students to make contact as they require.

The most frequent criticism of academic advising arrangements relates to variability in their operation. Inconsistent provision should be avoided and an equitable experience for all students delivered.

The role of the academic adviser should include:

- actively reviewing and monitoring academic performance;
- helping students to identify the skills being acquired;
- assisting students with reflecting on their learning and in developing educational plans/targets;
- assisting students in understanding academic policies/procedures;
- helping students to access campus resources;
- assisting students to overcome educational/personal problems;
- enabling students to engage with and develop an understanding of the factors which contribute to academic success.

Student engagement

Academic advising needs to be a process in which students actively participate: successful support and development is reliant on this. The 2009 United Kingdom National Student Forum report (produced by a diverse range of undergraduate and postgraduate students) acknowledged that to be successful, students need to:

- be an active partner in learning;
- strive for excellence in all academic achievements;
- view learning whilst in higher education as broader than just academic achievements;
- take seriously the feedback provided.

(National Student Forum Annual Report, 2009)

The concept of student engagement and students as 'co-producers' or partners with their institution in their learning experience, is now widespread. There is insurmountable national and international evidence demonstrating that students are engaging in enhancing the student experience and assisting with the support of other students in the provision of both pastoral and academic support and development.

Students can, and do take, an active and powerful role in improving the educational experience of others through structured approaches, including: Students' Union involvement; student partnership and consultation; student representation; residential academic support; peer support; and peer education. The use of peer education in various forms has a long and rich history in providing academic support and development. Ender and Newton argue that peer educators are 'students who have been selected, trained, and designated by a campus authority to offer educational services to their peers. These services are intentionally designed to assist peers toward attainment of educational goals' (2010:6).

There are many reasons why peers produce positive results in assisting student success. Higher level students are able to share their experiences; identify with and understand the transitional stages and academic journey of other students; assist with addressing academic adjustment challenges; support the development of study and learning strategies and act as a broker and signpost to other academic services as well as providing feedback and informing institutional strategy and policy.

The four case studies in this chapter are initiatives involving high levels of student engagement and peer interaction.

Case Study 25 by Andrew Casey explores student course representation structures at Kingston University, UK, and highlights the need to address the local academic home unit structures in tailoring student and staff engagement in order to maximise the benefit of the engagement of course representatives.

Case Study 26 from Marcia Ody and William Carey explores the benefits of peer-assisted study sessions in supplementing academic support, providing an opportunity for students to deepen their understanding of fundamental academic principles and developing intellectual and professional competencies within an informal environment.

Case Study 27 by Louise Livesey provides a unique example of highly structured one-to-one mentoring based primarily on academic tutor referrals at Stockport College, UK.

Case Study 28 from Ian Munton outlines the experiences and support needs of students during and returning from a leave of absence at Keele University, UK. It serves as an excellent example of the use of peers to complement the work of academic colleagues.

Case Study 25

Name and university
Andrew Casey, Academic Quality and Student Support Officer, London South Bank University, UK.

Title of project/initiative
A student voice in learning and teaching at Kingston University: the importance of an effective course representation scheme.

Who was involved in the initiative
Students' Union Student Support Coordinator (SSC), Peer Assisted Learning Scheme Coordinator, Director of the Academic Development Centre (ADC), Faculty Student Support Officers, Faculty Senior Management, academic staff across faculties, current and former Student Course Representatives (SCRs).

Reason for the project/initiative
A course representative is a student who represents their cohort on the same course and level of study at faculty/school meetings in order to provide input with the aim of improving their academic and social experience whilst at university. They should exist in all faculties and across all courses at the university. Student numbers and courses have steadily increased at Kingston University over the years.

However, research had shown that, whilst there had been a growth in SCRs at Kingston, there were still inconsistencies in terms of representation across all courses and all levels.

Also, the Students' Union (SU) is the key body for independent support and advice for students in the UK, was not engaging with SCRs at faculty level. This resulted in SCRs not having the same access (via committees and other feedback mechanisms) in voicing their concerns and opinions at a faculty or university level about their academic and social experiences.

Why it was developed
The aim was to develop a rigorous and effective scheme which engaged SCRs with key stakeholders, accommodated each faculty's uniqueness and empowered and equipped SCRs with a range of transferable skills. The project had a number of aims and objectives.
The aims were to:

*   understand the nature of and procedures relating to SCR activity across the faculties;
*   understand the level of student engagement in the scheme;
*   evaluate the resources offered by the Students' Union and the long-term support provided.

The objectives were to:

*   develop a scheme involving all key stakeholders that supported SCRs and helped them engage at faculty and university level with an effective voice;
*   accommodate the diversity of the faculty structures;
*   provide the SCRs with the opportunity to be involved in the evaluation of their own scheme;
*   consider the possibility of accrediting the scheme.

The project was partly driven by the forthcoming institutional audit, along with an overall aim from both the SU and the university to be able to demonstrate student engagement especially within existing learning and teaching quality mechanisms.

The target group
SCRs across all faculties.

How it was developed, what it included and how it was implemented

How it was developed
The SSSC met with key staff in the ADC to outline broad strategic aims for the scheme and the current situation. Together, we conducted the research into how the scheme was operating. The working relationship helped give the project credence within the faculties which was important as some had experienced little interaction with the SU.

Those involved or who should be involved in the scheme at both university and faculty level were identified and interviewed, allowing us to gain a full understanding of the operation of the scheme across the university. They included faculty staff with responsibilities towards SCRs (academic and support staff) and SCRs themselves. They were asked a range of questions looking at:

- how the scheme was marketed;
- the training provided;
- how engaged the course representatives were with the scheme;
- the formative and on-going support they received;
- whether personal development planning could be more closely integrated within the scheme.

What it included
After consultation, a broad scheme was developed and included:

- Information and advice for the faculties on how to effectively recruit SCRs. Information was sent out to students both by the SU and the faculties.
- The training of SCRs and information and advice for staff. The training was streamlined, focused and emphasised skills rather than procedural knowledge, with the session reduced from two hours to 90 minutes. A second session was developed for representatives who had been in the role for a year or more; this was more reflective, could be run in the first or second semester, encouraged representatives to identify gaps in the scheme and in their own skills base and informed the union and university on areas to address. All key stakeholders received information and advice on the scheme with key dates.
- A personal development requirement that was trialled in two faculties, with representatives having to submit a 500-word reflective statement at the end of the year.
- Faculties having responsibility for ensuring SCR attendance at relevant meetings and for reporting forward issues and feeding back responses from the relevant committees. This would ensure that students had a voice in the policy and strategic discussions at senior university meetings and that the university would be able to demonstrate (to external bodies such as the Quality Assurance Agency and to the students themselves) student involvement in these mechanisms.

How it was implemented
The broad aims of the scheme were agreed by the senior management of each faculty who then agreed a faculty contact who would look after the scheme within the faculty.

Analysis and feedback

Analysis was undertaken by both the SU and the ADC. Changes were then fed through the key contact staff in the faculties and then disseminated among SCRs. Establishing a more formalised dialogue and having specific points of contact within the faculties allowed central departments to have a more formalised approach to supporting the scheme. The scheme was refined and further development was undertaken in the training and building of individual portfolios for SCRs.

The cost and timeline

The initial cost was purely in terms of time. The research was undertaken jointly by the ADC and the SU and carried out over two summers.

How it is/was monitored

Elected union staff were required to attend the relevant faculty meetings where SCRs would build a picture of representative involvement. Training was monitored using modified evaluation forms.

The outcome

The SU and the ADC have jointly agreed to share ownership of the development of the scheme and continually monitor it. The SU has replaced the SSSC role with two new membership service staff allowing for strategic focus on representation within learning and teaching.

Has or could the initiative be used for a different group?

Aspects of the initiative, such as the formative training could be used for other student groups, such as student ambassadors or mentors.

Advice and guidance

- Identify all stakeholders.
- Encourage buy-in at every level across the institution and university body (students and staff).
- Develop a clear understanding of the current situation and avoid 'top-down' strategic goals before understanding the current processes and practices.
- Support front-line staff.
- Aim to empower SCRs.

Contact details

caseya2@lsbu.ac.uk

Case Study 26

Name and university
Marcia Ody, Teaching and Learning Manager, and William Carey, Teaching and Learning Adviser. Students as Partners, Teaching and Learning Support Office, University of Manchester, UK.

Title of project/initiative
PASS: supporting transitions, supplementing core curriculum, stimulating learning.

Who was involved in the initiative
A range of academic and professional support services colleagues and students including Teaching and Learning Manager, Teaching and Learning Advisor, Sabbatical Interns, Student Coordinators, PASS Leaders and students (Figure 9.1).

Reason for the project/initiative
The transition into and within HE is challenging and complex for the student body and there is the growing argument that students are less equipped with the learning strategies required to be higher level learners.

Evidence suggests that students desire opportunities to engage as co-producers in their learning, as co-developers with the institution and as leaders in co-curricular and extra-curricular activity.

Peer Assisted Study Sessions (PASS) create partnerships across the institution. The programme is centrally coordinated and each scheme is discipline-owned and student-led.

PASS is the UK adaptation of the well-established and internationally successful Supplemental Instruction (SI) model which has goals including:

- improving student performance;
- increasing continued enrolment/retention;
- improving student performance.

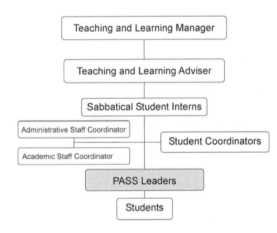

Figure 9.1 PASS structure

These goals should be achieved without:

- lowering academic standards;
- inflating grades;
- spending lots of money.

The expansion of PASS supports the University of Manchester's strategic priority to enhance and personalise the student experience by supporting transitions, supplementing the core curriculum and stimulating learning.

Why it was developed

PASS was developed to provide an additional opportunity for students to:

- discuss learning strategies in small groups;
- promote the concept of community within disciplines and programmes;
- develop links with peers;
- provide an opportunity to deepen the understanding of fundamental academic principles and develop intellectual and professional competencies within an informal, social environment.

The target group

Students who are studying the programme or unit to which PASS is attached (generally Level 1 and 2 students).

How it was developed, what it included and how it was implemented

How it was developed

The international SI model was developed at the University of Missouri, Kansas City, in the early 1970s (Hurley et al., 2006) and adapted in the 1990s for use in British HE.

Initial implementation at the University of Manchester was through enthusiastic staff and the delivery of training by an externally trained SI supervisor. The subsequent development of the programme led to internal central staff being trained as SI supervisors by the International Centre (www.umkc.edu/cad/si).

What it included

- Volunteer higher year (Level 2 and above) students trained as PASS leaders to facilitate small groups of lower year students to explore 'already delivered' academic material.
- Academic integration was encouraged through pastoral support, orientation assistance and socialisation.
- PASS groups (two leaders assigned approximately 15 students) met during welcome week as part of induction. Activities included: campus tours, team building, city treasure hunts and/or a student-led social activities.
- One hour weekly timetabled sessions usually taking place in flat teaching rooms.
- Sessions are student-led with leaders encouraged to be creative and arrange 'additional' sessions where needed.

PASS is voluntary but it is timetabled thus making it available to all, so those choosing not to attend are electing to 'opt-out'.

PASS integrates study skills and learning strategies with PASS leaders trained to embed skills into sessions within the context of their discipline.

How it was implemented

It was essential to get both student/staff to buy-in and ensure the scheme was shaped by the discipline. The stages included:

- consultation with staff/students;
- staff awareness and training;
- agreement of roles and functions and identification of academic and administrative leads;
- scheme administration, including timetabling and room bookings;
- recruitment and training of leaders;
- provision of on-going leader training and support;
- observation and debriefs;
- recognition and reward for leaders;
- reviewing, monitoring and evaluating.

Analysis and feedback

Qualitative and quantitative analysis was undertaken and included:

- attendance at sessions correlated against academic performance;
- questionnaires distributed to attendees/non-attendees and leaders;
- use of Participation Response System (PRS) in target group lectures;
- leader feedback through debriefs (scheme development and leader benefits);
- focus groups.

The cost and timeline

Costs vary according to scheme size but include:

- centralised costs:
  - training costs (refreshments, lunches, etc.);
  - leader resource folder and stationery;
  - recognition of leaders.
- localised costs:
  - session resources (paper, pens, text books, biscuits);
  - leader reward (lunch/evening meal);
  - student coordinator honorariums.
- staffing costs:
  - academic/administrator time;
  - students as partner faculty sabbatical interns;
  - central support (SI supervisor trainers, quality assurance, consultation).

In the initial implementation, the consultation period is recommended to be one semester to a full year. The annual activity for a scheme is:

- April/May: recruitment of leaders for the following academic year;
- September: training;
- welcome week: initial leader meeting with students (particularly for Level 1 schemes);
- start of teaching period: study sessions commence.

On-going activity:

- PASS leader support (regular debriefs, observations and on-going training);
- regular staff and student coordinator network meetings;
- end of academic year: annual leader awards evening.

How it is/was monitored

PASS is a quality-assured model and monitoring is undertaken at varying levels:

- central/faculty;
- comprehensive facilitator training (delivered by SI supervisors);
- annual monitoring (Faculty Teaching and Learning Committee and Institutional Teaching and Learning Group);
- local;
- regular observations of leaders;
- sabbaticals interns meet and support coordinators to disseminate good practice;
- session attendance collected.

The outcome

Many benefits of PASS have been recognised by different stakeholders and the original aims and purpose for development have expanded in recognition of the wider benefits.

Evaluation has shown that there is a strong correlation between students regularly attending PASS and an increase in academic performance (approximately 10 per cent), a lowering of the failure rate and an increase in high achievement (three-fold increase of more than 70 per cent) (Fostier and Carey, 2008).

Leaders develop graduate skills and have the opportunity to engage in a PricewaterhouseCoopers skills development course to enhance their employability skills.

PASS is a strategic priority for the University of Manchester as one vehicle to enhance and personalise the student learning experience.

The University of Manchester has long been recognised as the National Benchmark for PASS given its structured and coordinated approach to the adaptation of the SI model. Consequently in April 2009, it became the UK National Centre with responsibility for training PASS/SI supervisors, facilitating a network of practitioners and assisting in collating national research (see http://www.pass.manchester.ac.uk).

Has or could the initiative be used for a different group?

Schemes already exist in all faculties but plans are in place to explore further expansion across discipline areas and into higher years including postgraduate study.

Work is being undertaken to look at implementing the international SI model in activities including:

- industrial placement/year abroad/distance learning;
- health sciences and work-based learning to develop professional clinical skills.

Advice and guidance

PASS/SI is built around core principles that allow flexibility to ensure a 'good fit' for your students. Ensure that you:

- involve or train SI supervisors;
- allow enough time and resources for implementation;
- undertake staff and student consultations;
- know why you are doing it;
- determine evaluation criteria;
- establish internal quality and monitoring processes.

PASS has had a dramatic impact on student engagement at the University of Manchester. We have seen a real change of culture since PASS was introduced. Students become very engaged (e.g. producing pre-arrival material) and enthusiastic about pedagogy. They are committed and many develop a desire to work in partnership to enhance the wider student experience.

References

Fostier, M. and Carey, W. (2007) 'Exploration, experience and evaluation. Peer Assisted Study Scheme (PASS), sharing the experience of The University of Manchester: 480 1st year bioscience students'. Paper presented at the Science, Learning and Teaching Conference, Staffordshire: Keele University.

Hurley, M., Jacobs, G., Gilbert, M. and Stone, M. (eds) (2006) 'The basic SI model', *Supplemental Instruction: New Visions for Empowering Student Learning: New Directions for Teaching and Learning*, 106(2), 11–22.

Contact details

marcia.ody@manchester.ac.uk
william.carey@manchester.ac.uk

Case Study 27

Name and university
Louise Livesey, Widening Participation Officer, Stockport College, UK.

Title of project/initiative
Academic and welfare support delivered through the individual mentoring of students on Higher National Certificate (HNC) or Higher National Diploma (HND) engineering courses by an non-academic mentors.

Who was involved in the initiative
Widening Participation (WP) Officer, Careers Service and Younger Learner Mentor Managers, Curriculum Area Managers for Higher Education (HE), Adult Education and Construction and Engineering, Advanced Learner Manager (ALM) Engineering and HE engineering tutors.

Reason for the project/initiative
In August 2008, we identified HE engineering as having a retention rate of below 70 per cent, a status triggering intervention measures.

Why it was developed
To improve the retention rates of HE engineering courses.

The target group
The group consisted mostly of part-time day release students.

How it was developed, what it included and how it was implemented

How it was developed
We piloted a mentoring programme for the academic year 2008–9 with the WP officer acting as mentor. Meetings were held with the ALM and HE engineering tutors to discuss implementation. Support service managers were consulted on production of paperwork and logistics.

What it included
The overarching aim was to improve retention rates. However, the mentoring sessions in themselves would not achieve this; the mentees needed to engage in the whole process by accessing all additional curriculum and specialist support services available, and adopting time management techniques agreed with the mentor.

There needed to be student awareness of the programme; via oral, paper and electronic information and an understanding of the referral system; students could self-refer by email, telephone or visiting the information and advice centre where I am based. Tutors referred students by emailing a completed referral form.

The referral session content included an initial session where the mentee and I discussed:

- reasons for referral;
- the nature of mentoring, including the voluntary involvement of staying on the programme and acting on any suggestions made by myself;
- structure of the sessions;

- motivational and practical support available during sessions, including time management;
- signposting students to other internal specialist services for additional study skills or personal support, or to tutors for extra academic assistance;
- confidentiality relating to session content, paperwork and computer logs, including circumstances under which I must disclose information standards of behaviour and attendance;
- possible areas of goal and deadline setting;
- average length and number of sessions;
- exit session and paperwork if the student wanted to participate in the programme.

A checklist on the above was completed and signed by both parties as well as a confidentiality contract, and a session record sheet including actions agreed by me and the mentee. The date and time of next session was agreed.

The subsequent structure of the sessions discussed:

- the efficacy of actions completed by mentor and mentees, and any other possible solutions to problems or concerns not addressed;
- any new worries or issues incurred since the last session and to seek solutions;
- motivatating the mentee to stay on course and succeed to the best of his/her ability;
- completion and signing by both parties of a session record sheet.

Between the sessions, contact was maintained between mentee and mentor via telephone and email. This was either to provide information requested by the mentee within a session or to confirm a time for the next session if this was not possible during the last one. Mentees contacted me with any additional queries or concerns they had or to re-appoint a session. The frequency of this contact varied depending on the mentee's given situation and the actions I was to fulfil.

In the exit session, all aspects of the mentoring process and programme were discussed. A paper exit form was completed by each mentee. The form asks for information relating to time and date of first contact and first session, and the total number of hours spent with the mentor; issues covered over the whole of the length of the programme; if these issues have been dealt with and what methods were employed in doing so; and if mentoring has been helpful.

How it was implemented

Within one month of starting their course, students attended short introductory talks within their teaching areas, which I delivered. My contact details were distributed for self-referral or queries. If a student was referred by a tutor, initial mentoring sessions were mandatory. Information was also available to students via the college's virtual learning environment, Moodle. Mentoring sessions started in October 2008.

Analysis and feedback

- All tutor-referred students attended the initial sessions and none complained of their mandatory nature.
- The first students to be referred were not made aware of the reason for tutor referral prior to attending the initial session. This was rectified to ensure all students knew why the tutors referred them.
- Holding sessions in the course area caused no reported stigma problems.
- Timetabling constraints, session length and number may not have been deemed sufficient contact time within the mentoring arena. However, no students complained that a lack of attention caused them any problems.

- Few students were tutor-referred later in the academic year. This was highlighted to tutors who subsequently referred students throughout the following academic year.
- It was difficult for mentees to provide anonymous evaluation of their experience due to the low number of mentees, having a single mentor and forms being submitted by hand to me. For the same reasons, impartiality was a concern. For subsequent years, an online form was placed on Moodle ensuring anonymity.
- The top three disclosures related to difficulties with time management, lack of study and mathematical skills and difficulties with the course subject. These were dealt with by creating study timetables, referring students to our specialist study and mathematical skills tutors based in our StAR Centre (now called Study +) and to tutors for one-to-one help or attending an extra evening tutorial available to all students.
- Seven out of 13 mentees completed the evaluation form due to either disinclination or unavailability due to completing course work off-campus. There is an intent to improve the numbers of mentees completing questionnaires by contacting students via telephone and email with reminders.

The cost and timeline
The programme attracted no additional funding except minimal expenditure for photocopying. Mentoring started within two months of HE engineering being chosen as the pilot course area.

How it is/was monitored
Students completed an evaluation questionnaire. Tutors completed feedback forms to comment on any perceived changes in attitude or work content.

The outcome
- Primary: retention improved and was reported at senior management level in October 2009.
- Unforeseen: I was invited to attend HNC/D internal board meetings which determine if students are given extensions to assignment deadlines, repeat years, etc.
- Closer working relationship between support services and curriculum area.

Has or could the initiative be used for a different group?
The initiative can be applied to any given course area or specific issue, and also can be adapted for e-mentoring.

Advice and guidance
- Ensure all colleagues are engaged.
- Could be costly when expanded as mentors are employed.
- Start as a small pilot programme to ensure processes and procedures in place before expansion.
- Provide senior leadership team with regular updates.

Contact details
louise.livesey@stockport.ac.uk

Case Study 28

Name and university

Ian Munton, Head of Student Support Services, Keele University, UK.

Title of project/initiative

Supporting students returning from a leave of absence at the University of Sheffield.

Who was involved in the initiative

Student Development and Support Manager and team colleagues, colleagues from teams across student services, Students' Union representatives and student peer helpers.

Reason for the project/initiative

The university has robust administrative procedures in place to support students wishing to take a leave of absence (LOA). However, the overall experience of taking a leave of absence was relatively unknown. We wanted to gain more of an understanding of what our students were experiencing in this period in their student journey and, in particular, we wanted to refine the support and advice offered to students as they returned from their period of leave.

Why it was developed

Information about the experience of students on a LOA and their subsequent success when returning to the university was limited. Whilst many students met with their personal tutors to discuss their intention to take a LOA, the majority of reasons cited for this choice were only captured with a tick in a box on a change of status form. The understanding of the personal experience was therefore limited and as such so was the approach to supporting our students through these experiences.

The challenge for us was to develop an intervention that would support students returning to multiple departments across an expansive campus with a sensitive and consistent level of service that recognised the transitions that they had negotiated and moved through.

The target group

The project aimed to address the multiple issues, experiences and needs of all of our students both whilst on a LOA and throughout their transition back into study at the university. These students had taken this often difficult decision for a variety of reasons, such as a change in family circumstances, financial difficulties or health concerns.

How it was developed, what it included and how it was implemented

How it was developed

A project proposal was presented at the university's student support forum for discussion and approval.

The aims and objectives of the project were to:

- provide an opportunity to discuss issues of concern by staff and students;
- give tailored information dependent on a student's circumstances;
- increase the use of related support services;
- engender students with the sense that the university is interested in their return to study;

- ease transition back to university (and also transition of withdrawal from university);
- identify early those students wishing to withdraw from university.

What it included

From this, several meetings were arranged with service providers across the university to work out how to balance the various support messages we were wishing to address through this intervention.

Peer supporters, who were trained students (paid), made contact via telephone and email with students on a LOA at two specific points; two months prior to their return to study which is at a point when students are preparing for the transition, and one month after they have returned to the university. For continuity and to provide some personal familiarity, the contact was made on both occasions by the same peer supporter.

In preparation for return

A leaflet was sent to students on a LOA with information and advice about what they needed to do while preparing to return to the university. This was sent in conjunction with general welcome material. The letter sent to accompany this information specifically addressed the student's experience of taking a LOA.

In conjunction with this mailing, students were telephoned by a peer supporter. If the supporter could not make contact by telephone, they sent an email to the student with support information and contact details for them to reply to.

Upon return to university

Within a month of returning to study, the student was contacted again by the same peer supporter to see how they had settled back into university life and to see if their expectations had been met.

How it was implemented

A member of staff within the student development and support team coordinated the project in collaboration with various support partners across the professional services. Faculties were provided with a list of students and asked for information and permission to contact them.

Analysis and feedback

The project has provided us with a better understanding of the challenges faced by students on a LOA. Peer supporters recorded the issues and concerns of LOA students. These were reported to the student development and support team. In several cases students had indicated that they were expecting more information and at an earlier stage from the university and their academic department. Financial concerns were also apparent with some students explaining that they purposefully needed to take a break from being a student but that they were not prepared for the pressure to support themselves financially whilst on a leave of absence; this was particularly noticeable with students who were not able to return to their family home.

The project has led us to consider the experience of students on a LOA in more detail. We are looking at other opportunities to further enhance the experience of these students and to develop the support provided to them. A range of material was developed for dissemination to returning LOA students.

The cost and timeline

This very practical intervention was both cost-effective and straightforward to implement. The project took three months to develop and implement.

How it is/was monitored

Monitoring is on-going through reports and regular meetings with the student helpers and key stakeholders.

The outcome

Feedback about the service from many of those students returning from a LOA has been very positive. For many students an email in their inbox to acknowledge their return to study was unexpected and very satisfying:

> Thank you for your concern, I continue to be impressed by the devotion to students' welfare shown by all members of the university staff. I am doing well and am finding the return to student life to be a pleasing return to normality. Whilst I do not fore-see any problems, it is excellent to know that these services are on hand (Level 1 Student).

The project has been refined through student feedback and from the hard and involved work of our peer supporters who have driven forward the project out of recognition that students on a leave of absence do require additional and a more personalised form of support.

The project which is intended to compliment the work of our academic colleagues is recognised as a positive tool to support the transition of students returning to the university and those who make alternative choices, such as to extend their leave or to withdraw from the university.

Has or could the initiative be used for a different group?

The initiative has been successfully adapted to support students who have entered the university through clearing. We are looking at extending the support and advice to students before they go on a LOA, further into their LOA and for a longer period after they return.

Advice and guidance

- Develop a flexible approach to supporting students because no-one's experience of a LOA is the same.
- Involve colleagues from across the institution in the development of the project and the delivery of the training to peer helpers.
- Be realistic and stay positive as students will not always have updated their contact details, will not always have replied and might not always appear grateful.
- Distribute feedback and let your colleagues know what students are telling you – the good, the bad and the ugly!

Contact details

i.munton@acad.keele.ac.uk

Conclusion

There is no universal academic support and development model that suits the entirety of higher education. The case studies illustrate that institutions have established a plethora of forms of academic support to supplement the core activity delivered by academic advisers and centralised services.

Responsibility for academic support is typically dispersed across a number of services as well as the home unit and requires significant project management to overcome the 'silo' mentality and ensure a holistic approach.

Advice and guidance provided by the case study authors include:

- encourage buy-in at every level;
- ensure all colleagues are engaged;
- provide senior leadership;
- develop a flexible approach;
- provide training and support for staff and students.

To achieve excellence, joined-up practice is required in which strategies and providers are connected. Practitioners need to work innovatively across service boundaries to develop systematic and interlocking support arrangements which enable students to derive maximum benefit from a supportive and collegiate culture of academic support.

References

Cuseo, J. (2002) *Academic Support Strategies for Promoting Student Retention and Achievement During the First Year of College*. Online. Available at: http://www.ulster. ac.uk/star/resources/acdemic_support_strat_first_years.pdf (accessed 17 October 2010).

Ender, S. and Newton, F. (2010) *Students Helping Students: A Guide for Peer Educators on College Campuses*, San Francisco: Jossey-Bass.

McCaffery, P. (2010) *The Higher Education Manager's Handbook: Effective Leadership and Management in Universities and Colleges*, London: Routledge.

National Student Forum Annual Report (2009). Online. Available at: http://www.bis.gov. uk/assets/biscore/corporate/docs/n/10-p83-national-student-forum-annual-report-2010 (accessed 29 October 2010).

Chapter 10

Supporting staff to be supporters

Glyn Jones, Kingston University, UK

Introduction

As explained in the opening chapters, the dual impact of the 'massification' and the 'wide-ification' of higher education (HE) presents challenges for us as practitioners in helping students make both the transition to HE from school, college or return to study and then support students through the respective stages of the student lifecycle as described in the Practitioner Model. A number of factors, which are driven both by the reality of the student experience and the expectations of the students themselves, necessitate supporting staff to be supporters. This chapter will look at ways in which staff themselves can be supported in supporting the student experience through drawing on the experience of practitioners involved in this process. There is limited literature on supporting staff to support students except for those produced 'in-house' by staff engaged in such projects in their respective higher education institutions (HEIs). Accordingly, the case studies in this chapter provide examples of initiatives that can readily be applied to the reader's own institution.

The student lifecycle comprises distinct stages through which the student needs the appropriate support and assistance to facilitate their progression. It is important for staff to support students through each stage and for these staff to receive the support and training from the institution to assist them in this process. The focus of improving the student experience has very much been on the student, with staff support being neglected.

With students paying more money for their studies across the international HE sector and a corresponding growing 'consumer' culture in HE, students are expecting and demanding a quality service from HEIs in terms of facilities and support. For example, the immediacy of modern communication, such as texting and social networking sites, generates an expectation for students to receive instant responses to queries and to be signposted to the relevant support services by staff. Students will therefore assume that staff will possess the relevant knowledge and expertise to provide the relevant support for their student experience.

Furthermore, as explained in the Practitioner Model, students tend to identify more closely with their 'home unit'. As a result, staff in the home unit will often be the first port of call for students with an enquiry about their studies, facilities or support provision. Therefore, it is important that all staff in the home unit are informed about the range of home unit and university level services and facilities available to support students at the various stages of their student lifecycle. To facilitate this process, there needs to be a close collaborative partnership between the home unit and central departments who are normally responsible for student support provision.

A cultural change may be required for all staff within HE to view themselves as stakeholders in supporting and enhancing the student experience and this needs to be underpinned by appropriate staff development. From this perspective, the traditional dichotomy between academic and non-academic staff could be viewed as artificial due to all staff having a role as both practitioner and educator in the student lifecycle. For instance, due to the fact that social, personal and financial factors can impact on a student's ability to study, teaching staff providing academic advice and support should be aware of all other support provision for students. In this way, the academic role becomes akin to that of an academic and welfare tutor. Similarly, professional and support staff, traditionally categorised in the non-academic bracket, make an important contribution to a student's education through their respective interactions with the student body. For example, student funding advisors can teach students about money management whilst staff responsible for disciplinary procedures can encourage the student to reflect and learn from their behaviour as part of the process of becoming responsible citizens.

As the Practitioner Model shows, all staff have a key role in supporting students through the various stages of the student lifecycle. However, staff will need to be suitably trained and supported in order to make a valid contribution. Awareness of student support provision for staff tends to be covered generally in postgraduate teaching qualifications undertaken by academic staff without the rationale and importance of possessing this knowledge being fully articulated. Similarly, where courses are provided in HEIs, these will be normally be attended by staff who are already active practitioners which may be 'preaching to the converted'. Furthermore, HEIs often do not provide the opportunity for staff to reflect on how they can support the student experience. The case studies below provide templates of best practice to support staff in supporting students. The case studies are based on the respective authors' own experiences of training which has served to encourage and to empower staff in enhancing the student experience.

In Case Study 29, Andrew West outlines a project at the University of Sheffield, UK, where the student services department has provided information and training to staff across the university in supporting the student experience. The training programme and information are designed to make staff aware of the support provision available to students and the ways in which staff can engage with this process to support the student experience.

Case Study 30 from Maia Ibsen and Karen Clarke describe a scheme where students are trained to support their peers in developing academic skills at Kingston University, UK. Located in a home unit-based drop-in centre, these student staff members assist their fellow students in addressing any academic skills shortfall which facilitates the transition to HE and enables them to become more independent learners.

Case Study 31 by Lynn Burnett looks at an initiative to support and enhance the first-year experience at the University of Western Sydney, Australia. The focus of the project is to provide training and support for the university's first-year advisors (FYAs) who are a key point of interaction with the first-year students. Training includes keeping FYAs updated on good practice and research to both inform and to resource their role.

Case Study 32 from Clare Philp describes an initiative to support and to empower staff in faculties and departments in handling and addressing complaints and disciplinary issues at Kingston University, UK. The project acknowledges the student's close identification with the home unit through providing staff with the tools and training to take greater ownership of managing their students' expectations.

Case Study 29

Name and university
Andrew West, Director of Student Services, University of Sheffield, UK.

Title of project/initiative
Supporting the supporters.

Who was involved in the initiative
Director of Student Services, heads of teams in student services, personal tutors, academic department administrators, Students' Union representatives.

Reason for the project/initiative
The University of Sheffield is a large institution with around 24,000 students. We believe that effective student support underpins academic success, and that student support is appropriately a partnership activity involving staff across the university, in professional teams, in academic departments and in the Students' Union. 'Supporting the supporters' is an explicitly staff-facing programme, which is designed to complement the university's range of support offered direct to individual students and student groups. 'Supporting the supporters' provides training, support and development primarily to staff based in academic departments who have a student support or student administration role.

Why it was developed
'Supporting the supporters' has the aim of better connecting the services and support provided by central professional teams, with student support provision in academic departments. The intention is a sustainable student support network or matrix across the institution which makes a reality of partnership working, increases the confidence and expertise of all involved and brings service benefits in terms of improved support for students.

The target group
The initiative is aimed at staff based in departments across the university (outside the student services department) who have a student support or student administration role. Primarily the target group is staff based in academic departments – both academic staff and support teams. Other staff, including those based in the library, IT services and the student accommodation service, have also benefited from the programme.

How it was developed, what it included and how it was implemented

How it was developed
The overall 'supporting the supporters' concept has been developed incrementally over a period of years. During the 2007–8 academic session the approach was systematically reviewed, steered by a project group comprising representatives from student services, academic departments and the Students' Union, and drawing in views from around 500 staff across the university. Following on from this review, the programme was re-launched in 2008, at which point a part-time role was created within our student services 'one stop shop' to coordinate the programme.

What it included
'Supporting the supporters' is a broad ranging staff support programme. There are four key elements:

1   Staff-facing publications, in particular a 20-page 'supporting our students' booklet. This is principally aimed at staff in academic departments. It contains information for staff on the services available within the student services department, with a particular focus on helping staff to better support students. We also include an issues-based flow chart to help staff work through student concerns, such as health or personal problems. There is a specific page of information on helping students with mental health difficulties and brief guidance on matters, such as making effective referrals, confidentiality and dealing with parents. Accompanying the booklet is a summary poster (intended for staff notice boards) with key contact points.

2   A regular bulletin for staff covering student support issues. This is issued four to five times over the academic year with a range of articles covering matters, such as international student support, student well-being issues and student financial support. We also use the bulletin to issue service updates from the student services department and we include reminders about key administrative dates and deadlines. Articles are deliberately kept concise (c.100–200 words) and we try to ensure that items have particular relevance to readers in academic departments.

3   An annual programme of training and development sessions, workshops and events. These range from one hour 'bite-size' lunchtime sessions to half-day events which might be designed and tailored for a particular audience or department. There are around 40 events over the academic year. Topics include disability awareness; 'this student's worrying me' – a workshop for staff dealing with difficult student situations with an emphasis on sharing good practice, practical support and sign-posting; student finance update sessions; and a workshop on supporting Muslim students.

4   A staff-facing website which underpins the whole programme. This includes the facility to download the publications and bulletins mentioned above, and there is also an online booking screen for the various training sessions and workshops. The site includes a staff-facing A–Z reference page; a set of 'frequently asked questions' and a range of more detailed resources on matters, such as immigration issues, mental health and complaints and appeals. Some of this material is intended as a further reference point to augment the practical training and workshops referred to above.

How it was implemented

A member of staff based in our front-line student services information desk acts as the overall coordinator for the programme. This includes editing the various publications and maintaining the staff-facing website. She liaises with colleagues throughout the student services department which contributes to the programme in different ways, for example as workshop leaders.

Analysis and feedback

Feedback on the training and support sessions is obtained routinely as part of the process of organising and delivering the events. Participant views are used to inform improvements to the programme and as the basis for new sessions. Other elements of the programme are evaluated periodically, for example a reader survey to obtain feedback on the staff-facing bulletin.

The cost and timeline

The overall programme and publications are reviewed annually. Revised publications are produced in line with the start of the academic year. We have a small budget to support specific elements, for example printing costs for the booklet (around £2,000).

How it is/was monitored

We have established a 'supporting the supporters' management group to oversee the development and operation of the programme. This is a light-touch structure and the group meets twice annually to receive progress reports and to plan for future developments. After the re-launch of the programme in 2008, we witnessed a 250 per cent increase in participation by staff in academic departments within the refreshed training and support programme.

The outcome

'Supporting the supporters' is now an established part of our student services provision, with a reach across the university. Every year we are working with more staff groups and teams to develop and improve the programme.

Has or could the initiative be used for a different group?

We are currently using the model of 'supporting the supporters' as the basis of an equivalent programme under development to support staff across the university who have responsibilities relating to student recruitment and admissions. This new 'recruitment matters' programme will include similar elements of support (publications, websites, workshops and other networking events). We intend to cross-refer between the two programmes as a means of strengthening our network of partnerships across the institution.

Advice and guidance

* Build a genuine partnership by involving colleagues across the institution.
* Adopt a 'building block' approach and do not try to implement everything at the same time.
* Ensure that communications are balanced across a range of media, to ensure interest and engagement from as many staff groups as possible (e.g. hard copy publications, websites, events and workshops).
* Assign coordinating responsibility to an individual, but draw in other colleagues to ensure a comprehensive scope.
* Consult with and involve the Students' Union.
* Ensure you have an evaluation plan – and follow it through.

References

Our staff-facing website can be found at http://www.shef.ac.uk/ssd/welcome.html.

Contact details

a.west@sheffield.ac.uk

Case Study 30

Name and university
Maia Ibsen, Senior Lecturer, School of Civil Engineering and Construction, and Karen Clarke, Senior Lecturer, School of Surveying and Planning, Kingston University, UK.

Title of project/initiative
Construction Academic Skills Centre (CASC): a drop-in centre to support students with their academic skills, run by trained student advisors in the schools of Civil Engineering and Construction, and Surveying and Planning.

Who was involved in the initiative
Two members of staff and four trained student staff when the project was initiated in January 2007. Now it involves four academic staff and 14 trained student staff members.

Reason for the project/initiative
There were a range of reasons behind this initiative. We recognised the increasing diversity of entry level skills to the university due to the different educational backgrounds and ability levels of our students. In addition, we had experienced a rapid growth in our international student body. As a result we were concerned about the level of academic skills support our students were receiving. Due to the high student-to-staff ratio in our departments, this type of guidance was not being given sufficient attention. Poor progression rates and the potential to enhance achievement were an important part of the rationale for this project.

Why it was developed
The original aims of this project were to:

*   encourage and enhance confident interpersonal and communication skills among all construction-based students;
*   help bridge the gap from dependent to independent learning and enhance progression and achievement.

The target group
All students studying construction based subjects in the schools of Civil Engineering and Construction, and Surveying and Planning.

How it was developed, what it included and how it was implemented

How it was developed
Two staff members initiated the scheme by selecting four existing students (two from each department) who had achieved exceptional academic attainment along with the ability to communicate. These students were already involved in the peer assisted learning scheme within the university and, therefore, had a skills base prior to their involvement with CASC. The training was implemented through the association with the Academic Development Centre (ADC) and the manager of the Academic Skills Centres (ASCs) across the university. Student staff members now have to apply for positions at the beginning of an academic year and are chosen according to their academic abilities, track records within the faculties, as well as their personal aptitudes for dealing with others.

What it included

CASC opened in February 2007 and it was based in a room along a main corridor close to the library. It has since moved location, but is still in a highly visible position in a central point of the university within the same building as most of the lectures and near the laboratories. Since its inception, CASC has opened daily from 11am–3pm and offers one-to-one advice on assignments prior to their hand-in date. Sessions are normally staffed by two student staff members with a member of academic staff being on call. In conjunction with the drop-in sessions workshops are organised on specific subjects at relevant times of the year. For example, exam techniques are held near the end of both semesters. There is also a CASC email address that students can use to send queries or ask for advice on their work which is monitored by a senior student staff member.

How it was implemented

The management of CASC has adopted a number of approaches. Initially, members of university academic staff were in charge of all aspects of the day-to-day running and organi-sation of CASC. However, due to other commitments and schedule conflicts, we decided to hand over the majority of these responsibilities to two student staff members that had been involved in the project from the start. In doing so, we created the position of 'senior CASC student member'. This allowed them to run the programme under the guidance of the academic staff and included timetabling and organising cover of sessions at short notice if required.

The training that the student staff members are given involves:

* a brief outline of their responsibilities and what the CASC scheme is trying to provide for students;
* a clear outline of the dos and don'ts with the advice that should be given to students;
* guidance on understanding the social and psychological aspects when dealing with students seeking help.

These aspects of training are structured around various different role play situations which highlight particular aspects of the job. All CASC staff members whether academic or student staff members participate in the annual training. It not only acts as a refresher course but it provides a positive start to the academic year and a good basis for those who are new to the team.

Workshops are normally given by staff with the relevant expertise. However, senior CASC student staff are now being trained to take on some of the workshops by themselves, with the intention of also developing their range of skills.

Analysis and feedback

The reshuffling of responsibilities early on in this project and the development of the senior CASC position has proven to be very successful. These positions have allowed the academic and senior student staff members to more actively plan and organise workshop events and concentrate on the expansion of the centre. It has also helped provide and enhance student staff members personal development and key employability skills. When there is a significant attendance of students at CASC sessions, the flexibility of academic staff to provide assistance by always being on call has meant that there has been the capac-ity to accommodate increased numbers of students seeking support.

Over the duration of this project the facilities have changed. Our recent room provides excellent lighting and a good working ambience as well as sharing the facility with maths aid and other ASCs across the university. Due to the success of the ASCs, this room is being converted into a skills only location from 11am–3pm with the introduction of private booths.

The cost and timeline

Each year the staff involved in the project bid for funds from the ADC to cover the costs of employing students for the centre. Workshops are offered voluntarily by academic staff. Initially some funds were used for advertisements, such as posters and leaflets but email and the university's StudySpace on the internet have shown to be far more effective.

How it is/was monitored

Annual reports are written for the ADC along with ideas for improvement for the following year. The senior CASC members liaise on a weekly basis with the academic staff to ensure the smooth running of the centre.

The outcome

CASC has been running constantly and successfully since its inception as well as expanding continuously. The long-term intention is for it to become a sustainable resource within the university.

Has or could the initiative be used for a different group?

The initiative has already been extended to cover all the civil engineering students based at a different site within the university, EnASC (Engineering Academic Skills Centre).

Advice and guidance

*   Using trained students as staff helps to bridge the gap between those students asking for advice and the academic staff.
*   Need to have a very clear outline of what the service does and does not offer along with distinct guidelines for the advisors.

Contact details

m.ibsen@kingston.ac.uk
k.clarke@kingston.ac.uk
casc@kingston.ac.uk
enasc@kingston.ac.uk

Case Study 31

Name and the University

Lynn Burnett, Teaching Development Unit, University of Western Sydney, Australia.

Title of the initiative or project

Enhancing the first-year student experience by supporting staff through the first-year advisor (FYA) initiative at Griffith University.

Who was involved in the initiative

Academic members of staff who had taken on the role of FYA at programme/degree level, FYA Coordinator, Deans and Deputy-Deans (Learning and Teaching) (eight senior members of staff: level C, D or E), and Deputy Vice-Chancellor (Academic) [DVC(A)].

Reason for the initiative

The FYA initiative developed as part of a strategic whole-of-institution approach to enhancing the first-year student experience in the face of spiralling attrition rates, major changes to government funding and widening participation rates. The FYA coordinator role was developed alongside the FYA role as a means of supporting and growing FYAs beyond a pastoral-care function to a motivated network of staff engaged in reflective, evidence-based practice (Scholarship of Learning and Teaching (SOLT)) willing to take on active leadership roles within the university.

Griffith University is a multi-campus university in south-east Queensland, Australia. There are over 30,000 students enrolled across five campuses. Each campus is diverse in relation to its location, programme offering and student cohort. There is a high percentage of first-in-family, mature age, low-socio-economic and international students. Each of these cohorts brings unique perspectives and issues, hence the need for a first-year experience contact for students in the form of a FYA.

Why was it developed

As a result of the reasons described above, the university decided to take a pro-active stance to enhance the quality of the first-year student experience and improve learning and teaching within the institution through its support of staff with face-to-face responsibility and interaction with first-year students. There was an understanding that 80 FYAs could not keep abreast of innovative practice, nor could they sift through first-year experience research without assistance, support or coordination; hence the important role performed by the FYA coordinator.

The target group

Academic members of staff undertaking the FYA role.

How it was developed, what it included, how it was implemented

How it was developed

The FYA role and FYA coordinator are unique and the first of their kind. Initial work began with the Griffith Retention Project (Lizzio and Peters, 2004) and the instigation of multiple FYA roles in 2005/2006 (Lizzio, 2006a; 2006b). The case study author's previous role as FYA coordinator was a new on-going academic appointment based in the university's learning and teaching unit, prior it was a short-term two-year project position seconded to the Office of the DVC(A).

What it included

The FYAs work directly with first-year students and are responsible for leading a team of people (both academic and professional staff) at their local level to help students settle into their first year, become self-managed learners and take responsibility for their studies and careers. The FYAs do this by facilitating orientation and developing sustained engagement practices which are meaningful to their cohort and discipline area. FYAs also collect and evaluate data to inform their evidence-based practice.

The FYA coordinator role was focused on supporting and providing leadership for capacity building of the FYAs to enhance practice and wider understanding of the role. Each of the groups established the FYA role within different time frames and had a variety of different needs, issues, and student cohorts which shaped the role at the local level. At an institution-wide level, the coordinator position informed policy and institution-wide cultural change and worked towards increasing visibility, understanding and career advancement of the FYAs and improved student experience.

How it was implemented

The FYA coordinator was responsible for the development and implementation of a broad range of support mechanisms and practices, for example, a FYA induction folder which contained a wealth of practical resources for FYAs to dip in and out of. The folder also served as a hard-copy resource for local and long-term contingency planning and development. A series of visual FYA identity items (bookmarks, posters and water bottles) were designed and distributed to ensure a common language and understanding about the role.

Among other responsibilities, the coordinator designed and implemented local level FYA forums each semester and two annual whole-of-institution events. The first annual event was held in June and theme-based around leadership and capacity building. The second annual event was held in November as part of celebrating teaching week. It was designed as an innovative and interactive showcase to highlight and share good FYA practice, initiatives and strategies occurring across the institution. It also honoured excellence in learning and teaching, encouraged professional networking across groups and disciplines, and facilitate the sharing of original and innovative practice between presenters and participants.

The cost and timeline

The whole initiative was part of a long-term whole-of-institution cultural change process. It required serious additional central funds in its initial stages to support development and implementation and then on-going high-level strategic centralised support to maintain the momentum. The FYA coordinator position was funded at a lecturer B level and was provided with a small annual budget to facilitate local and whole-of-institution events and resource development.

How it is monitored, analysed and feedback

Evidence-based practice is highly valued within the institution, hence a number of monitoring and reporting mechanisms are embedded internally within the institution. For instance, all commencing students are invited to participate in an online Starting@Griffith survey during weeks 4–7 of first semester each year. This information provides timely and informative information about students' early experiences and connectedness with the university. It also provides information on the visibility, effectiveness and connectedness of FYA role and first-year students.

A variety of FYA feedback was systematically sought from the FYA coordinator at regular intervals to gauge on-going support requirements.

The outcome

As with any large-scale process, measurable outcomes are not always immediate. Continual improvements have been visible in the results of a series of large-scale monitoring tools over the past few years and student retention rates have improved or held in what has been an otherwise volatile economic climate. Overall global performance indicators are trending upwards and demonstrate increased persistence and satisfaction of commencing students at the university.

Has or could the initiative be used for a different group?

Small pilots have been initiated in some colleges of the University of Western Sydney over 2009/2010 under the auspices of a FYE programme convenor based in the Student Learning Unit (SLU).

Advice and guidance for others facing similar issues

There are many strategies which one can use to bring about positive, long-lasting support and capacity-building for staff engaged in enhancing the first-year student experience. These include:

- a coordinated activity and authentic communication to grow and inform top-down and bottom-up initiatives;
- an evidence-based approach is essential for monitoring, documenting, reflecting and evaluating activity and engaging in SOLT;
- recognition and visibility of people working at the local level;
- funding for supporting and growing local level activity;
- a visible champion in a position of power and authority.

References

Lizzio, A. (2006a) *Designing an Orientation and Transition Strategy for Commencing Students. A Conceptual Summary of Research and Practice. First-Year Experience Project.* Brisbane, Australia: Griffith University.

Lizzio, A. (2006b) *Enhancing the Early Learning Environment for Commencing Students at Griffith University. A Degree Programme Based Planning Process. First-Year Experience Project.* Brisbane, Australia: Griffith University.

Lizzio, A. and Peters, J. (2004) *The Retention Project.* Brisbane, Australia: Griffith University.

Contact details

l.burnett@uws.edu.au

Case Study 32

Name and university
Clare Philp, Student Affairs Advisor, Student Services and Administration, Kingston University, UK.

Title of project/initiative
Faculty complaint and disciplinary coordinators.

Who was involved in the initiative
Student Affairs, Faculty Complaint and Disciplinary Coordinators (FCDCs), University Secretary's Department.

Reason for the project/initiative
Student complaints and disciplinary issues were historically the responsibility of a central student services department. We were responsible for conducting investigations, interviewing students, issuing penalties and dismissing or resolving complaints. This created a cultural perception that these issues were neither the problem nor responsibility of the faculties. Faculties would be consulted during the respective processes but the outcome was the sole responsibility of a central department. Staff in faculties were not empowered to deal with situations and lacked the confidence to tackle issues as they arose. Increasing numbers of students were submitting formal complaints and being referred to the disciplinary process. Faculties had insufficient involvement in the process to incentivise them to rebuild relationships with the students.

Why it was developed
It became apparent that complaint and disciplinary issues were escalating through the respective procedures too quickly even though most complaints were often easily resolved and poor behaviour easily remedied. Removing ownership of these issues from faculties resulted in a detachment between the student and the faculty in terms of the outcome of the process.

   The introduction of FCDCs aimed to provide an effective process through which faculties could manage both the student experience they were providing as well as the way in which their students interacted with that experience. It empowered staff to deal with issues through being better informed about the latest developments and sharing best practice.

The target group
Faculty staff.

How it was developed, what it included and how it was implemented

How it was developed
Proposals for amendments to the student complaints and disciplinary procedures were included in the annual reports to senior management. The proposals set out the reasons why faculties needed to take ownership of these issues at the first stages and outlined the way in which this could be achieved.

What it included
It included:

- revisions to the student complaints and disciplinary procedures;
- redefining roles within the faculties to introduce greater responsibility;

- development of a first stage that was the responsibility of the faculty;
- guidance and training on how complaint and disciplinary investigations should be conducted;
- guidance on the range of outcomes available.

How it was implemented

It was implemented by:

- faculties nominating faculty-based complaint and disciplinary coordinators;
- FCDCs attending an initial meeting to discuss the respective procedures;
- the development of shared online resources to facilitate communication regarding procedures, training material, internal and external reports;
- the introduction of training throughout the first year to enable staff to feel confident in dealing with the issues.

The training programme was designed to cover the following:

- Best practice in conducting investigations providing parties with an opportunity to respond to issues.
- Not making judgements.
- Considering the information provided prior to and during the course and whether this is clear, accurate and reflects reality.
- Considering mitigating circumstances presented in respect of poor behaviour and the underlying problems that might be contributing.
- Looking at situations from the student's point of view.
- Outcomes and recommendations – considering the financial costs or impact on progression/completion that an error has had.
- Resolving the issue via ex-gratia offers and alternative resolutions. The legal implications of offers of resolution. Issuing penalties that are fair, proportionate and consistent.
- Consideration of case studies – identifying areas for improvement and patterns of problematic behaviour. Consideration of Office of the Independent Adjudicator (OIA) cases. The OIA is an external agency that makes judgements on non-academic complaints which cannot be resolved by the university.

Analysis and feedback

The central student services department maintain overall responsibility for the operation of the student complaints and disciplinary procedures. We also remain responsible for complaint investigations at the second stage and serious incidents of misconduct. Regular feedback between the FCDCs and the central department is facilitated at meetings throughout the year.

The cost and timeline

All FCDCs were nominated and appointed from existing staff. Staff have been required to attend training sessions and meetings.

FCDCs were implemented at the beginning of the academic year with a review of the process at the end of the first year.

How it is/was monitored

Annual reporting of the cases dealt with at the respective stages of the student complaints and disciplinary procedures and the outcomes. Monitoring is on-going and undertaken by the central department responsible for the procedures. This has allowed analysis of how successfully faculties are dealing with and resolving issues involving their students.

The outcome

Complaints and disciplinary issues involving students need to be dealt with quickly and effectively at the point at which the issue occurs. Those responsible for conducting the initial investigations into complaints or disciplinary issues are familiar with the service area or staff involved. FCDCs are able to conduct investigations within a shorter time frame, they have faculty documentation to hand and are often already familiar with how processes and procedures operate, meaning that they are not spending time getting to grips with what should have happened before comparing it to what actually happened. FCDCs are well placed to recommend outcomes and resolutions to complaints that are appropriate and deliverable as well as being in the ideal position to issue penalties that can be monitored and enforced over a period of time.

Resolving complaints at this level has the added benefit of restoring the student's faith in the faculty they are dealing with. Students are more confident that their concerns have been listened to. This has reduced the opportunities for deterioration in the everyday relationship between a student and the staff they deal with.

In respect of disciplinary issues, faculties are becoming increasingly aware that standards of behaviour are the responsibility of all staff, not just one central department. Responsibility for dealing with low-level misconduct highlights areas where additional support or training are required, resulting in staff feeling confident in tackling problem behaviour immediately and before it becomes established as the norm. Although still a formal stage of the disciplinary procedure, faculty staff are dealing with issues quickly and without the formality and bureaucracy of referring the matter to a central department. Students now have more respect for the process and outcome as the approach is proportionate to the misbehaviour. This has reduced the opportunity for on-going resentment between student and staff member.

Has or could the initiative be used for a different group?

Central student services and support departments will be provided with the same level of training and information.

We are also looking at implementing the principle of FCDCs in partner institutions to help staff deal effectively with complaints.

Advice and guidance

Devolving responsibility for dealing with complaints and disciplinary issues at the early stages does mean relinquishing some control over how these are investigated, the penalties applied and which complaints will be dismissed or upheld. Complaints and disciplinary issues must be dealt with consistently if appeals are to be avoided. It is important to:

- provide thorough guidance and training in respect of investigations and outcomes, particularly during the first year;
- ensure senior staff are on board with the implementation of these roles;
- ensure FCDCs are free to recommend the resolution or penalty that is most appropriate and that they are not constrained by faculty management views.

Contact details

c.philp@kingston.ac.uk

The above four case studies have common themes which link to the respective stages of and support the Practitioner Model. Integral to the initiatives described above is the importance of staff viewing themselves as key stakeholders in supporting and enhancing the student experience. At the core of all the case studies is a recognition that staff will need to be appropriately trained and supported to fulfil this role. Regular monitoring and evaluation of the case study projects to ensure information, training and support remains relevant, current and meets students' requirements is also essential. This is an area where central departments have an important role to play in informing colleagues of latest research developments and sharing best practice from across both the institution and the sector.

Conclusion

Key determinants to the successful application and implementation of the above initiatives to support all staff in enhancing the student experience can be summarised as follows:

- The provision of a coordinating role to champion the initiative and to provide relevant support and training to staff at all levels across the HEI. This role will normally be fulfilled by staff in central departments.
- Ensuring projects remain current and relevant to the requirements of staff and informed by both operational experience including student feedback and relevant research undertaken in the field. This is a role to be fulfilled by the project coordinator.
- Regular communication and training opportunities for staff throughout the academic year and not just confined to when new students arrive.
- The support and commitment of senior staff to such projects. Senior staff should support initiatives through allocating the necessary resources and time to encourage staff attendance. The presence of a Dean of Faculty or departmental head at a training event will also convey to staff the importance attached to an initiative.
- A variety of media to be employed for training and communicating to staff. The above initiatives drew on a combination of approaches ranging from training events, websites, email forums and periodic bulletins to convey messages to staff and to keep them informed. This takes into account the busy schedules of staff and the need for accessible materials to support them in their roles.
- Students being trained to support staff in supporting students to facilitate their peers' transition to HE. This recognises the value of peer support to enhance the student experience.

Hopefully, the current financial constraints affecting the HE sector worldwide will not impact on initiatives to support staff to be supporters. With HEIs having to minimise expenditure, there is a risk that faculties and departments could focus more on their traditional academic activities and exclude or abandon a holistic approach to support as a result. Such a scenario would be detrimental to staff perceiving their roles as supporters and champions of the student experience. From this perspective, the case studies play an important role in encouraging collaborative working and the pooling of resource for the collective institutional benefit.

Chapter 11

Supporting learning and teaching

Improving academic enagagement

Liz Thomas, Edge Hill University, UK

Introduction

This chapter focuses on supporting the student learning experience in higher education (HE) through improving student engagement. Learning and teaching is at the heart of the student experience and, indeed for many, constitutes the bulk or even the totality of their student experience. Furthermore, students' experience of the curriculum has a profound influence on their retention and success in HE. Curriculum in the HE context is open to interpretation but it is used here to cover programme contents, pedagogy, academic development, feed-forward and feedback and assessment (see Crosling *et al.* 2008 for a fuller discussion). This chapter argues that the curriculum can be designed and delivered to promote the engagement, sense of belonging and retention of students. It does not, however, focus on assessment issues.

Academic transition

Transition to HE is challenging for many students, but particularly those who are the first in their family, community or social network to attend. The academic transition from school or college into HE can be particularly problematic, resulting in 'academic culture shock' (Quinn *et al.* 2005). Students often find the teaching methods to be unfamiliar, and the teaching staff unapproachable, and this can result in them feeling like outsiders, or not belonging in HE.

> The language they used and the structure of the teaching was a lot more in-depth and complicated, it felt a lot more adult.
>
> (first-year first-generation entrant who withdrew from university)

> When I did drop out it was mainly the teaching methods that were off-putting coming from college to university. They were so suddenly academic that it was a real shocker!
>
> (second-year male first-generation student who withdrew from university and entered another one)

> They just talk. That's about it, it's a lecture, you listen and take notes. When you take notes you forget what they are saying. When you go back to your notes you wonder what you have written down. You don't know whether to take notes or listen.
>
> (first-year female first-generation entrant who withdrew from university)

I didn't feel comfortable approaching lecturers and asking how I did some of the work. I didn't want to feel like an idiot.

(male first-generation working class entrant who withdrew from university in his first year)

I found I could never really talk to the lecturers, there were so many people in our class. The lecturers were always busy doing something else. They never had time. There was always someone else talking to them.

(male first-generation entrant who withdrew during semester 2)

Academic engagement and belonging

In an on-going programme of research about student retention and success, we found that if students are able to engage with their peers, academic teaching staff, other institutional staff and the institution per se, then they are less likely to feel like outsiders and more likely to feel like they belong in HE – and to be retained and fulfil their potential (Thomas and May 2011). In summary:

Student engagement lies at the heart of retention and success and therefore offers institutions the answer to their improvement. Essentially institutions need to attend to not just the number and range of interventions or services they provide, but the quality and extent of the students' interactions with those as well as the institution more broadly. Successful higher education depends on a partnership between a student and the institution they attend.

(ibid.)

Although engagement takes place across higher education institutions, the academic sphere is of central importance. Some institutions have revised curriculum contents to improve engagement retention and success, but research with students identifies relational and pedagogical issues as more crucial to enabling them to successfully engage in HE (Thomas 2002).

Academic engagement is characterised by:

- staff having a good understanding of the previous experiences, current interests and future aspirations of their students and making learning relevant to them;
- students having opportunities to develop relationships with academic members of staff who can be engaged to enhance the learning experience;
- students actively engaging with the discipline to construct meaning and promote deep learning;
- academic and social interaction between peers to check meaning and understanding and promote greater engagement with the learning process;
- feed-forward and feedback to support students to better understand course material and assessment requirements, and to enable staff to gain a better understanding of their student cohorts;
- the provision of student capacity building to enable students to participate fully in their learning experience, including: developing personal confidence; improving understanding of academic expectations and conventions; enhancing academic skills; and encouraging individual responsibility for learning.

Student-centred learning

Academic engagement is promoted by student-centred approaches to learning. These facilitate staff and student interaction, enabling students to develop academically and staff to have a better understanding of their students. These learning approaches also promote peer interaction and the development of long-lasting friendships. Student-centred approaches can be contrasted with teacher-led approaches to learning. Student-centred approaches acknowledge and build upon the knowledge, experience and ways of understanding that students bring with them, and recognise their different learning styles. Students construct their own meaning by talking, listening, writing, reading and reflecting on content, ideas, issues and concerns. Student-centred learning makes use of group learning in particular, which requires the lecturer to provide the learning resources and guide and support students through their use, and thus to be the organiser and facilitator of learning. Students have greater responsibility for their learning and must engage and work collaboratively with their peers, allowing them to check understanding, clarify meaning and engage more deeply with the topic. Learning is an active, dynamic process in which connections are constantly changing and their structure is continually reformatted.

Practical ways of promoting academic engagement to improve the student learning experience

Practical ways to improve academic engagement include:

- Comprehensive and required academic induction to explain norms and expectations of HE, which is integrated into the core curriculum.
- Small group teaching or compulsory, structured personal tutoring, to develop relationships between staff and students and with peers, especially in the first year. This may require a redistribution of resources towards the first year, but this will be recouped through greater student progression.
- Mechanisms to check that students are coping and which demonstrate that the institution is concerned about them. This may include attendance registers and follow up of students who are not attending. Follow up can be done by academics, support staff or peers (with different resource implications).
- Development of collaborative learning strategies to help students form peer relations and to build their confidence.
- Provision of development and support for academic staff to develop more student-centred approaches to learning and teaching.
- Greater emphasis on feed-forward and formative assessment to assist students to understand the processes of higher education.
- Staff development and alternative career progression structure to reward staff who spend time on student support, and to signal that this is an important activity valued by the institution.
- Use of new technology to assist students to keep in touch, remain up to date and engage with course materials and learning.

About the case studies

The case studies in this section of the book provide specific examples of ways in which staff and institutions have sought to enhance the engagement of students in the academic experience.

Case Study 33 by Marcia Ody and William Carey from the University of Manchester focuses on the provision of peer academic support. It presents three examples in different discipline areas of how students have collaborated to engage peers. This case study provides engagement opportunities and associated benefits for the students delivering the peer academic support, and for those in receipt of it, as well as for staff. Students who provide the academic support benefit from: more meaningful relationships with staff and students; enhanced capacities as learners and facilitators of learning; a deeper level of engagement with their discipline as they are involved in facilitating the learning of peers; and they are more likely to feel like they belong within the institution as they are acting on behalf of the institution.

For the students who are supported by peers, learning is more relevant as it is student-led and they have opportunities to develop relations with peers in other levels. Staff benefit from better understanding of their students' needs and interests and enhanced relationships with the students delivering academic peer support.

Case Study 34 by Brad Garner from Indiana Wesleyan University is about the 'teaching toolbox newsletter', which offers staff ideas to enhance their teaching. While it is not explicit from the case study that these are student-centred tips, a review of the website confirms that this is the case. This is an innovative way which has proved effective at communicating ideas to staff which they put into practice in their teaching. A focus on staff development is essential to ensure that they have the knowledge and skills to change their teaching and learning approaches. Staff benefit from being inspired to try out new teaching methods which are likely to be more engaging. Students benefit from innovative teaching which is aimed at stimulating their interest and promoting their engagement.

Case Study 35 from James Denholm-Price is about electronic voting at Kingston University. Academic staff pose problems during the course of a (large) lecture, and students can indicate their response with their hand-held electronic voting systems (EVS) clickers. This is an innovative electronic solution to help improve student attendance and engagement in the classroom. This approach allows students to check their understanding during the lecture, and provides feedback to the lecturer about student understanding which can be acted on immediately, or in a subsequent teaching session.

Case Study 36 by Beverley Matthews shows how the University of Derby implemented an institution-wide electronic attendance monitoring and standardised follow-up system. A prerequisite for student engagement is attendance, and non-attendance provides an indicator of students who are disengaging and at risk of withdrawing. Furthermore, attendance not only improves retention, but this case study demonstrates that it also improves achievement. This institution-wide approach enables staff to monitor attendance and have a better insight into their students. Simultaneously, it demonstrates to students that the institution is aware of when they do not attend, and cares about them. Follow-up action enables relationships to be developed between support staff and students at risk of withdrawal. Students can be referred to appropriate support services and enabled to re-engage, or if necessary they can be supported to withdraw from the programme if this is the most appropriate outcome.

Case Study 33

Name and university
Marcia Ody, Teaching and Learning Manager, and William Carey, Teaching and Learning Adviser – Students as Partners, Teaching and Learning Support Office (TLSO), University of Manchester, UK.

Title of project/initiative
Academic peer support beyond the first year: a trio of examples.

Who was involved in the initiative
Central staff based in the Teaching and Learning Support Office (T&L Manager and Adviser), sabbatical interns and a range of champions (coordinators) at a local level including:

*   faculty associate deans;
*   programme directors;
*   module leaders;
*   senior tutors;
*   teaching fellows;
*   administrators.

See Case Study 26 (page 152) for structures diagram.

Reason for the project/initiative
The University of Manchester's undergraduate review of education recognised the significant impact of peer support on the Level 1 student experience and recommended that its implementation across all programmes and all years be considered. Student demand for peer support activity beyond Level 1 had significantly grown since 2007.

Why it was developed
It was important to tailor peer support to the needs of each year cohort and discipline area. This case study provides three different examples of peer support in higher years.

Example A: Peer Assisted Study Sessions (PASS) (see Case Study 26) for basic econometrics, a complex concept module which is a compulsory new topic for Level 2 BEconSci pathway and necessary for progression in many other economics programmes.

Example B: peer mentoring for geography dissertations as many students found the initial dissertation period quite daunting given the nature of such extensive independent study (25 per cent of a student's final mark). Previous students were to act as mentors thus sharing their experiences.

Example C: final year structured informal discussion groups in life sciences to help students manage their own learning, become more self-reliant and get the opportunity to form new peer study groups to discuss course material and extra reading outside of lectures.

The target group
Example A: primarily Level 2 but also some Level 3 taking this as an optional unit. Open to all in a timetabled slot.

Example B: Level 2 students entering semester 2 at the stage of exploring and 'researching' for their dissertation. Open to all students with Level 3 mentors assigned based on nature of dissertation topic (human, physical) and attached to staff-led groups.

Example C: self-selecting final-year students identifying study topics/modules and establishing study groups.

How it was developed, what it included and how it was implemented

How it was developed

Central support and consultation provided expert advice in establishing the objectives of the schemes and some consistency across all examples. However, each example was driven at a local level (e.g. module or programme) by students and/or staff.

Example C required leadership and development to come directly from students. Only structural support was provided by staff.

What it included

Example A: 24 final-year students who had previously taken the module voluntarily trained as PASS leaders to support Level 2 and final-year students in 12 study groups. PASS operated as a weekly, one-hour timetabled session across both semesters. PASS leaders worked with academic staff coordinators and central support to:

- provide feedback on the way in which module material is being received and processed;
- support leaders in their professional development;
- develop supplementary materials for use in sessions;
- recognise additional needs resulting a series of 'add-on' workshop sessions, e.g. computer lab work.

Example B: 67 final-year students were recruited and trained as mentors. Two to three mentors were allocated per dissertation tutorial groups on the basis of broad academic and research topics. Approximately three 'formal' meetings (weeks 6, 9 and 12) were planned with encouragement for Level 2 mentors to be in contact with their second-year mentees outside of this period.

Example C: self-selecting final-year students identified modules for which they would like to have inter-peer discussion groups. Students volunteered to be the group coordinator and initiate the group. Consequently, sessions varied from module to module. The groups planned their own sessions using lecture notes and intended learning outcomes, recommended reading and past papers as a guide. They decided what would be covered for each session, the way in which they would approach the information and how the responsibility/workload would be spilt between group members.

How it was implemented

The implementation of any recognised peer support schemes requires a strong partnership between students and staff.

Example A: the same implementation process for PASS was used (see Case Study 26). It was essential that the training was tailored to consider the transition from Level 1 to Level 2, rather than the transition into university.

Example B: final-year student opinion and feedback was ascertained at the 'dissertation hand-in session' at the end of semester 1 on the use of the scheme and topics for Level 2 students. Potential mentors volunteered at the same time. A small group of students/staff from geography worked with TLSO and faculty staff to develop the scheme's structure. The pilot scheme attracted around 30 mentors who, having received training and based on their previous dissertation experience, were allocated groups of Level 2 students.

Example C: the development of this scheme was entirely student-led. Once a module discussion group had been identified and a group coordinator volunteered, the students informed staff of a convenient time (often coordinated via a Doodle Poll) and a room was booked for them. However, modules operating discussions groups could change each year based on student uptake.

Group coordinators were supported in their role through a short briefing meeting led by TLSO and faculty staff. All students attending the group received a 'Starter Pack' that was discussed at their first meeting when they agreed, as a group, how to work together.

Analysis and feedback

Example A: attendance at sessions was monitored to enable a correlation against academic performance. An online questionnaire was distributed to all students on the module.

Example B: a review of the scheme is conducted on a yearly basis at dissertation hand-in time.

Example C: an online questionnaire of participating students and interviews with group coordinators and non-attendees were conducted.

The cost and timeline

Each of these schemes utilise structures that exist for Level 1 peer support programmes. At a local level the cost of materials to support these schemes does not exceed £500 per scheme. From the point of the decision being taken to develop any of the schemes, it was quite quickly implemented (with existing structures this is approximately a semester).

How it is/was monitored

Example A: PASS is a structured quality-assured model where there is comprehensive monitoring through observations, debriefs and evaluation.

Example B: in addition to a yearly review mentors discussed current issues with the group's tutor.

Example C: group coordinators were encouraged to produce summaries of session discussions and unresolved feedback issues to the module leaders.

The outcome

Student feedback for all of these schemes was incredibly positive and each year students continue to enhance and develop the schemes. Staff at various levels have recognised the wider benefits of peer support in higher years.

Has or could the initiative be used for a different group?

A roll out of the use of PASS in higher years is intended across the institution. We recognise that mentoring can be creatively adapted in higher years to support recognised key transitions at both UG and PG levels. Example C for final-year discussion groups is already being adopted for Level 2 students within the same faculty but could also be used in other discipline areas.

Advice and guidance

- Get students on board.
- Encourage discipline staff to look at key transition points.
- Provide support and training for students taking leading roles.
- Be creative!

Contact details

marcia.ody@manchester.ac.uk
william.carey@manchester.ac.uk

Case Study 34

Name and university

Brad Garner, Assistant Dean for Teaching and Learning, Indiana Wesleyan University (IWU), USA.

Title of project/initiative

Opening *The Toolbox*: a newsletter to help faculty gain enhanced teaching skills.

Who was involved in the initiative

I started *The Toolbox* newsletter in 2003 as a resource for faculty members at Indiana Wesleyan University in the United States where I serve as a facilitator in faculty development.

Reason for the project/initiative

The aim of this project was to provide academic colleagues at my institution with guidance, support and advice on how to improve their teaching skills through teaching styles and innovative teaching methods. I hoped that it would help colleagues feel more engaged and more confident and that it would improve the learning and teaching experience of our students thus aiding our persistence rates (retention).

Why it was developed

For some of us, the decision to pursue a teaching career in higher education was a natural transition from the role of a graduate assistant while pursuing a terminal degree (e.g. a doctorate). For others, the decision to teach at the university level was made well after pursuing an advanced degree in a chosen field of study (e.g. business, education, nursing, art, music). My research and experience as well as that of other respected colleagues in the field found that regardless of the path of entry into teaching and although highly qualified as experts in their chosen areas of academic passion, faculty across the sector often received little preparation for the process of teaching. Quite often they would arrive on the college campus, be handed a syllabus and placed in front of a group of students with little guidance or support.

Observations by researchers, such as Reder (2007) highlighted that:

- faculty do care about the quality of their teaching;
- the enhancement of teaching skills requires time and commitment;
- the gap continues to widen each year as technology begins to play in increasing role in the lives of our students;
- we must find ways to run faster in order to keep pace with a rapidly changing world.

The newsletter would be a tool to support staff in their teaching.

The target group

All faculty and those interested in learning and teaching.

How it was developed, what it included and how it was implemented

How it was developed

I wanted faculty to gain new skills in teaching via a quick and usable format. This led to the development of *The Toolbox* newsletter. The idea was to create a newsletter of no more than two pages that:

- identified critical and practical concerns in teaching;
- provided a brief literature-based connection to best practices;
- offered the directions for two or three easily implemented skills in the classroom.

The specific issues addressed were based on, and informed by, the latest research and examples of good practice in learning and teaching across the sector.

The process has evolved over the years. I have found that the use of new teaching strategies is greatly enhanced by personal contact and conversation. To this end, I have initiated lunchtime conversations with faculty around specific topics in teaching and learning (e.g. assessment, syllabus development, problem-based learning). Faculty members who may not know one another very well get together and share ideas and also begin to talk about ways that they can collaborate in interdisciplinary teaching.

What it included

There are currently over 40 issues of The Toolbox now archived on the website hosted by the National Resource Centre for the First-Year Experience and Students in Transition (NRC). Topics include a variety of issues that faculty frequently cite as frustrations of teaching (e.g. strategies for encouraging students to read assigned texts, creating a course syllabus, mentoring students, cooperative learning strategies, effective organisation of classroom learning sessions). I am always on the lookout for new topics that are on the cutting edge of teaching as well as those identified as challenges in the classroom. Just the process of writing the newsletter has been a motivation for me to always be on the lookout for new classroom strategies and to be more adventurous in the classroom by trying out new approaches to teaching.

How it was implemented

From the beginning, the newsletter has been delivered electronically, via email, six times per year.

Analysis and feedback

Since initiating the newsletter, as each issue is distributed, I typically receive emails from colleagues thanking me for the ideas and suggestions for future topics. For me, the most important encouragement for me to keep the newsletter going is that colleagues inform me that they plan to try out the new techniques in their classroom. Even better, these comments typically come from different faculty members each time. This encourages me to believe that the topics being covered each month appeal to different groups of colleagues who are at different places on their journey to excellence in teaching.

The most gratifying moments come when I meet with a colleague and they greet me with these words: 'Hey, I tried one of The Toolbox techniques and it was highly successful!' Even better, it is satisfying when faculty create iterations to the strategies in the newsletter and make adaptations specific to their academic discipline.

The cost and timeline

The only cost of this initiative has been the time and energy involved in gathering new types of teaching strategies and summarising them in a manner that will be meaningful and useful to faculty. At the present time, I do the initial writing. Editing and layout work is done by members of the NRC staff.

How it is/was monitored

Newsletter content is reviewed by members of the NRC staff for clarity, compatibility with best practice and for accuracy of references, etc.

The outcome

The Toolbox has helped colleagues improve their teaching skills. There is more creativity and innovation within the classroom at IWU. In 2009, *The Toolbox* newsletter gained an international audience when the NRC agreed to take over from me the tasks of editing and layout. It was given to a team of experts who engage in these tasks every day. As a result, the readership has increased exponentially. Records kept on the number of website hits indicate a continuing growth trend in readership. This is very gratifying. This move has also allowed me to spend more time on developing and seeking out new tools for colleagues to adopt and adapt. Initial responses from the field to the newsletter on the NRC site have been very favourable (Bloom, 2010).

The newsletter can be accessed at http://sc.edu/fye/toolbox.

Has or could the initiative be used for a different group?

The newsletter could be developed for particular academic disciplines (e.g. the sciences, the arts).

Advice and guidance

Always look for ways to engage in conversation with colleagues about the joys and challenges of teaching. I guarantee that you will walk away with a concept, idea or strategy to use in your classroom.

References

Bloom, J.L. (2010) 'The Toolbox newsletters', *Journal of Student Affairs Research and Practice*, 47(1), 132–4.

Reder, M. (2007) 'Does your college really support teaching and learning?' *Peer Review*, 9(4), 9–13.

Contact details

brad.garner@indwes.edu

Case Study 35

Name and university
James Denholm-Price, Principal Lecturer and Learning and Teaching Coordinator, Faculty of Computing, Information Systems and Mathematics, Kingston University, UK.

Title of project/initiative
Using electronic voting systems to enhance the student learning experience.

Who was involved in the initiative?
The module leader.

Reason for the project/initiative
The module leader's desire to improve students' engagement with relatively technical material and to experiment with electronic voting systems technology (EVS).

Why it was developed
The module where this development occurred aims to get students comfortable with the technologies behind the 'client-side' web experience (i.e. what they see and interact with when browsing the web). Typically, this means learning how to write programmes that use JavaScript code to interact with HTML and CSS, which are the web's most common languages for mark-up and presentation. These activities are best-suited to computer lab-based teaching but due to increasing class sizes, timetabling and other infrastructure-related issues it is not always possible to move entirely out of the lecture theatre, so I was looking for ways to improve student engagement within the traditional classroom.

The principal aim was to improve the student experience of learning the 'dry' side of programming the web, where students must learn to select appropriately from a large set of concepts in response to changing scenarios online. It would utilise 'concept questions' (Nicol, 2007), which focus on the application of concepts rather than simple recall of definitions, similar to the 'Force Concept Inventory' (Hestenes et al., 1992) where the questions are based on concepts from Newton's laws of motion.

Who was the target group?
Students in a 'web technologies' module within a modular, joint honours programme from a variety of backgrounds and courses. In the past five years, the class size has varied between 50 and 240 students.

How it was developed, what it included and how it was implemented

How it was developed
There is a regular review process before any module starts each year. Before implementing EVS, I reviewed the module's curriculum. I estimated that using the EVS would occupy approximately 30 minutes of each 100-minute lecture (within a two-hour timetable slot) and so some of the lecture material had to go. This was a healthy process as it involved identifying out-of-date material or material that students could learn outside of the lecture, and refocused the lectures on appropriate learning outcomes.

What it included

Each week I used the EVS to:

- Remind students that they were expected to do weekly reading/preparation by asking an EVS question like 'How much of the reading have you done?' Asking students to self-evaluate each week helps to focus their minds on the task as well as re-emphasising its importance. It also had the beneficial side-effect of testing the system at the start of each session before the higher-stakes interaction with concept-based EVS questions.
- Present between 1–3 EVS-based concept questions designed to elicit students' comprehension of material before moving onto the next topic. The number varied depending upon the perceived difficulty of the material, based on experience from the previous year.

How it was implemented

I prepared EVS activities on a weekly basis in order to allow for flexibility in the speed of consumption of topics. This added to weekly preparation time but the process became somewhat more sustainable after the first iteration of the module as 'good' questions can be recycled.

In most cases it's useful to have a concrete (yet reasonably generic) example for students to latch onto. For example, when discussing web-based forms it's fun to use Facebook as an example:

> Question: When you sign-in to a website like Facebook there's quite a lot going on. What event(s) are triggered in the web browser when you click on the 'log in' button after having filled in your email and password?

> Answers: blur, change, click, submit, mouseover, mouseout, mousemove.

In fact, all of the above are reasonable responses and they can be used to draw out important concepts in the module.

The real purpose of a question like the example is not to award points for correctness but to recognise students' ideas, provide an opportunity for interaction with and among students, and to enable even the weakest student to make a response they're comfortable with. In the above example, 'click' or 'submit' are the ones that everyone should get and they can be discussed in meaningful ways to provide a positive, reinforcing experience.

Analysis and feedback

All students who attended classes using EVS questions seemed to be excited by the technology and generally were happy to answer questions anonymously with the clickers. There was no change in the module's results that was identifiable as being statistically significant (there was a 5 per cent increase in the average mark compared to the previous year, but there has been a ±5 per cent fluctuation before then) but attendance was improved and there seemed to be no mid-semester dip that usually occurred after our mid-semester 'reading week'.

There were 16 written comments in the module evaluation questionnaire responding to 'I think the best features of this module were ...' and six of those were about the level of interactivity in the classroom sessions, e.g. 'The interaction between lecturer and students. James always tried to get us involved as much as possible'.

There was evidence of 'question fatigue' occasionally (where response rates became slower), but the students remained interactive even during the session where the subject matter lent itself to more short EVS 'retention' style questions; in that session 17 questions were posed rather than the usual three or four.

The cost and timeline

The cost for 200 hand-held EVS clickers and associated equipment was approximately £6,000. Setting up the activities in advance of each week's lecture and distributing the handsets is slightly time consuming for the lecturer and there is an up-front cost in the time needed to become comfortable using the system.

How it is/was monitored

The continuous in-class engagement of students with the activities was immediately apparent and the overall engagement of students with the technology was evaluated as part of the usual module evaluation process.

The outcome

The module's content has been transformed from a fairly traditional interactive lecture into a more problem-based class using electronic voting to provide interactive in-class feedback. This 'EVS enhanced' approach to teaching has proved to be popular with students and has had some positive side effects without significant drawbacks to the lecturer. It can be seen as an interim way of improving lecture-style classes whilst infrastructure catches up with the need for flexible space. For me, I hope it's a stepping-stone towards adapting Mazur's 'peer instruction' teaching style, if time allows (Mazur, 2009).

Has or could the initiative be used for a different group?

The general principle of identifying concepts for discussion in mini problem sessions within a longer lecture could be adapted elsewhere (indeed, it's a popular use of EVSs in the literature).

Advice and guidance

* Get comfortable with the EVS and software before using it live.
* Questions based around concepts are better for learning, interaction and feedback than memory-based questions.
* Equality among students facilitates discussion. Most questions should include responses suitable for all levels of understanding, although difficult concept questions that the majority will get wrong are great discussion starters!

Contact details

j.denholm-price@kingston.ac.uk

References

Hestenes, D. Wells, M. and Swackhamer, G. (1992) 'Force concept inventory', *The Physics Teacher*, 30 (3), 141–58.

Mazur, E. (2009) 'Farewell, lecture?' *Science*, 323, 50–1.

Nicol, D. (2007) 'E-assessment by design: using multiple-choice tests to good effect', *Journal of Further and Higher Education*, 31 (1), 53–64.

Case Study 36

Name and university
Beverley Matthews, Student Support and Information Services, University of Derby, UK.

Title of project/initiative
Student attendance monitoring.

Who was involved in the initiative
Student Support and Information Services (SSIS), Programme Advisory Service (PAS), Heads of Faculties, academic staff, Student Experience Strategy Group (SESG), Student Liaison Officers (SLOs) and Learning and Information Services (LIS).

Reason for the project/initiative
We believe that a change in the patterns of student attendance is an excellent indicator of the risk of withdrawal from the university and that student participation in timetabled sessions increases achievement.

Why it was developed
We wanted to be able to monitor student attendance by introducing a transparent and consistent approach across the institution which would enable us to quickly identify and reach out to support students who might be experiencing difficulties.

The target group
On-campus undergraduate students initially, developing to encompass all on-campus teaching.

How it was developed, what it included and how it was implemented

How it was developed
We wanted academic staff to be at the centre of our approach, and to enhance their relationship with students where it might have appeared to have broken down. We needed academic buy in. We also wanted to relieve some of the administrative burden previously associated with following up student non-attendance through offering a centralised service which met academic and student needs and could work across the diverse delivery of our taught sessions.

We drew together information on the disparate attendance monitoring activities across the university, identified best practice and introduced a unified approach.

In 2006 attendance monitoring became a discrete function of the Programme Advisory Service (PAS). Through collaboration and consultation with academic staff, a system of centralised notification asking students about their non-attendance was introduced.

We ensured that supportive messages and support service signposting was communicated to the students, along with stressing the importance of regular attendance to students. We also had mechanisms for follow-up messages to students explaining the possible consequences of persistent non-engagement.

Our current student record system was introduced in 2005, and we have exploited its capabilities to enable our academic staff to report student non-attendance.

An academic-led, small-scale pilot in 2007 investigated the potential for barcode scanning to collect attendance data. Its successful outcome led to the widespread adoption of the system.

What it included

It included:

- A system for academic staff (module leaders) collecting data (barcode scans or registers) and notifying PAS of student non-attendance.
- PAS using the notification data to make quick contact with the student through text message and email initially. This communication outlines support services available, and encourages students to talk to their module leader about the reason for absence;
- Follow-up processes for students who do not respond (formal letter explaining consequences of not engaging).
- A process of deregistration of a student from a module for persistent non-attendance.
- Data collected on students not attending a range of modules in a semester so that intervention from the student liaison officer (SLO) or course leader can take place, and withdrawal actioned in a timely way if necessary.
- Key performance indicators (KPIs) developed for faculties to analyse engagement with and outcomes of the system.

How it was implemented

Two systems were implemented:

- submission of notifications through our student record system called Peoplesoft;
- gathering and downloading data from hand-held barcode scanners in lectures.

An academic interface for our student records system already existed. Within the interface, we developed functionality for module leaders to call up their module list, check a box against non-attending students and submit an email notification to PAS for follow up. This allowed for mass reporting if it was necessary.

Our student ID card had a barcode and we saw the potential in using barcode scanners to collect attendance data. Our module leaders scan the student ID card, download the data, and notify PAS about non-attending students. The scanner download links to our student record system.

Notifications from either method immediately come through as workflow for PAS with a one-day turnaround for contacting students.

Our regulations about student engagement with taught sessions were revised in 2007. The student participation policy that is part of our regulations and which students sign up to at enrolment, has become embedded in all module and programme handbooks.

Heads of faculties saw the benefits of centralised student attendance monitoring for staff and students through the KPI data and fully support and encourage its use across the academic community.

Analysis and feedback

A workshop with student representatives highlighted that students believe attendance is important and should be monitored. Academic staff are invited to feedback on the processes and to offer suggestions for enhancements. Academic staff and students regularly communicate that they value the support.

Regular monthly KPI data shows:

- academic engagement with the process across faculties;
- the outcomes for students successfully re-engaging;
- the number of registration corrections;
- the number of de-registrations which the process identifies.

From 2006, we have consistently achieved a 70 per cent student re-engagement rate.

The cost and timeline

The process has grown since 2005 and has become the university's core method of dealing with student non-attendance in taught sessions. The electronic capture of attendance data was introduced in 2008. The cost of the barcode scanners for approximately 500 members of academic staff has been £45,000. The cost of IT development time was subsumed through the recruitment of a member of staff whose remit included developing IT systems to aid retention.

How it is/was monitored

The monthly KPIs identify the level of staff engagement. Faculties can report on usage of the process and encourage staff to use it fully. We can cross-reference notifications with student achievement on modules.

The outcome

- Increased retention rate.
- Relationship building with students who may be experiencing difficulties.
- Increased awareness and take up of support for students.
- Increased module completion rates.
- Timely withdrawal of students where appropriate.
- Systems development that benefits academic staff and students.
- Students knowing that we notice when they're not there – and that we care.

Has or could the initiative be used for a different group?

The process can be developed for online learning student engagement, where the 'attendance' is engagement with virtual learning environments.

Advice and guidance

- Get colleagues on board by clearly explaining the benefits for their work with students.
- Get an in-depth awareness of what additional support can be made available to students – you'll be key in signposting them.
- See student attendance monitoring as a positive, supportive process and not a negative one.
- Support from faculty and university senior teams will help you embed the process.
- Use your data sets as key performance indicators – they're the evidence that what you do is making a difference for the students and can be a useful tool for getting others on board.
- Collecting attendance data electronically can be quick and easy but think about the IT support you'll need to develop the system to meet your needs.

Contact details

b.j.matthews@derby.ac.uk

Conclusion

The academic experience is central to the whole student experience. An engaging academic experience has positive outcomes for student satisfaction, retention and success. Relationships – with peers, academics, other institutional staff and the institution – are at the heart of engagement in HE – and are effectively nurtured in the academic sphere by student-centred learning. Thinking about the examples above and reflecting on the following questions may help you to ensure that you deliver a more engaging academic experience:

- How do academic staff get to know students?
- When do students have opportunities to work closely with academic members of staff?
- How are students encouraged to work with and get to know each other?
- How could learning and teaching be more student-centred?
- How do students develop their understanding of learning and teaching expectations, conventions and approaches to assessment?
- How are students enabled to develop their capacity to engage in their learning experience?

References

Crosling, G., Thomas, L. and Heagney, M. (eds) (2008) *Improving Student Retention in Higher Education*, New York: Routledge Falmer.

Quinn, J., Thomas, L., Slack, K., Casey, L., Thexton, W. and Noble, J. (2005) *From Life Disaster to Lifelong Learning: Reframing Working Class 'Drop Out'*, York: Joseph Rowntree Foundation.

Thomas, L. (2002) 'Student retention in higher education: the role of institutional habitus', *Journal of Education Policy*, 17, 4: 423–42.

Thomas, L. and May, H. (2011 forthcoming) *What Works? Student Retention and Success Programme*, London: Paul Hamlyn Foundation.

Chapter 12

Student evaluation and feedback

Duncan Nulty, Griffith University, Australia

Introduction

Many moons ago, the importance of feedback for improving student performance and achievement was recognised and originally known as 'The Law of Effect' (Thorndike, 1911). Since then, our understanding of this 'law' has been substantially increased through research and experience. We now have a better appreciation of the role of feedback, the importance of timeliness in providing it, the role students' motivation has on whether feedback is used and the need to close the loop to demonstrate responsiveness to feedback (McKeachie, 1990; Race, 2005).

Improving performance and achievement is accomplished by obtaining and evaluating feedback on performance, and then adjusting one's performance in ways that are informed by that evaluation. As noted elsewhere in this book, student evaluation and feedback is a critical activity in the toolbox of the practitioner. This chapter will discuss the importance of evaluating student comments and opinions, how practitioners use that information to inform the development and implementation of initiatives to improve and enhance the student experience and explicitly feeding back the results to students.

Defining student evaluation and feedback

First, it is important to understand and define what we mean when we talk about student evaluation and feedback.

On the one hand, we may mean feedback from students that helps us evaluate and improve the educational experience. This is the deliberate focus for this chapter and a critical facet of the Student Experience Practitioner Model. As noted in Chapter 1, this happens on a daily basis at different levels of scale.

On the other hand, 'student evaluation and feedback' could relate to the feedback provided to students that informs their study behaviours and patterns of engagement, or more directly responds to their performances on tasks they have completed for the purpose of assessing their learning progress and achievement.

The case studies reported in this chapter reflect both meanings, although (deliberately) none focus on the assessment of student learning directly. Thus, for example, you will see that in Case Study 39, feedback provided by students is used to both improve teaching and programme design through targeted interventions, and to feed information back to students in ways designed to help guide and support their learning. In contrast, Case Studies 37, 38 and 40 report on a feedback process primarily from students to academics.

Although the direct assessment of student learning is not covered by these case studies, this is a particularly rich source of data that can help us to improve the student learning experience (Meyers and Nulty, 2009). One just has to have an open mind to such possibilities.

Second, the design, development and implementation of initiatives needs to be informed by students' experiences if those initiatives are to actually result in improvements to the student experience. For this activity to happen, student evaluation and feedback is essential.

General points about student evaluation and feedback

Before presenting the case studies for this chapter, there are two important points about evaluation and feedback that I think are worth making explicit, because they will increase your appreciation of the case studies and will enhance your general ability to design and make good use of evaluation and feedback mechanisms yourself.

The first is about the validity of student evaluation and feedback. There is a lot of research literature on this issue, and not all of it reaches the same conclusions. A good colleague and friend once said to me, 'Duncan, there is evidence to support almost any proposition you would care to make, but what's important is where the weight of the evidence lies' (Zimmitat, 2004, personal communication). The weight of evidence strongly suggests that student evaluation and feedback is valid (Cashin, 1995; Marsh, 1987).

As a sector, we should accept and embrace this and get on with meaningful evaluation and use of the students' feedback to develop appropriately informed responses to everyone's mutual benefit.

The second point is a question I would like to pose: Where does the 'value' in the word 'evaluation' come from? My answer is that it comes from the use of feedback in conjunction with some well-founded 'theory' about causes and effects. What I mean by this is that when thinking about improving the student experience, we should preface our efforts on evaluation and feedback with the development of a well-articulated suite of evidence-based and interlinked questions that allows us to be more purposeful in seeking and using feedback in meaningful and theoretically well-founded ways. This will provide a framework for student views and allow you to use your data to good effect. My call to you is this: be scholarly in your collection and use of student evaluation and feedback.

The following case studies provide illustrations of how some institutions have developed initiatives to collect from, and provide feedback to, students.

Case Study 37 is by Akbar Aboutorabi from Kingston University, UK. It describes an approach to obtaining student feedback at the mid-point of their study of a module so that this can be used in ways that are demonstrably more responsive to students' needs.

Case Study 38 by Barry J. Beggs and Elaine Clafferty describes a novel approach to effectively, but rapidly, engaging students in the provision of very focussed student feedback on specific learning and teaching issues at Glasgow Caledonian University, UK.

Case Study 39 by Sherry A. Woosley and Darlena Jones from Educationl Benchmarking Incorporated (EBI), USA, outlines the development and use of a suite of survey tools across 80 institutions, the use of which has improved student retention rates through a 'risk indicator' and targeted interventions.

Case Study 40 from Duncan Nulty details the development and use of a simple but effective evaluation tool that has been systemically embedded as an institution-wide quality assurance processes to improve the quality of teaching and courses – and to close the student feedback loop at Griffith University, Australia.

Case Study 37

Name and university
Akbar Aboutorabi, Deputy Dean and Head of the Student Experience, Faculty of Engineering, Kingston University, UK.

Title of project/initiative
Mid-module (course) student evaluation and feedback in the Faculty of Engineering.

Who was involved in the initiative
Faculty staff: Deputy Dean for the Student Experience, Learning and Teaching Coordinator and Student Experience Manager (LTCSE), Blended Learning Coordinator, Associate Dean for Quality, Student Course Representatives (SCRs) and Student Office Manager. Central staff: Academic Development Centre.

Reason for the project/initiative
University requirement and faculty desire to improve learning and teaching processes for students and staff.

Why it was developed
Most of the modules (one unit) that make up a degree programme in the faculty operate on a semester basis with only a few being year-long. A team of academics often teach on the module with the module leader taking responsibility for the management of the module. Comprehensive module student evaluation and feedback was traditionally undertaken at the end of the semester in which it ran. This meant that:

- we were unable to effectively identify any learning and teaching or curriculum design issues until the end of the module through the module evaluation process;
- students did not benefit from the evaluation and feedback they provided;
- it was often difficult to identify if the issues were a team or individual related.

The aim of this initiative was to be able to identify any easily resolvable issues or problems and address them appropriately and accordingly half-way through the module. These could include the speed and the delivery of lectures or the quality of and access to lecture notes. This would demonstrate to our students that their voice could make a difference to their learning experience, we could address any teaching issues and, hopefully, we could improve the module grades and pass rate.

Who was the target group
All students undertaking modules at all academic levels of full- or part-time study at the university.

How it was developed, what it included and how it was implemented

How it was developed
The faculty looked at various methods of data collection and piloted a number of processes in collaboration with academic colleagues and students. The relevant committees in the faculty then decided which method should be adopted. The faculty decided against collecting feedback via an online survey on StudySpace (Blackboard) because it had not achieved a good level of engagement by students even with active encouragement from module leaders and the LTCSE during the pilot.

It was agreed that the student evaluation and feedback had to be:

- quick and easy to collect;
- collected anonymously to encourage honest feedback and participation by students;
- fed back to the students within one week of collection with a response.

For it to be quick and easy to collect, the survey needed to be short.

What it included

It was agreed that students half-way through a module would be asked two questions:

1   Which three things do you consider are good about this module?
2   Which three things would improve the module?

SCRs identified 14 typical problems students could experience coming up to the mid-module point.

How it was implemented

It was decided that the SCR would ask these two questions and collect the responses at the end of a module once the module lecturer had left the room.

They would ask their peers for verbal responses. If students were not responsive, the SCR would use the 14 issues identified by SCRs in their 'start-of-year' SCR training as a prompt guide. The top three responses provided by the majority of students present in the lecture for each question would be written on a feedback module template (FMT). Any extra comments that the SCR felt were important would also be recorded. The contents of the FMT would be read back to the students by the SCR for confirmation.

The SCRs were trained to effectively facilitate and undertake this activity as part of their course representative training at the start of the academic year.

Analysis and feedback

The SCR would deliver the completed FMT to the student office where it would be photocopied; one copy was given to the module leader, one to the relevant head of school and one placed on the mid-module feedback file. Module leaders were then required to provide verbal feedback to the comments the following week or put them online on the module Blackboard site.

The cost and timeline

The process was developed over an academic year. The primary cost was the time of the SCRs and the LTCSE.

How it is/was monitored

The module leader was required to include both the mid-module and end-of-semester module evaluation and feedback in their annual module reports and feed the results into their module team meetings. Feedback on the process was obtained from SCRs at student and staff consultative committees.

The outcome

The feedback from the SCRs via the mid-module feedback process, and the various faculty committees, is that students do appreciate the opportunity to give feedback halfway through their module. It has helped staff improve their teaching methods and has identified staff development issues. It has also shown where we need to manage unrealistic student expectations.

Has or could the initiative be used for a different group?

The next stage is to see how the mid-module evaluation and feedback survey can be rolled out across partner institutions and those studying on distance or work-based learning courses.

Advice and guidance

- It is important to get all students and staff on board.
- Support and training should be provided in the collection of feedback, responses to feedback and the use of any equipment and software.
- Students are often 'surveyed out' in terms of evaluation and feedback so it is critical for them to see how their evaluation and feedback can help them.
- Make sure the responses available for each question are applicable to the faculty, student body and subject.
- Close the loop by publishing the results.

Contact details

a.aboutorabi@kingston.ac.uk

Case Study 38

Name and university
Barry J. Beggs, Senior Lecturer and Elaine Clafferty, Head of Learning, Teaching and Quality, Glasgow Caledonian University, UK.

Title of project/initiative
Student opinion gathering using 'Lifterviews'.

Who was involved in the initiative
Senior Lecturer, School Head of Learning and Teaching, AV technician, administrator.

Reason for the project/initiative
For many years now there has been a desire by those working in and responsible for the higher education sector to seek and gather information about the extent to which students are satisfied with the learning experience they have whilst enrolled on a programme of study. We have developed an innovative, accurate and efficient student opinion gathering technique that has evolved in an attempt to discover what students really think about what is going on with respect to their experience at university.

Why it was developed
We believe that one of the most accurate and best ways of discovering the true opinion of students is to speak to them. For this reason the concept of conducting Lifterviews was developed.

The target group
The target audience was a random selection of students enrolled in programmes in the School of Engineering and Computing. This was an appropriate group in this case due to the very generic and non-programme-specific nature of the questions asked. The target group needs to be selected carefully and according to the area/topic about which feedback is being sought.

How it was developed, what it included and how it was implemented

How it was developed
Lifterviews are an innovative and efficient way of interviewing students and capturing their opinions. The methodology we used was to 'ambush' students in lifts when they were leaving a class and were on their way to another floor of the building. No prior warning that the interviews were going to take place was given to the students. As groups of students waited in the stairwell they were asked if they would agree to a brief interview being conducted and recorded when they went into the lift. The agreement of students willing to participate was noted at this stage. The interview team lying in wait in the lift were informed of any students willing to be interviewed and then conducted the interviews as the lift was moving from floor to floor.

What it included
Students were asked if they would be prepared to answer a couple of brief and very simple open-ended questions relating to coursework and if they would give their permission for the video footage recorded and results data to be published. Most of the students approached were happy to be involved and many were quite amused by the unusual

request. Students were then filmed identifying which programme they were studying and answering the following two questions:

1   What was the main problem with or worst aspect of your coursework this year?
2   How could things be improved?

How it was implemented
We considered it best to avoid the use of any members of academic staff during the Lifterview process. A member of the administrative staff with previous interview experience was selected as the interviewer and a member of the technical staff was selected to perform the video and audio recording.

Analysis and feedback
The responses to the first question highlighted that the main concern of students in relation to coursework appeared to be time management. The majority of students seemed to consider that they had not planned their preparation time very well. Not surprisingly, the response to the second question was that, in the main, students believe that better time management will help them for future coursework submissions.

The cost and timeline
All equipment (very basic camcorder) and staff involved were already available. Approximate staff time used to conduct and analyse ten Lifterviews (involving 16 students):

* administrative/technical – three hours;
* academic – one hour.

Costs may be estimated based on staff time using the above.

How it is/was monitored
Although the Lifterviews were conducted by non-academic staff, the design and final analysis of the process and procedures used was under the control of senior academic staff members. The outcomes from the Lifterviews reported were presented to the School of Engineering and Computing Student–Staff Consultative Committee where the general opinion of the majority of class representatives was that the method was novel, useful and 'cool'. The outcomes were also presented to the School of Engineering and Computing Academic Practice Committee which then initiated and resourced the development of the online student time management support resource for use by students across the school.

The outcome
Using the Lifterview technique has allowed very timely and accurate snapshots of student opinion about aspects of their learning experience to be efficiently gathered. The technique is capable of producing highly relevant and important information that can assist those with an interest in and/or responsibility for continuous improvement of the student learning experience.

Has or could the initiative be used for a different group?
The Lifterview technique has been used a number of times within the School of Engineering and Computing and could also be used with other student groups in any discipline and in any university.

Advice and guidance
* Where there is a genuine desire to seek current, accurate student opinion relating to aspects of the student experience and where the more common methods, such as

paper or online questionnaires are not facilitating this activity adequately, it may be worth considering using the Lifterview technique to obtain an immediate and accurate impression of student opinion.

- The technique works best when it is implemented at a fast pace – everything needs to happen in the time taken for the lift to go from the departure to the destination floor.
- Only a very limited range of topics can be explored in any one Lifterview session due to the very short time available for each Lifterview. We prefer to explore only one topic during any Lifterview session.
- We have always used video recording during Lifterviews, but if a method of rapidly recording student responses by some other method (e.g. audio only or the use of shorthand) is devised then the use of video recording could be dispensed with.
- As is the case with any form of student opinion harvesting, if there is no follow-up action taken to address any issues or concerns consistently raised by students, then the exercise is worthless. In other words, the feedback loop must be closed.

Contact details

esm@gcu.ac.uk
bjbe@gcu.ac.uk

Case Study 39

Name and university
Sherry A. Woosley, formerly Associate Director of Institutional Effectiveness at Ball State University, currently Director of Analytics and Research at Educational Benchmarking Incorporated (EBI), and Darlena Jones, Director of Education and Program Development, EBI.

Title of project/initiative
MAP-Works: a tool for student self-evaluation and feedback.

Who was involved in the initiative
The original MAP committee had representatives from academic advising, academic assessment and institutional research, housing and residence life, the learning centre and university college. These areas crossed divisional boundaries (housing and residence life is in student affairs while the other units are part of academic affairs). The administration of the MAP-Works project has fallen largely to academic assessment and institutional research with much of the decision making being made locally in the various areas involved.

At Ball State University, over 7,000 first- and second-year students participate in this project. In addition, 64 faculty/staff are participating in departments including academic advising, housing and residence life, the learning center, student life, multicultural centre, academic assessment and institutional research, and university college.

Reason for the project/initiative
In 1988, Ball State University identified three main areas of concern regarding their incoming first-year students which it wanted to address.

* Unrealistic expectations: their first concern was that many incoming students had unrealistic expectations of what college would be like. For instance, many students expected to earn high grades without significant effort, they did not expect any roommate or social adjustment issues, and they did not seem to understand the extent to which or the amount of effort they needed to manage their time and their lives.
* Retention rate: Ball State's second concern was its retention rate which was not as high as desired. Although faculty and staff worked with students to address retention issues, those issues were often not identified until it was too late. Ball State utilised mid-term deficiency reports which would not become available until October or early November. Due to the late time frame most academic issues were so serious that it was often too late and too difficult to help students overcome those deficiencies by the end of the fall term.
* Better information: Ball State's final concern focused on better understanding the characteristics of the incoming class in order to identify needed programming changes and create new initiatives that would help those students succeed.

Why it was developed
The original project, a paper and pencil survey with paper feedback, was titled MAP (Making Achievement Possible) and was used on the Ball State campus from 1989–2004. In 2005, Ball State University partnered with Educational Benchmarking (EBI) to create the next generation titled MAP-Works.

The target group

We wanted to target all new first-year students including all new matriculating students and new transfer students. We also targeted all third-semester freshman (Level 1) and sophomore (Level 2) students as defined by credit hours.

How it was developed, what it included and how it was implemented

How it was developed

In 1988, the original MAP committee, with representation from a variety of campus constituencies, developed a survey focused on issues and concerns that are classic in the college student and first-year student transition literature. Their final instrument clearly reflects influences from Tinto, Astin, Gardner, Pascarella, Terrenzini and other experts in the field.

In 2005 when the MAP-Works project began, it built on the experiences and expertise gained at Ball State University with MAP. In 2006, a limited pilot was launched, survey and reporting changes were made and, in 2007, a larger pilot was implemented. Feedback from those schools led to further survey and reporting improvements and a full roll-out in 2008 occurred. By the fall of 2009, over 80 institutions used MAP-Works.

What it included

MAP-Works includes:

- Four surveys (fall transition, fall check-up, spring transition and spring check-up) administered throughout the fall-to-spring academic year.
- Institutional data collected on participating students including admissions and demographic characteristics, mid-term deficiencies and fall and spring term outcomes, such as GPA, credits earned and retention.
- Individualised feedback to students includes a flash video on the results of their fall transition survey benchmarked against their peer group. Written and downloadable reports for all four surveys includes progress reporting, campus resource information and action planning for their personal improvement.
- A risk algorithm to identify students who may be likely to leave the institution and/or likely to struggle academically.
- Faculty/staff reporting includes easy-to-use reporting that locates at-risk students, individual student talking points and dashboards, as well as aggregate student reporting to identify group-wide issues.

How it was implemented

MAP-Works implementation:

- Prior to the beginning of the fall term, institutions upload to MAP-Works the list of participating first- and second-year students and key student characteristics as well as faculty/staff information.
- Three weeks into the fall term, institutions initiate the fall transition survey and all reporting occurs simultaneously.
- Faculty/staff intervene with students identified at risk.
- Institutions upload mid-term deficiencies and faculty/staff meet with students.
- Approximately ten weeks into the fall term, institutions initiate the fall check-up survey, the list of at-risk students is updated and students receive additional feedback.
- At the beginning of the spring term, institutions upload fall term grades, credits earned and spring persistence.

- Three weeks into the spring term, institutions initiate the spring transition survey, the list of at-risk students is updated and students receive additional feedback.
- Faculty/staff intervene with students identified at risk.
- Institutions upload mid-term deficiencies and faculty/staff meet with students.
- Approximately ten weeks into the spring term, institutions initiate the spring check-up survey, the list of at-risk students is updated and students receive additional feedback.

Analysis and feedback
Analysis throughout the 20+ years of MAP-Works indicates the predictive validity of the risk indicator, improved retention, and targeted interventions.

The cost and timeline
Cost of participation is dependent on the number of students. Timeline is a full academic year.

How it is/was monitored
A survey of participating faculty/staff is conducted every fall to provide information for improving MAP-Works. In addition, on-going data analysis supports improvement in the survey instrument and risk algorithm. Also, implementation is monitored through faculty/staff usage reports as well as student response rates and viewing records of the student reports.

The outcome
As stated above, retention rates have improved, faculty/staff usage has improved, and the number of students viewing their reports has increased

Has or could the initiative be used for a different group?
In the fall of 2009, over 80 institutions utilised MAP-Works.

Advice and guidance
It is important to think about MAP-Works as a complete student success project, not just a series of surveys and a risk algorithm. Therefore, to implement MAP-Works means thinking about which faculty/staff have direct connections to students and what information might be useful to them to improve their ability to efficiently and effectively intervene.

Contact details
swoosley@webebi.com
darlena@webebi.com

Case Study 40

Name and university
Duncan Nulty, Senior Lecturer in Higher Education, Griffith University, Brisbane, Australia.

Title of project/initiative
Using student feedback in an evidence-based approach to improving the quality of teaching and courses.

Who was involved in the initiative
Faculty Deans, Heads of Schools, Course Coordinators, the University Secretariat and the CRIR Working Party (WP) who reported to the University Learning and Teaching Committee (ULTC).

Reason for the project/initiative
Griffith University uses a standard survey-based approach to the collection of student feedback about teaching (Student Evaluation of Teaching (SET)) and courses (SEC). Two concurrent issues emerged from the implementation and use of this system. First, a desire to ensure academic staff made good use of the data to improve their teaching and their courses. Second, to ensure that students were informed about this use (i.e. giving students feedback on what was done in response to their feedback).

Why it was developed
We wanted to develop a process that could be used by all academic staff to ensure that student evaluation data was properly used (with other data) to improve teaching and courses. We also wanted to 'close the loop' by appropriately informing students of the responses made to their feedback. This activity is regarded as a component of good practice in evaluation that can help to engender greater student commitment in the evaluation process – thereby ensuring that the feedback obtained in the first place is more considered and useful (a win–win).

The target group
The project targeted course convenors in the production of 'course review and improvement reports' (CRIRs), heads of schools in reviewing those reports and students as 'consumers' of the student summary portion of the CRIRs.

How it was developed, what it included and how it was implemented

How it was developed
A CRIR template was developed through consultation between the chair of the university academic committee (the body responsible for quality assurance and accreditation of all university degree programmes) and a curriculum and assessment design expert (me) from the Griffith Institute for Higher Education (GIHE), which is an educational development institute with a university-wide mandate. The report template was used and refined through three repeat trials involving a large number of volunteer schools and courses over 18 months.

What it included

The single-page CRIR template prompted course convenors to write:

- a brief summary of students' feedback;
- a brief response (for students);
- a longer response about course issues (for an academic audience);

and state:

- the ways in which student feedback had been obtained;
- where the response for students was published.

Data from the SEC and SET was integrated within the CRIR.

How it was implemented

For each trial, the working party devised a schedule of activities (for all involved) associated with obtaining student feedback, producing CRIRs, quality assurance of these by heads of schools and publishing the response to students. This schedule took account of key dates in the academic calendar. The academic secretariat then liaised with volunteer heads of school and school administration officers (SAOs) to establish a list of courses to take part. From there, SAOs liaised with the course convenors and acted as the single point of contact between them and the heads of school.

Analysis and feedback

The evaluation included: what proportion of course convenors participated; the quality of the reports they wrote; and what the convenors, heads of schools and students had to say. We found that participation was good throughout the trials due to:

- participation requests to selected colleagues;
- colleagues realising the benefits associated with writing the CRIRs.

Through the trials, the report template was simplified to minimise workload while maintaining its functional integrity. The final template was simple (little more than the headings above in the 'what it included' section). Most academics responded in a meaningful way, not merely in a compliant manner. Academics commented on workload and time pressures (inevitably) but, as the trials proceeded, this became less significant and the benefits more notable. It was clear that gradual culture change was occurring and that improvements would continue as people experienced the benefits of engaging with this process. Report writing guidelines were developed and the quality of reports improved. Some CRIRs were detailed and longer than others but, in all cases, all sections of the CRIR were completed to the required standard.

The cost and timeline

The main 'cost' of the project was the (un-costed) time participants invested in it (course coordinators, WP members and committee time). We had minimal funding for a research assistant who aided the working party in designing, conducting surveys and analysing the responses. The time invested was considered by academic colleagues and the ULTC as time well spent.

How it is/was monitored

The development of the CRIR template, and the associated trials were conducted like three successive small-scale learning and teaching development projects (in the style of action research). These were co-managed by the members of the working party and the academic secretariat. After each trial, a report was prepared for consideration by the ULTC. Each report contained several recommendations, most of these were accepted.

The outcome

It is clear that most participants regard the process as very worthwhile. Accordingly, the university is now adopting this model on a university-wide basis. However, additional considerations are being worked through, which other institutions will also have to face.

Clearly, there is workload associated with the CRIR process. Like all institutions ours seeks to minimise the impost of new work requirements by integrating them with existing processes. It also seeks efficiency by targeting such requirements to where they are most likely to be beneficial.

Some systemic integration has been achieved by adopting a new electronic course profiling system. This system includes a dedicated section that, for each course, explicitly requires the convenor to provide students with feedback on changes made in response to previous evaluations. Consequently, at the minimum, all course convenors are required to reflect on evaluative data and to author a response. The CRIR trials have helped to develop guiding notes and examples that illustrate how to do this well.

The workload issue is being managed by selectively targeting only some courses for the CRIR. This is consistent with the selective nature of the three trials themselves. The process is that only the convenors of courses that score below 3.4 on a 5-point scale in their SECs are required to complete a CRIR. This criterion corresponds to about 20 per cent of courses with the lowest course evaluation scores. Thus, the CRIR is used were it is most clearly justified, and where benefit is most likely. Another effect of this selectivity is that our improvement efforts are more efficiently targeted: the GIHE is better able to support educational development with convenors of 20 per cent of the courses than it could if all courses were involved.

In conclusion, the CRIR is a key aid to course quality improvement. It is an easy and standard way of helping convenors to formulate their analysis of course performance and to articulate improvement plans. By its nature, it also encourages a somewhat more thorough and informed analysis than might otherwise occur.

Has or could the initiative be used for a different group?

The CRIR has been adopted as described above. Its simplicity belies the potency of its effectiveness, and also means a similar approach could be readily adopted elsewhere.

Advice and guidance

- Carefully timed collection of data and feedback.
- Secure appropriate participation though scrutiny of CRIRs by heads of school.
- Use the CRIR to help promote the integration of multiple data sources.
- Require meaningful analysis and interpretation, not merely compliance.
- Tie the process in to broader QA processes (like the SEC 20 per cent).
- Provide guidance on the production of good reports.
- Commit to developing the ability and culture in which this can be done.
- Appreciate that it takes sustained effort over at least a couple of years.

Contact details

d.nulty@griffith.edu.au

Conclusion

All the case studies in this chapter illustrate great ways to embed the collection and use of student feedback to improve courses, programmes, teaching and conceivably every aspect of a student's experience. All can be adopted widely, even if some local adaptation might be required. Take home learning points from me include:

- Embedding the collection of feedback from students into courses and modules while they are running. Doing so in ways that engage the students is a good way to ensure the feedback you obtain is considered, meaningful and of mutual benefit.
- Making systematic multi-institution processes for gathering student feedback that can be used in multiple ways to inform multi-pronged and extended interventions that improve students' experiences.
- Utilising these mechanisms in ways that include personal and useful feedback to individual students in an effective way to get much greater engagement – and better outcomes for all.
- Thinking systemically about simple ways to incorporate the collection and use of student feedback into existing institutional practices and procedures. This is a good way to negate some of the resistance of staff engaging with student feedback that often comes simply from issues associated with workload.

So to summarise, the design, development and implementation of any student experience initiative needs to be informed by student experiences provided by effective feedback if those initiatives are to actually result in improvements to the student experience.

References

Cashin, W. E. (1995) 'Student ratings of teaching: the research revisited', Idea Paper No. 32, Kansas State University: Center for Faculty Evaluation and Development.

Marsh, H. W. (1987) 'Students' evaluations of university teaching: research findings, methodological issues, and directions for future research', *International Journal of Educational Research*, volume 11, issue 3, 253–388.

McKeachie, W. J. (1990) 'Learning, thinking and Thorndike', *Educational Psychologist*, 25(2), 127–41.

Meyers, N. M. and Nulty, D. D. (2009) 'How to use (five) curriculum design principles to align authentic learning environments: assessment, students' approaches to thinking, and learning outcomes', *Assessment and Evaluation in Higher Education*, 34(5), 565–77.

Race, P. (2005) *Making Learning Happen*, London: Sage Publications.

Thorndike, E. L. (1911) *Animal Intelligence: Experimental Studies*, New York: Macmillan.

Chapter 13

Future developments in higher education and the student experience

Michelle Morgan and Glyn Jones,
Kingston University, UK

Introduction

Practitioners can make a genuine difference to the workings of a university, as outlined throughout this book. Their roles will become even more crucial as the student experience becomes a critical selling point for institutions in attracting applicants who are likely to continue to have plenty of choice about where to study. Now that social networking by applicants and students is so ubiquitous, it is imperative that institutions do really focus on the student experience in all publicity material, in prospectuses and on the university website. They need to make it the main driver of their business rather than just paying lip service to it. In the future, the quality of the student experience will make or break an institution and hence its reputation and survival.

In this concluding chapter, our aims are three-fold. First, we will discuss what institutions need to consider when shaping their future. Second, we will review the aims behind the Practitioner Model in light of the experiences described by the chapter and case study authors and summarise the advice provided by them. And third, we will look at the future challenges practitioners face in developing a modern and robust student experience suitable for a diverse student body. These challenges must not only be manageable by staff and fit for business, but they must meet the imperatives of government policy in the twenty-first century.

Challenge for HE institutions: which direction?

Institutions need to honestly discuss and consider a range of questions when shaping and developing strategies for their future. For some institutions, this may require a major shift in their thinking and behaviour as well as the allocation of resources.

Embedding the concept of the student experience

Although the student experience movement is well established widely across the Western world and internationally, institutions have adopted the concept of the student experience in various ways. Whilst some are very engaged and committed to the delivery of a high-quality student experience, others just talk rhetoric and deliver the minimum service standards required. Some colleagues do not fundamentally believe that the focus on the student experience is valid. They argue that students at university should learn in a traditional way, fitting around the needs of the university and, if they fail, it is merely a way of sorting the strong students from the weak. Some universities which have an established stronghold in terms of student recruitment, and are at the top of the chain of HE institutions, may feel that the demands of delivering an excellent student experience are not critical to their survival. However, if the quality and standards of higher education are to be maintained, then this attitude must change. No vice-chancellor or senior manager of any institution can afford to take a cavalier attitude or negative approach towards the student experience. Institutions need to recruit senior staff who are practitioners with a thorough understanding of the student experience, and they need to be prepared to invest the necessary resources to enhance it. Funding for the student experience should be seen as a positive investment and thus be the last area to be reduced if financial constraints must be be imposed.

Choosing a direction in a changed landscape

As a sector, we need to formally acknowledge that the landscape of higher education, as described in Chapter 1, has changed and that these changes will continue to impact upon the delivery of our provision. We cannot educate and support a massified and diverse student body in the same way we did 40 years ago when just seven per cent of the population went to university. In recent years, there has been a push by governments for HE institutions to move away from undertaking and delivering specific roles and services (e.g. offering either academic or vocational programmes) and to engage in a broad range of activities. However, with continuing massification and diversification, HEIs should be looking at their strengths and focusing on creating unique offers to the sector. But these niches must be informed by knowledge from a broad range of activities: academic, vocational and research-led and they must focus on being expert in the area of learning and teaching. An educated population provides a multitude of benefits for society but institutions will need to create learning environment niches that are suitably matched and fit the needs of their particular cohort of students.

Repositioning of the undergraduate degree

An undergraduate degree is a rung on the ladder of lifelong learning. The value of most modern undergraduate degrees within a mass system means that they cannot be regarded with the same gravitas as they were 40 years ago when a small percentage of the population achieved the accolade. Students' expectations must be managed so that when embarking on their university life they do not think that an undergraduate degree is an immediate and guaranteed passport to a good career and high salary. By managing student expectations, we are more effectively able to minimise student complaints and, hopefully, avoid later disappointment and recrimination relating to their experience.

Sustaining our future

If you are reading this book, you are more than likely to be among those already converted to the student experience. For colleagues who do not share these views, it is worth emphasising that most students will chose the institution that provides best value for money, a high-quality student experience and a degree that is current and recognised in their potential workplaces. They expect and deserve a quality experience. If an institution does not provide these criteria then they will not attract students, at a time when students, particularly in the UK, are going to be making tough decisions about whether to study at university or not. The equation for university staff is very simple: no students, no job.

The benefits of the Practitioner Model

The Practitioner Model can support institutions in shaping the student experience they deliver. The case studies outlined in the previous chapters demonstrate the appropriateness and relevance of the Practitioner Model in ensuring that the necessary support throughout the respective stages of the student lifecycle is embedded across an institution. The model:

- helps deliver interlinked academic, welfare and support activities;
- supports both students and staff;
- can be used in either a top-down or bottom-up approach.

The model is most effective where an institution has in place a clear mission, vision and strategy which has had input and guidance from practitioners across the institution and that has been ratified by the university governance with the engagement of all university staff. A management structure that encourages the proactive and creative participation of staff in developing new processes provides a sound foundation on which practitioners can develop effective initiatives based on increased student engagement and staff cooperation and participation. The absence of such a vision and strategy, or a weak and unstructured management, can hinder the work of the practitioner in implementing suitable models of practice as well as critically undermining the institution and its mission.

The key to the Practitioner Model, and the success of the case studies in this book, is that it requires key players at all levels across an institution to proactively interact and link their skills and activities. Fundamental to accomplishing this objective is good communication which informs and empowers university staff. This has been a recurrent theme integral to the success of many of the case studies in the previous chapters.

Advice from the chapter and case study authors

Throughout the book, the chapter and case study authors have provided valuable advice and insights into improving the student experience in the current higher education environment. A summary of 'themed' advice provided by the authors in their role as practitioners follows.

Management

- Accept that one size does not fit all, and that initiatives need to be developed for diversity to ensure inclusion.
- Provide a student-centred approach to students and their support networks.
- Recognise the importance of 'buy-in' by senior managers, accompanied by well-placed student experience champions at all institutional levels, who actively encourage the participation of everyone in supporting the institution's vision and strategy.

Integration and collaboration

- Ensure that theory and practice are interlinked and do not operate in isolation from each other.
- Integrate and coordinate the work between central departments and the departmental study units to ensure processes and support provision are streamlined in order to attain a more holistic student experience.
- Have an integrated and coordinated approach to support inclusion activities targeting specific groups as appropriate (e.g. mature students, first-generation immigrants, etc.);
- Ensure that centre and departmental units are aware of each other's respective roles, in order to provide seamless integrated provision for students and staff.
- Engender greater flexibility from academic and support staff in terms of providing course and qualifications outside traditional delivery modes.

Training

- Ensure that all staff understand the need to engage in the student's educational process irrespective of their institutional role or position.
- Provide further training and development to empower staff to be creative when looking at the needs of the modern learner.
- Broaden the knowledge base of staff to heighten awareness of the impact of previous educational experiences (e.g. school/further education, workplace, independent study) especially if they are involved in the application, orientation and induction stages of the student lifecycle.

Resources

- Provide adequate and dedicated resources to support all aspects of improving and enhancing the student experience.
- Utilise different forms of resources to inform and train all staff whether that is face-to-face or via online and downloadable resources.

Communication

- Employ varied, relevant and accessible communication media (e.g. use of social networking sites) to encourage the academic and social integration of students with their peers and university staff.
- Recognise the need for good communication networks both internal and external to the university.
- Engage and communicate with students as partners in their own learning in order to create effective peer support and student support networks to facilitate this process.

Review, evaluation and development

- Learn from past and present experiences by listening and responding to students and colleagues communicating about their requirements.
- Positively embrace internationalisation and globalisation throughout all the university's processes.

- Continually review and evaluate the support provision to ensure that all support remains relevant to the students' requirements at all stages of the student lifecycle (e.g. via student surveys, student feedback mechanisms, etc.).

Challenges facing the practitioner

In light of the directional choices institutions should consider, some of the challenges that practitioners need to start thinking about, and planning for, are set out below.

Funding for higher education

With the reduction in public expenditure for higher education, especially across Europe, practitioners will need to be more creative in developing cost-effective initiatives that provide outstanding value for money. Future funding for higher education will be generated from a range of sources and will place extra pressure on the practitioner to deliver a high-quality student experience. They will include:

- universities increasing student fees for specialised short courses and abbreviated or full-length degree courses;
- introducing subject fee differentiation without impacting on the university brand;
- universities increasing the recruitment of international students inline with visa requirements;
- collaborative arrangements with business and research organisations thus making them stakeholders within the HE sector;
- increasing student participation at undergraduate level through the delivery of flexible study modes, such as part-time study, distance learning, work-based/work-related learning and shorter, more intensive degree courses;
- the recruitment of new learners from non-traditional markets, such as the early retirement populace;
- targeted training schemes for those wishing to retrain or who are seeking work opportunities;
- continued expansion of postgraduate level courses that meet the needs of the economy and are supported by the business sector and industry.

Student expectations

In the UK, the increase in student fees to compensate for the reduction in government/state funding will have a number of effects on the attitude of the student. As student fees and their associated study debt increases, so will student expectations both in terms of the quality of the student experience they expect to receive at university and their perceived value of their degree in the employment market. A significant motivation for many undergraduates, as mentioned elsewhere in this book, is that a degree will greatly enhance their employment prospects. With an increase in student fees, and the concept of students being clients and partners in their learning becoming embedded in university culture, we can expect to see a justifiable increase in student complaints if we do not deliver an excellent quality experience. In order to attract students and to manage their experience, institutions may decide to offer 'added value' benefits on courses giving students immediate financial benefits through discounts, such as subsidised accommodation and free field trips. This will allow an institution to maintain the fee level and protect its brand whilst students will feel that they are receiving added value on a product they will pay for in the future.

Changes in teaching, learning and assessment environments

As the student body continues to increase and diversify, creative and innovative teaching and learning approaches, such as problem- and enquiry-based learning, will need to be developed by institutions to enable students to learn in the most effective way. Relevant development and training for staff, coupled with the necessary resources, will need to be provided to effect this process and ensure that learning outcomes, standards and quality are maintained and enhanced. The curriculum needs to be responsive to students' expressed needs in order for them to engage fully. It needs to align with the cultural values of the student body, the institution and a multicultural society in order to equip students with the necessary skills for work and to be active citizens. The need for HE to produce multi-skilled graduates in terms of transferable skills and flexibility means that personal development and employability activities need to be fully embedded within the curriculum.

The progressive move towards providing flexible study modes to enable students to engage in the type of learning that meets their need, is likely to have a major impact on how we organise our academic year, our practices and the delivery of learning, teaching and assessment.

Changes in the delivery of services

In the future, universities may decide that the most cost-effective way to fund infrastructure developments, services and welfare support is to contract them out to the private sector and other HEIs which have developed specialisms in particular areas. This is already the case with, for example, English language provision for international students. In some institutions, services such as cleaning, catering, accommodation and maintenance are already being partly or wholly contracted out. Other support services, such as disability and welfare support may be areas universities consider contracting out. It is likely that institutions will be expected to pool and streamline departmental and central services. This could be in the form of centralising welfare and support services to create 'one stop shop' services, as is the case in a number of universities already, or the disbanding of large central units and the placing of specialists within the home unit with satellite management (e.g. a career unit placing an employability coordinator at school level). The efficient pooling of resources could be extended to include universities within a region in an attempt to achieve maximum savings, although this must never be allowed to compromise the quality of the delivery.

Staffing issues

To embed an excellent quality student experience for a diverse student body with complex demands will require staff to receive training in the area of enhancing the student experience and not just in their own subject specialism. All staff at every level in an organisation from the car park attendant to the vice-chancellor should recognise that the student experience is integral to their role and responsibilities within their institution. To facilitate this process, relevant and continuous training should be provided to equip them with the knowledge and skills to enable them to be active participants in the enhancement of the student experience. Accordingly, training should not be limited to the champions of the student experience, senior managers or those who are passionate about it, but to all staff. To accomplish this goal, a key requisite will be the provision of affordable access to good practice both locally, nationally and internationally. Case studies, such as those outlined in this book will assist in this process. Strategies could include more locally based conferences and networking, shared web-based training materials to support staff in this process, shared training amongst institutions in the region and even perhaps a'university TV' service (concept similar to Teachers TV).

The training of staff must also be linked to the recruitment of the right kinds of staff in the first place. Higher education on a global scale has an ageing academic population. If HE is to survive and continue to expand and the next generation of academics and support staff are to fully understand the needs of a diverse student body, we need an immediate informed rolling recruitment and training programme to ensure that we have the right staff in place.

Creation of university and wider communities

Institutions should aim to create not only university communities but also to engage the wider community or 'society' in its activities. This can be achieved through providing skilled graduates: knowledge transfer, student volunteering and purchasing from local businesses. These activities can open up a range of possibilities, such as encouraging local businesses to offer placements to students; to employ new graduates from local institutions; to get local business involvement in the curriculum; and to help develop work-based or work-related courses.

Internationalisation and globalisation

As internationalisation and globalisation of higher education increases, it will be critical for universities to fully integrate internationalisation within their institution and to become global by recruiting international students and staff; by developing the curriculum to reflect international discourse; and to undertake joint research overseas and ensure that international students feel part of their new learning community. It is important for universities not to see internationalisation and globalisation as merely an income stream. Income should be seen as a by-product of this dimension in HE.

Conclusion

Higher education is at a crossroads in terms of how it addresses the student experience. The way in which institutions respond to government policy for the continued massification and wide-ification of HE; supply an appropriately educated workforce for business needs; and increase expectations of students due to rising tuition fees and an aging academic body, will all shape the future of the sector. These are already challenges but they will become more acute given the changes in the economic climate and the financial constraints facing many of our institutions.

Further reading
Information and practical advice

Assessment and feedback

Gibbs, G. (2010) *Using Access to Support Student Learning*, Leeds: Leeds Metropolitan University.

Race, P. (2009) *The Lecturer's Tool Kit: A Practical Guide to Assessment, Learning and Teaching*, Oxon: Routledge.

Irons, A. (2008) *Enhancing Learning through Formative Assessment and Feedback*, Oxon: Routledge.

Academic support

Carlson, G. and Scarbrough, J. (2009) 'Holistic intervention programme for at-risk students', in D. Nutt and D. Calderon (eds) *International Perspectives on the First-Year Experience in Higher Education*, monograph 52, Columbia, SC: University of South Carolina, National Resource Center for the First-Year Experience and Students in Transition.

Hixenbaugh, P., Pearson, C. and Williams, D. (2006) 'Student perspectives on personal tutoring: what do students want?' *Personal Tutoring in Higher Education*, London: Trentham Books.

Hunter, M.S., Wriggins, B.M. and White, E.R. (2007) *Academic Advising: New Insights for Teaching and Learning in the First College Year*, monograph 46, Columbia, SC: University of South Carolina, National Resource Center for the First-Year Experience and Students in Transition.

Thomas, L. and Hixenbaugh, P. (2006) *Personal Tutoring in Higher Education*, London: Trentham Books.

Employability

Callender, C. (2008) 'The impact of term-time employment on higher education students' academic attainment and achievement', *Journal of Education Policy*, 23 (4), 359–77.

McInnes, C. and Hartley, R. (2002) *Managing Study and Work: The Impact of Full-Time Study and Paid Work on the Undergraduate Experience in Australian Universities*, Canberra: Department of Education, Science and Training.

Yorke, M. (2006) *Learning and Employability Series One: Pedagogy for Employability*, York: Higher Education Academy.

Yorke, M. and Knight, P.T. (2006) *Embedding Employability into the Curriculum*, York: Higher Education Academy.

Finance

Callender, C. (2009) *Awareness, Take-Up and Impact of Institutional Bursaries and Scholarships in England: Summary and Recommendations*, Bristol: Office for Fair Access. Online. Available at http://www.offa.org.uk/wp-content/uploads/2009/12/OFFA-2009.07-summary-and-recommendations.pdf (accessed 8 July 2010).

Callender, C. and Jackson, J. (2005) 'Does the fear of debt deter students from higher education?' *Journal of Social Policy*, 34 (4), 509–40.

Purcell, K. and Elias, P. (2010) *The Impact of Paid and Unpaid Work and of Student Debt on Experience of Higher Education: Working Paper 3*, Warwick: HECSU.

First-year experience

Krause, K. and Coates, H. (2008) 'Students' engagement in first-year university', *Assessment and Evaluation in Higher Education*, 33 (5), 493–505.

Krause, K. (2007) 'Social involvement and the transition to higher education', *The Journal of the First-Year Experience and Students in Transition*, 19 (1) 27–45.

Mullendore, R.H. and Banahan, L.A. (2005) 'Designing orientation programs', in M.L. Upcraft, J.N. Gardner and B.O. Barefoot, *Challenging and Supporting the First-Year College Student: A Handbook for Improving the First Year of College*, San Francisco, CA: Jossey-Bass.

Thomas, L. and Quinn, J. (2006) 'First generation entry into higher education: an international study', *Learning and Teaching in Higher Education*, 3 (8), 113–16.

Upcraft, M.L., Gardner, N.J. and Barefoot, B.O. (2004) *Challenging and Supporting the First-Year Student: A Handbook for Improving the First Year of College,* San Francisco, CA: Jossey-Bass.

Yorke, M. and Longden, B. (2007) 'The first-year experience in higher education in the UK: Report on Phase 1 of a project funded by the Higher Education Academy', York: The Higher Education Academy. Online. Available at www.heacademy.ac.uk/assets/York/documents/ourwork/research/FYE/FirstYearExperienceRevised.pdf (accessed 4 November 2010).

Gender

Leath, C. and Read, B. (2009) *Gender and the Changing Face of Education*, Maidenhead: Open University Press.

Learning and teaching

Crosling, G., Thomas, L. and Heaney, M. (2007) *Improving Student Retention in Higher Education: The Role of Teaching and Learning*, London: Routledge.

Hunter, M.S. (2006) 'Fostering student learning and success through first-year programs', *Peer Review*, 8 (3), 4–7.

Krause, K. (2007) 'E-learning and the e-generation: the changing face of higher education in the 21st century', in J. Lockard and M. Pegrum (eds) *Brave New Classrooms: Educational Democracy and the Internet*, New York: Peter Lang Publishing, 125–40.

Krause, K. (2011) 'Using student survey data to shape academic priorities and approaches', in L. Stefani (ed.) *The Effectiveness of Academic Development*, New York: Routledge.

Mazur, E. (1997) *Peer Instruction: A User's Manual*, Upper Saddle River, NJ: Prentice Hall.

Race, P. (2010) *Making Learning Happen*, 2nd edn, London: Sage Publications.

Lifelong learning

Schuller, T. and Watson, D. (2009) *Learning Through Life: Inquiry into the Future for Lifelong Learning*, Leicester: NIACE.

Mature students

Pritchard, L. and Roberts, L. (2006) *The Mature Student's Guide to Higher Education*, Maidenhead: Open University Press.

Parental support

Keppler, K., Mullendore, R.H. and Carey, A. (eds) (2005) *Partnering with the Parents of Today's College Students*, Washington, DC: NASPA.

Mullendore, R.H. and Banahan, L.A. (2007) *Empowering Parents of First-Year College Students: A Guide for Success*, Columbia, SC: National Orientation Directors' Association and the National Resource Center for the First-Year Experience and Students in Transition.

Part-time study

Callender, C., Wilkinson, D. and Mackinon, K. (2006) *Part-Time Students and Part-Time Study in Higher Education in the UK: A Survey of Students' Attitudes and Experiences of Part-Time Study and its Costs*, London: Universities UK/GuildHE.

Callender, C. and Feldman, R. (2009) *Part-Time Undergraduates in Higher Education: A Literature Review*, Manchester: HECSU.

Callender, C., Hopkin, R. and Wilkinson, D. (2010) *Futuretrack: Part-Time Students Career Decision-Making and Career Development of Part-Time Higher Education Students*, Manchester: HECSU.

Raising aspirations and widening participation

Duke, C. and Layer, G. (2005) *Widening Participation: Which Way Forward for English Higher Education*, Leicester: NIACE.

Gorard, S., Smith, E., May, H., Thomas, L., Adnett, N. and Slack, K. (2006) *Review of Widening Participation Research: Addressing the Barriers to Participation in Higher Education*, Bristol: HEFCE.

Shaw, J., Brain, K., Bridger, K., Foreman, J. and Reid, I. (2007) *Embedding Widening Participation and Promoting Student Diversity*, York: Higher Education Academy.

Thomas, L. and Slack, K. (1999) *Evaluation of Aiming High*, Stoke-on-Trent: Institute for Access Studies, Staffordshire University.

Watson, D. (2006) 'How to think about widening participation in UK higher education', discussion paper for HEFCE. Online. Available at: http://www.hefce.ac.uk/pubs/rdreports/2006/rd13_06 (accessed 15 February 2011).

Returning students' student experience

Hunter, M. S., Tobolowsky, B., Gardner, J.N., Evanbeack, S.E., Pattengale, J.A., Schaller, M.A. and Schreiner, L.A. (2010) *Helping Sophomores Succeed: Understanding and Improving the Second Year Experience*, San Francisco, CA: Jossey-Bass.

Gardner, J.N. and Van der Veer, G. (1998) *The Senior Year Experience: Facilitating Integration, Reflection, Closure and Transition*, San Francisco, CA: Jossey-Bass.

Student retention

McGiveny, V. (2003) *Staying or Leaving the Course: Non-Completion and Retention of Mature Students in Further and Higher Education*, Leicester: NIACE.

Tinto, V. (1983) 'Defining dropout: a matter of perspective', in E. Pascarella (ed.) *Studying Student Retention*, San Francisco, CA: Jossey-Bass.

Tinto, V. (1993) *Leaving College: Rethinking the Causes and Cures of Student Attrition*, 2nd edn, Chicago, IL: University of Chicago Press.

Tinto, V. (2003) 'Establishing conditions for student success', in L. Thomas, M. Cooper and J. Quinn (eds) *Improving Completion Rates Among Disadvantaged Students*, Stoke-on-Trent: Trentham Books.

Yorke, M. and Longden, B. (2004) *Retention and Student Success in Higher Education*, Maidenhead: SRHE/Open University Press.

Yorke, M. and Longden, B. (2008) 'The first-year experience of higher education in the UK', York: The Higher Education Academy. Online. Available at: www.heacademy. ac.uk/assets/York/documents/ourwork/research/surveys/FYE/FYEFinalReport.pdf (accessed 11 January 2011).

University management

Denton, S. and Brown, S. (eds) *Beyond Bureacracy: A Practical Guide to University and College Management*, London: Routledge.

Kamenetz, A. (2006) *Generation Debt: Why Now is a Terrible Time to be Young*, New York: Riverhead Books.

McCaffery, P. (2010) *The Higher Education Manager's Handbook: Effective Leadership and Management in Universities and Colleges*, New York: Routledge.

Stefani, L. (2011) *The Effectiveness of Academic Development*, New York: Routledge.

Stuart, M. (2003) *Collaborating for Change? Managing Eidening Participation in Further and Higher Education*, Leicester: NIACE.

Watson, D. and Amoah, M. (2007) *The Dearing Report: Ten Years On*, London: Institute of Education.

Watson, D. (2010) *The Question of Morale: Managing Happiness and Unhappiness in University Life*, Maidenhead: McGraw-Hill/Open University Press (accessed 10 January 2010).

Useful websites

The 1994 Group
www.1994group.ac.uk/publications Admissions to Higher Education Review
www.admissions-review.org.uk

Aimhigher
    www.hefce.ac.uk/widen/aimhigh

Council for the Advancement of Standards in Higher Education (USA)
    www.cas.edu/index.php/index.php/index.php

Department for Business Innovation & Skills (UK)
    www.bis.gov.uk/policies/higher-education

Department of Education, Employment and Workplace Relations (AUS)
    www.deewr.gov.au/Pages/default.aspx

European Access Network
    www.ean-edu.org

European First Year Experience
    www.efye.blogspot.com

The Higher Education Academy (UK)
    www.heacademy.ac.uk

Higher Education Statistics Agency (UK)
    www.hesa.ac.uk

The Improving the Student Experience Website by Michelle Morgan
    www.improvingthestudentexperience.com

National Resource Centre for the First-Year Experience and Students in Transition (USA)
    www.sc.edu/fye

The Practitioner Model
    www.practitionermodel.com

Universities Australia (AUS)
    www.universitiesaustralia.edu.au

Index